ADVANCE REVIEWS

"The more you actually know, the less confident you become. I advise you not to read any books. Including this one." —Charles Dow

"I did not learn how to trade the markets from reading this book. It is a rip-off." —Jesse Livermore

"The author should not have gotten back up on her horse when she fell off." —Richard Wyckoff

"I did not understand the angle this book was taking. Clearly, the author is making this up." —William Gann

"The sequence of stories in this book is confusing, it just doesn't add up. Retrace your steps directly out of the bookshop." —Leonardo Fibonacci

"How dare this author write about a woman trader! Her credentials make her unqualified to write on this subject. Besides, I made more money than she ever did." —Hetty Green

"This chick is ballsy—she's cornering the market in books about women traders. It won't end well." —The Hunt Brothers

"The only market women belong in is the supermarket, and this book belongs firmly in the discount bin." —Bernard Baruch

"I experienced only waves of nausea reading this book. It has no forecasting value." —Ralph Elliott

"This author needs to learn how to write. She sure can't trade. Cut your losses immediately." —George Douglass Taylor

TRADING SARDINES

TRADING SARDINES

LESSONS IN THE MARKETS FROM A LIFELONG TRADER

LINDA BRADFORD RASCHKE

Daughters Press

Copyright © 2018 by Linda Bradford Raschke

Published by Daughters Press, Florida

All rights reserved. No part of this book may be reproduced, scanned, photocopied, or distributed in any printed or electronic form without permission. For information, please contact Daughters Press at Lindaraschke.net. Please do not participate in or encourage piracy of copyrighted materials in violation of the author's rights.

This book reflects the author's recollection of events over time. Some experiences have been compressed, and some dialogue has been recreated. My mom disputes the Scrabble story. And she says I did not actually sleep in a converted tool shed off the garage. But I have done my best to make this a truthful story. No names have been changed to protect the innocent. There was no need to make up events either since truth is stranger than fiction.

Limit of Liability

This book is sold with the understanding that the author and publisher are not engaged in rendering investment planning, trading or other professional advice. The author and publisher cannot be held responsible for any loss incurred as a result of specific investments, trades, or decisions made by the reader.

Charts courtesy of CQG
311 S Wacker Dr., #6100
Chicago IL 60606

Library of Congress Cataloging–in-Publication Data

Raschke, Linda Bradford

Trading Sardines: Lessons in the Markets by a Lifelong Trader

ISBN Hardback: 978-1-5323-9562-8

Printed in the United States of America

Book Cover and Interior Design: Creative Publishing Book Design

"The Edge... there is no honest way to explain it because the only people who really know where it is are the ones who have gone over."
—Hunter S. Thompson

CONTENTS

Introduction 1
1. A Less Than Auspicious Start 5
2. It Did Not Seem Prudent 15
3. Sneaky Tricks 21
4. Tater Tots 25
5. Land of Cheesesteaks 33
6. Lessons from Philly 37
7. Pipeline to God 49
8. Upstairs Trader 57
9. Oops 63
10. Insight 67
11. Danishes 73
12. Trying to Keep the Ball in Play 77
13. Market Technicians 83
14. Working the System 95
15. My Trading Program 99
16. Jigsaw Puzzles 109
17. Queen of Spades 111
18. My Name is in the Phone Book 119
19. It's a Profit Deal! 125
20. Synchronicity and the Morgue File 133
21. MRCI 141
22. Moving up to the Big Leagues 147

23. Orange Juice and Leo........................... 161
24. TAG.. 167
25. Florida...................................... 173
26. Making Waffles............................... 179
27. The Y2K Bug.................................. 185
28. Mr. Bill..................................... 193
29. Animal Kingdom............................... 201
30. Generic and Big Daddy........................ 209
31. Enter Enter Enter............................ 217
32. Mike Epstein................................. 221
33. Burning Dog.................................. 229
34. Nigel.. 235
35. War Horse.................................... 241
36. Hurricane Francis............................ 245
37. Travels with Erika........................... 249
38. Girls' Night Out............................. 253
39. Damon.. 257
40. Judd and the Start of Really Big Things..... 261
41. Bulls and Bears Make Money, Pigs Get Slaughtered..... 273
42. Jinx... 281
43. A Walk in the Park........................... 287
44. The Biggest Loss is Yet to Come.............. 291
45. What Do You Do For Fun?...................... 297
46. Full Circle.................................. 303
Epilogue... 305
Parting Shot..................................... 307
Acknowledgments.................................. 309
Glossary of Trading Lingo........................ 313

INTRODUCTION

I wrote this book because nobody could believe all the crazy things which have happened to me in the financial trading industry. When I was a market maker on the Philadelphia Stock Exchange, the specialist in the pit where I stood said, "Truth is stranger than fiction." It is impossible to make these events up. I started out trading in San Francisco on the Pacific Coast Exchange where there was one of the best business libraries in the country. The first book I checked out was about catastrophe theory. This is a concept used to show how gradual changes to a system can produce sudden drastic results. A stock market crash is an obvious example. It never caught on as a legitimate model of price behavior because it had no predictive value. But it opened my eyes to the fact that there is so much that we can't model. We live in an abstract nonlinear world that is in conflict with our human biases.

Despite the increased awareness over the past two decades of black swans, fat tails, and chaotic events, otherwise known as "outliers," people tend to be more comfortable engaging in straight lined thinking. Fuzzy variables are messy. The unknown is uncomfortable.

Yet trading is about decision making under uncertainty. This is my journey as a trader where my knack for being on the wrong side of outliers and unforeseen events is well beyond random. Some of the challenges and obstacles along the way were self-created. Some were plain old bad luck. But part of this story is about how to pull yourself up by the bootstraps yet one more time and keep a positive attitude. How to persevere, the work and single-mindedness required to succeed, and above all, how to maintain a healthy sense of humor to keep one's sanity.

It was not my intent to write an autobiography but to share some of the more interesting and useful lessons I learned on my journey. Hopefully, an astute trader will get some ideas to further their own research or see different ways of looking at things. For those who are newer to the financial trading industry, it might be an eye-opener as to how many potholes can pepper the road to success.

***

Nothing is ever as it seems. This was one of the first stories I heard on the trading floor:

"Trading Sardines"

An older gentleman was walking along the wharf watching the fishing boats return from a hard day's work. Hands clasped behind his back, he inhaled the salty air into his lungs and listened to the seagulls' caw as they chased after the fishermen. When he opened his eyes, he saw a group of men crowded at the end of the wharf about 50 yards away. They were raising their hands in a hurried commotion. Curious as to what the fuss was all about, the man moved closer and closer until the caws from the crowd overtook the caws from the seagulls. He slid between the men until he was in the middle of the action. An Asian man perched on top of a box in the middle of the crowd. He was a small man, with dark leathery skin, and deep wrinkles around his eyes. His sleeves were rolled up, and he was pointing at different members in the crowd. The older gentleman looked around and saw they were bidding on a rare can of sardines. "Hundred dollar bid, hundred dollar bid, now one ten, now one twenty, will you give me one thirty?" The energy from the crowd was infectious. Overcome with emotion, the gentleman started raising his hand too, driving the bid even higher.

"One sixty bid, now one sixty-five, will you give me one seventy? One seventy bid. Going once, going twice." Heart racing and determined not to be outbid, the gentleman raised his hand a shouted, "One seventy-five!" The auctioneer twirled around and said, "Sold!" The gentleman could hardly believe it. He was the winner. He tried to catch his breath as the other men patted him on the back and dispersed back to their homes for supper. The gentleman couldn't wait to get back home to show the prize to his wife.

Beaming with pride, he presented the rare can of sardines to his wife. She smiled at him and brought the tin over to the dinner table. They both sat down, preparing to feast on the delicacy the gentleman won. He hooked his finger around the tab and pulled the lid open. An awful stench hit him in the face. The can of sardines was rotten! The wife cried out as the gentleman jumped to his feet and raced out of the house back down to the wharf. He found the auctioneer cleaning up from the day and explained to him what happened, demanding a refund. The old man let out a laugh and said, "You silly fool, those were trading sardines, not eating sardines."

Don't place valuations on the things you are trading.

1

A LESS THAN AUSPICIOUS START

I lost everything.

Tears streamed down my face. I wondered, "How the fuck do I get myself out of this one?"

The year was 1982, and I was as wide-eyed as Dorothy first gazing upon the marvelous Emerald City. However, in this story, Dorothy ends up accosted by munchkins trying to outbid her every move and in debt up to her eyeballs to the Wizard of Oz after she had her ass handed to her by the Wicked Witch of the West. Unfortunately, no sparkly red shoes were going to save me from this one.

Having recently graduated college armed with a degree in economics and music composition in one hand and a chunk of student debt in the other, I moved to San Francisco to make my fortune as a stockbroker. I rented a tiny apartment with three girls who all thought it was a fantastic idea to paint our living room Pepto Bismol pink. We lived one block from the corner of Haight and Ashbury, so anything went.

Since I didn't have a last name like Rockefeller or Vanderbilt and thus zero access to a ton of ridiculously wealthy relatives who could become clients, I was rejected by every brokerage firm in San Francisco. Determined not to give up on my goal, but desperate to pay the rent, I ended up getting a job as a financial analyst at Crown Zellerbach. It happened to be across the street from the Pacific Stock Exchange. I didn't know what the Pacific Stock Exchange or "PCX" was at the time. I soon learned that it was one of four exchanges in the country that traded equity options.

Listed equity options had been around for less than a decade, so the trading floor functioned like the Wild West. Arbitrage opportunities were abundant. To oversimplify, arbitrage means exploiting a mismatch in price on different markets. Imagine you're grocery shopping and you see the cost of butter is $1.00 at Walmart and $2.00 at Target. You could buy the butter at Walmart for $1.00, walk across the street and sell it at Target and pocket $1.00. It was that easy. Of course, technology eventually led to efficient markets.

The building which housed the Pacific Stock Exchange was a product of the 1930s and fused together the previously standing classical architecture with the art deco style of the time. Ten imposing columns lined the entrance to the exchange giving it a stately appearance. A passerby would have no clue of the chaos that ensued inside.

Every morning, traders wearing jackets of green, orange, purple, some striped and all decorated with badges, streamed down the granite steps of the exchange in search of coffee, breakfast, and cigarettes. They resembled jockeys lining up before the next big race. Traders in New York stopped for lunch. With San Francisco three hours behind, this meant a pause for bagels and a game of backgammon. A friend introduced me to one of these colorful characters, a trader named Gerry.

Gerry was a lean, wiry man. He had a thin mustache that hid even thinner lips which were perpetually curled up like the Cheshire

Cat. Before becoming a trader on the floor, Gerry had been a mathematician. He drove an antique black Mercedes convertible with a license plate which read "THX TDY." TDY was the symbol for Teledyne, a high-flying tech stock in the early eighties. Gerry made handsome profits thanks to the volatility of Teledyne.

Eager to know more about precisely what Gerry did for a living, I invited him to play tennis. Gerry was a great tennis player. He had an intense focus and never took unnecessary risks to win a point. It was Gerry's turn to serve. Pivoting his weight to his back foot, he threw the ball into the sky and whacked it across the net in my direction. Right hand ready, I smashed the fuzzy yellow ball back over the net.

As we hit the ball around, I knew I had the opportunity to pick Gerry's brain about trading on the floor. Mind racing, where to begin... What do you do down there? *Too general.* How do you buy an option? *Too simplistic.* How do I unlock the mysteries of the universe to seize financial independence? *Too desperate.*

I inhaled deeply and paused. "What is a market maker?"

Gerry looked at me curiously. "A market maker provides liquidity," he said. "He quotes both a buy and sell price in whatever instrument is being traded."

I furrowed my brow trying to visualize what Gerry had said.

"How do you make money doing that?"

Gerry chuckled. "You make money on the difference between the bid and the ask which is called the spread."

Back and forth we went. I asked Gerry question after question, and he happily supplied me with answers. Our verbal volley mirrored our tennis match.

"Look, you seem pretty interested in this stuff," he said. "If you want, there is a series of tapes back at the clearing firm that covers the basics."

"Oh yeah?" This sounded promising.

"Yeah. Spend some time learning the ropes and then I'll bring you onto the floor."

I could hardly believe it. This was my chance to join the ranks of the colorful jacket gang of the Pacific Stock Exchange. I did not fit the image of a stereotypical floor trader. I gave off more of a Barbie vibe with my blonde hair, blue eyes, and slight Valley Girl accent. But was I going to let that get in my way? As if!

Gerry looked me straight in the eye as he was talking. He had stopped blinking, which was distracting. I refocused. This was business, not a game, and he was assessing my commitment. "I'll supply you with the initial capital and we'll split the profits 50/50."

"Deal." We shook hands and continued to play.

I created my first company and in true clueless form, I named it "Pyramid Trading Company." I was inspired by the pyramid-shaped Rubik's cube which dangled from my keychain. In hindsight, I realize how utterly insane a name that was for a company in the financial industry.

I had dedicated every waking moment of the past two months to the tapes Gerry had mentioned. The instructional videos covered topics ranging from how to price options to the intricacies of arbitrage strategies. They explained how a market maker buys and sells inventory and how to use hedging strategies in stocks and options to minimize risk. It was entirely mathematical and filled with dry terminologies like delta, gamma, theta, and implied volatility. I didn't fully understand all of it, but I took copious amounts of notes. Everything went out the window the first day I stepped foot on the floor. On that day, all I saw was a sea of faceless bodies. It was a twisted blend of *Joseph's Amazing Technicolor Dreamcoat* with Pink Floyd's *The Wall*. My throat tightened as I fought to steady my breath. "Here we go."

The original options floor comprised of 600 bodies pressed up against each other in a small, windowless room. There were 22 trading pits, each listing options on four to eight stocks on 15 screens dangling overhead. Each trading pit housed 15-20 regulars or "locals" and a handful of "boat people." These traders were called boat people because they would migrate to wherever the trading action was hot. They were at a slight disadvantage because the locals were reluctant to trade with them. If you formed solid working partnerships with the locals, you were more likely to participate in the order flow. It also behooved you to work a few individual stocks instead of trying to trade multiple stocks. If you had sizable positions on, it could be difficult to exit those trades unscathed.

I made my way through the bodies, wicking sweat off every trader I passed. I arrived at the furthest side of the exchange where a stock called Union Oil (UCL) traded. I strategically picked this pit because the volumes were excellent and the crowd was hospitable. Trading pit territories were fiercely protected so it could be difficult to break in as a new trader.

At the time, there was only one other female trader on the floor, a petite older gal named Kathy. I was the second female trader, recognized by my Dutch Boy haircut. Both of us were seen as a novelty, yet I always felt welcomed as part of the gang.

I stepped into the pit and the traders parted like the red sea. I gulped and walked to the center of the crowd. A ring of armpit sweat down to my waist left a dark stain on my emerald green jacket. As I stood there, I remembered going skinny dipping as a teenager. I snuck out of the house in the middle of the night and joined my friends at the community swimming pool by the Rose Bowl. There were three diving boards to choose from: small, medium, and tall. Unlike Goldilocks, I wasn't given the option of picking the one in the middle. Instead, my friends shoved me towards the ladder of the high dive. More afraid of letting the guys see me sweat than careening into the water below, I ascended to the top. I walked to the edge of the diving platform and peered out into the darkness. I couldn't see the pool below me. "This is it. This is how I die. Tomorrow the headlines will read: LOCAL GIRL PLUNGES TO HER DEATH, NAKED. What will mother think?" I took one last breath and jumped, not knowing what it would feel like to hit the water below.

* * *

A broker walked over with a sell order. Everyone in the pit turned to me and yelled, "Raise your hand! Bid for one!" My hand shot straight into the sky. Another broker rushed over with a buy order. Again, the crowd shouted, "Raise your hand! Offer it back out!" Like that, I completed my first transaction, flipping one option for a 1/8th profit. The pit applauded. For that one day, I was everyone's little sister. Every day after that, I was just another trading jacket and badge number.

San Francisco traders were true pioneers. In the early years of the PCX, trading volumes were light and volatility was low. An increase in trading volumes and volatility meant more opportunities to profit. In April of 1982, the Chicago Mercantile Exchange introduced what was to become the most popular contract on the CME—futures based on the SP 500. This new contract allowed us to speculate on the future value of the stock market. This piqued my interest. Following Gerry's lead, I picked up the phone and called an order to our floor clerk. "Rick, place a bid to buy one SP contract at 118.45." The SP futures had opened below 120. Today, they trade over 2,700. I closed my trade a whopping three ticks higher which yielded a gain of $75. It was a modest win, but I'm proud I can say I traded the SPs on the first day they were listed. I traded them every month after that for the next 36 years.

The secret to dealing with the unknown, whether it was walking onto the floor for the first time or trading a new market, is to clear the mind and make your body go through the motions. The sensation is like a tennis player relying on muscle memory. The moment the player starts to overthink the shot is the moment a mistake is made. As a newbie on the floor of the Pacific Stock Exchange with a couple of winning months under my belt, I was feeling confident and ready to take on the world. Or so I pretended. I had PTSD flashbacks to when I was a kid about to walk onstage for a piano recital. Heart racing, tunnel vision, and for some reason my right arm inexplicitly losing all feeling.

"Who can play the piano with a numb right arm?" I thought as I stepped closer to the worn baby grand in the middle of the stage. I knew my mom would be filling up the front row with a slew of my siblings, but I couldn't see them because everything was black in my peripherals. "Is this worse than death?" A bit melodramatic, but at 11 years old, it seemed true.

Now keep in mind, the DOW was trading below 1000 for most of 1982. Stocks had a daily range of half a point and volatility was nothing compared to what it's like now.

Gerry eyed the tape of stock prices scrolling overhead. "Rumor has it there might be a takeover of City Service."

"Oh yeah? There is definitely an increase in trading activity." I felt like I knew more than I actually did.

"It's a risky move, but it might pay off big to sell some straddles."

Without losing you in technical jargon about the intricacies of options and straddles, all you need to know is this: there is an unlimited amount of risk when you sell a straddle. And I was about to learn this lesson the hard way.

City Service stock was trading around $34. The options in City Service were marked up in price and the 40-level straddle was trading around $10. If the stock closed at $40 on options expiration, the trader would make $10. If the stock closed anywhere between $30 and $50, the trader could still make money. However, if the stock either closed *below* $30 or *above* $50, you could potentially lose unlimited amounts.

Remember what I've told you so far: the stock was trading at $34. In 1982 there wasn't significant price movement on takeover deals. The expiration for the option was at the end of the week and *it seemed as though I couldn't lose.* In a few days, I could collect my

$10 and chalk it up as a brilliant move from the surprisingly gifted new trader on the floor.

You ever get a little voice inside your head suggesting you ought not to do something but you go ahead and do it anyway because fuck that little voice, I'm going to make money...

I came face to face with my arch-nemesis: greed.

I sold some straddles minutes before the closing bell. "How can I lose?" I thought naively.

The next morning, I raced to the exchange, eager to check my position.

Trading on City Service had come to a halt. Gulf Oil bid for City Service at $63 and the stock opened 20 dollars higher than where it had closed.

"$63 bid? $63?!? How could this happen??"

This was completely unheard of. Such an outrageous takeover offer had never happened before. Mouth hanging agape, I was in shock. I'm sure everyone could see the panic streaked across my face.

"What have I done?"

I didn't have the capital in my account required to hold my positions. My clearing firm told me to go down to the floor and close out all my open trades. Humiliated, I started a walk of shame from trading pit to trading pit closing my positions, begging for fair prices. The sharks sensed blood and began circling. I could hear murmurs and snickers from the crowd, "We knew she wouldn't last."

This was one of the most embarrassing moments of my life, and it felt as though it would never end. In the midst of all the chaos, time ground to a halt. It was as if the universe was making sure I would always remember this moment.

Gerry had been selling straddles as well, but his trading account was 20 times bigger than mine. I was a mere peon. My total loss was $86,000, which doesn't sound like much now, but since I didn't have a nickel to my name, it felt like I had lost $86,000,000. This 23-year old had lost the cost of an MBA from Stanford in less than 24 hours.

As fate would have it, Gulf Oil, the company which set out to acquire City Service, backed out of the deal the next day. They realized their $63 a share deal was way too high and the stock opened down 20 points. Since I was forced to close my position the day before, the damage was done. I became an indentured servant to my clearing firm for the next six years as I worked to pay back my losses.

Years later, I became friends with Larry McMillan, a renowned expert on options. He started his career on an equity arbitrage desk. His firm had lost money speculating on Gulf Oil's bid as well except they got spanked when the price dropped. I got spanked when the price went up. As the saying goes, misery loves company.

Larry and I became fast friends as we bonded over our experience with Gulf Oil. I could appreciate that he was an excellent pianist as well. I found out over time that most every trader had experienced early fiascos in their careers. It simply was a matter of surviving.

2

IT DID NOT SEEM PRUDENT

It did not seem prudent to declare bankruptcy at 23 years old. After my blowout, I was in a predicament since I owed a substantial sum of money to my clearing firm. With my tail between my legs, I turned to my grandfather for a financial reprieve. He was the only one in my family who had the kind of money that could bail me out of my debt.

"Here you are, running around Wall Street, getting into trouble!" he said. My grandfather severely disapproved of my profession. He was a conservative man and didn't believe in making a fortune in the stock market. Who could blame him? He was born into a family of ten children. Each kid had one pair of shoes apiece. He survived the Great Depression and became a prominent attorney. My grandfather started a law firm in Seattle, Washington and formed a partnership with William Gates, Bill Gates' father. This is one of those degrees of separation the family likes to throw around at cocktail parties because it's fun to drop a name like *Bill Gates*. How bourgeois.

With martinis in hand, the conversation goes something like this: "You know, my mom grew up down the street from *Bill Gates*."

"You don't say!"

"Why yes! His father was partners with my grandfather."

"Get outta town!" My grandfather was so risk-averse that when his partner, William Gates, asked if my grandfather wanted to invest in his son Bill's company, my grandfather scoffed at the idea. "A computer! Who has a use for a *computer?*" he exclaimed.

If he only knew what he had passed up!

My grandfather made his decision clear by saying, "You got yourself into this mess and you are going to have to figure out a way to get out of it." I'm sure that was accompanied by a line about building character. He may have thrown in a "young lady" for good measure.

Fortunately for me, my clearing firm was in a predicament as well: they wanted their money back. They needed for me to stay in business so I could pay off my debt. Another firm in New York needed boots on the ground on the Pacific Stock Exchange, so my clearing firm found an opportunity to start collecting on my debt through indentured servitude. My new taskmaster was a trader named Morris. He was a well-educated, native New Yorker living at the Hotel Des Artistes on the Upper West Side. His great-grandfather made a fortune by inventing Christmas tree light bulbs. I was a deeply-in-debt California surfer chick. We made an unlikely pair.

Morris was at the forefront of trading technology. He was one of the first to develop software that scanned for mispriced options across the country's four major exchanges. Personal computers weren't even a thing yet, so this was cutting edge technology. It took a computer the size of a Volvo stored in Battery Park Plaza to run the proprietary software. This was a bit more advanced than Christmas tree light bulbs, but clearly, innovation ran in the family.

Morris had traders positioned on all the major exchanges ready to pounce on any arbitrage opportunity the computer spit out. I became his sole trader on the floor of the Pacific Stock Exchange. My trading badge was K91, so Morris nick-named me "Top Dog," which I took as a compliment.

We never met in person, but we spoke on the phone several times a day. Monday morning, 7:00 AM PST. "Hey Top Dog, it looks like the Wang April 30 call options are priced too high. Get in and sell some straddles!" 7:25 AM PST. "Hey Top Dog, the Zapata calls are priced too high. See if you can buy some calendar spreads to sell the expensive premium."

I rushed over to the Zapata pit, but the locals hissed at me. They knew my game and corrected the quotes before I could place the trade. There were no automated option pricing routines, so all the prices were updated by hand. Since the exchange was not specialist-run, it was up to the market makers to update the options in the pits. My days consisted of me running around the floor all day having quotes changed the minute I arrived.

According to Morris's models, every option on the floor was priced "too high." This was because the big bull market was off to the races, but the historical volatility models were still reflecting the doldrums of the preceding bear market. We didn't realize we were working off "outdated models." We had short straddle positions in most stocks. Thanks to my humbling experience with City Service, I knew that shorting straddles is an excellent strategy if prices stay in a contained range and I learned that doesn't always happen. Every day I came into work praying nothing would move.

As I was toiling away on the West Coast, there was a journalist named Robert Foster Winans on the East Coast making his last edits to my death warrant. Winans was notorious for his "Heard on the Street" column in the Wall Street Journal. Winans' words had power. What he wrote in his column could influence the market and knowing this, he took advantage of his position. Winans will go down in history as a sneaky little shit for running an insider trading scam with his long-term lover, David. The full story should be turned into an opera because it's filled with seduction, greed, and even a conspiracy to commit double suicide before the SEC SWAT Team comes flying through the front door. Winans leaked his stories in advance of publication to a retail broker with Kidder Peabody named Peter Brant. This allowed Brant to trade on the information a day before it was known to the public. And this left the rest of us selling options to someone with insider information.

Morris and I watched two companies trading on the Pacific Stock Exchange: Tie Communications and Key Pharmaceutical. Over a short period of time, the options for both stocks were heavily in demand. In fact, demand was so strong, the implied volatility on the options jumped like oil hitting a hot frying pan. Traders flocked to the action. Morris and I had sizable short straddles on these two stocks. That little shit Winans published one of his stories and then boom! One of the stocks gapped up big. I covered some short call options.

Morris called, "You wuss! Why did you adjust the position??"

Boom! The other stock gapped down big. I pondered what to do as the crowd was going crazy.

Morris called again. "Hey! What the hell are you doing? Get in there and adjust the position!"

I was damned if I did and damned if I didn't. Amidst all the chaos, I ran into the women's bathroom. Of course, no one was in there since the majority of traders used the men's bathroom. I closed the stall door and focused on the hexagonal patterns in the tiles until my vision clouded and two warm streaks grazed my cheeks. "What the hell am I doing?" I grabbed a wad of toilet paper and dried my eyes. I looked in the mirror to make sure my face wasn't red and puffy. I straightened my jacket, sighed, and threw myself back to the wolves. Again.

I am not sure how we survived the many landmines during the mid-eighties. There were hostile takeovers in the form of greenmail, salacious gossip, blackmail, and insider trading. Not only were we all screwed over by people like Robert Foster Winans and Peter Brant, but we had to deal with the actions of Michael Milken and Ivan Boesky. Michael Milken was known as the "Junk Bond King." A junk bond is exactly what it sounds like—a bond with a crap credit rating. It's the equivalent of lending your neighbor $20, except that your neighbor has a gambling problem and has already borrowed $200 from you. You're not so sure he's going to pay it back, but if he bets on the right pony at the tracks, you might win big. Junk bonds were conveniently renamed high-yield bonds to make it easier for investors to digest. It is nicer to think of a bond as giving you a high-yield rather than reminding you that what you are buying is actually junk. The finance industry has a funny way of renaming things to make them sound better to the public. Take the term "correction," for example. What a cute word for what actually represents a 10% drop in the market. "Oh, the market's just correcting itself." Like it made a boo-boo. Puh-lease.

Anyway, Michael Milken engaged in securities fraud and was partially responsible for the demise of Drexel Burnham, a major brokerage firm. Ivan Boesky, known for the start of leveraged buyouts and mergers, scammed the system as well. He was convicted of insider trading and ultimately ratted out Milken. The rest of us? We were doing our best to survive and, if lucky, thrive.

3

SNEAKY TRICKS

Most of the traders in San Francisco were doing very well. They owned racehorses, drove nice cars, and lived in beautiful houses which glistened like crown jewels atop the hills of the Bay Area. Gold was in—bracelets and necklaces and bags of gold coins stashed in closets. Even the clearing firms were swimming in the dough. They rented ski chalets in Lake Tahoe for traders to use. Free donuts and coffee greeted us in the morning. On Fridays, there was more pizza than anyone could eat. Tickets to the baseball games, racetrack outings, even free health insurance. All this to encourage the traders to stay at a particular clearing firm. One day I analyzed my commissions. Even with an exchange seat, I was paying 40% of my gross to the clearing firm in fees. This was true with most everyone. Each time a trader flipped an option, it was *ka-ching* for the clearing firm. But as traders printed money and spent the weekends at Lake Tahoe, it seemed like a fair cost to play the game.

Though most all the traders were good friends off the floor, a different set of rules applied in the pits. I watched one trader place orders through a broker on the other side of the exchange to pick off traders in his own crowd. He was standing next to the clerk who called our stock orders to New York. None of the other traders could see him. Dumping his inventory on his trading buddies—what a slime-ball tactic. This practice was soon ruled to be illegal, but it showed how ruthless traders were once the markets opened. Traders got picked off from many sources, including the person standing next to them.

A broker hollers, "What's the market on the UCL May 35 call options?"

A trader does not know if the broker is a buyer or a seller but has to make a two-sided market. "3 1/4 bid offered at 3 1/2, 500 up."

"Take 'em!" The broker buys 500 call options for his customer and before the traders have a chance to hedge the calls they sold with stock, a block of 500,000 shares prints up 1/2 point on the tape.

Picked off again by an institutional desk with big clients. No wonder it did not take long for a trader to become cynical.

There were two ticker tapes displaying news at the tops of the walls—one was Dow Jones, and the other was Reuters. Invariably, one of the news feeds would have a lead time of 1-2 minutes. The other feed was delayed while an upstairs firm tried to capitalize on the news first, sending orders to the pits before traders were aware of the event. The manipulation was blatant.

The Dow hit bottom on August 13, 1982. Incredibly, the Wall Street Elves also gave a perfect buy signal. The "Elves" was a name given by Louis Rukeyser to an index developed by Bob Nurock, a stock market analyst. Each Friday evening, 10 million viewers, (a lot back then), tuned in to watch this entertaining television show and learn the status of the market. Bob Nurock, a guest on the show for 19 years, had based his index on Market Momentum, Investor Sentiment, and Monetary Conditions. The timing of his buy signal at the bottom made quite an impression on me. I figured it would behoove me to figure out how to be an expert on his three main indicators as well. The track record for the Elves timing signals was close to 92% over one ten-year stretch.

Jiminy Criminy—92%! That is significant! Why pay attention to fundamentals or news when it's a liquidity game. Perhaps making money could be easy as long as one did not get caught on the wrong side of takeover deals.

4

TATER TOTS

I was 13-years old and I never wanted to eat another tater tot as long as I lived. My two younger brothers and sister were staring down at their plates. Day fourteen of eating tater tots for dinner and there was no end in sight. I pushed the little pieces of fried potato around with my fork. My brother, Steve, was the first one to put his fork up to his mouth. Crunch. He winced and put his fork back down. My sister, Anne, eyed the tater tots suspiciously and refused to touch them. My youngest brother, Roger, seemed content and was munching away. However, he was only 3 years old and hadn't refined his palate yet.

My mom walked into the dining room with scorecards in hand. "Okay, now everyone take a card and a pencil." There was a collective groan around the table. My mom sat at the head of the table and recited the questionnaire as if we were judging a fine dining experience.

"How did you find the consistency?"

Steve had his fingers in his mouth. "I think I cut my lip."

She ignored my brother and continued. "And how was the flavor? Linda, what did you think?"

I rolled my eyes like only a 13-year-old girl can do, huffed and said, "It tastes like sawdust."

My mom shot me a side look which hinted I should tone down the attitude or else. I was the oldest and was expected to lead by example. I swirled my tater tot in a path of grease. There wasn't enough ketchup in the world to get me to choke down another bite-sized piece of cardboard.

Mom had the brilliant idea of signing up our family to rate food products. A company sent us free samples in exchange for feedback on their products. Desperate to feed a family of six, my mom thought this was a savvy way to save money. Each family was assigned a different food item, and the options ranged from frozen chicken nuggets to frozen pizza. Unfortunately, we got stuck with frozen tater tots. An entire month of tater tots with dinner. It was enough to put me off the stuff for life.

My mom was the consummate penny pincher. If coupon clipping were a job, she'd win employee of the month every time. She would buy a whole cow at the butcher, split it with the neighbor, and then pack the body parts into the freezer like a morbid game of Tetris. That cow would last us a good six months before we could switch up our dinner menu options.

I'm sure my mom was concerned about money because my dad never had a steady job. Growing up, it was either feast or famine. In good years, we had ski passes, and in bad years, we lived off of hamburger helper. If I had to label my dad's profession, I would say "schemer." He found 21 ways of making money in 21 years. His desk was always covered with construction estimates or figures on his latest project. The majority of his ideas fell through, but it never stopped him from trying. He even tried his hand at trading. In the 1950s, he traded shell eggs based on lunar cycles. He never made any money at it, but he accumulated several books on the markets in his library.

One day after dinner, I slipped into the library hoping not to be summoned for dishwashing duty. I brushed my hand over the books, leaving a clear trail in the dust collected on the jackets until a title caught my eye: *Treasure of Wall Street Wisdom*. Curious. I pulled the book down and opened it up. It contained an exposé of the writings of technicians and traders including Dow, Rhea, Livermore, Gann, Schabacker, and Gartley to name a few. Everything you ever wanted to know about each master's method was summarized in ten pages or less. It was as if the heavens had opened up and the great traders of yesteryear were shouting out, "You can do it! Go forth and make money!" I found the Holy Grail.

I snapped back to reality when I heard Steve yelling for me to come to the family room. This could only mean one thing: game night. My eyes narrowed, and I put my game face on. Every night after dinner, my family circled around the living room to compete in an ultra-competitive game of Hearts, Scrabble, Parcheesi, Sorry, or Mastermind. We were ruthless and we were out for blood. Tonight's game was Scrabble.

Scrabble is not merely a game in the Bradford clan. It is an intense sport of wit and skill that could rival the likes of the Hunger Games. It is our family's form of Darwinism; we use it to weed out the weak links. My mom, Steve, and I positioned ourselves around the sides of the board, with Anne and Roger watching from the sidelines. Roger would eventually turn out to be a fantastic Scrabble player, which is painful to admit. However, at this point in his life, he was more likely to eat the letter tiles than form any high scoring words.

We each drew our seven tiles from the bag. My mom assessed the tiles she pulled. She picked up a few tiles and placed them in the center of the board.

"Prowl, 13 points. Steven, are you keeping score?"

"Yes, Mom."

"Okay, Linda's turn."

Eyeing the P tile, I placed my word horizontally under my mom's. "Pa + Aqua, 18 points."

My mom grinned. "Oh! Very good, Linda. What a clever word. And you used a Q."

I graciously accepted the compliment. I was pleased with my word.

Steve scoffed and puffed out his chest. "Oh yeah? Well, how about this: Za! Triple word, 33 points."

I scowled. "That's not a word, Steve!"

"Yes, it is, *Lin*-duh!"

I jumped up in indignation. "Mooooom!"

"Calm down! Please. As sneaky of a word Za is, it is, in fact, a word. Now sit down. It's my turn."

Steve stuck his tongue out at me while my mom pondered where to play her next word.

"Oh ho ho! Woodcut, 15 points. Thank you." My mom placed her letters vertically under the W tile of her first word and then waved acknowledgment at the imaginary applause.

I stared at my tiles. I was working with the following letters: I, E, S, S, N, T, and V. My mom had set me up perfectly for a triple word score, and I knew I had to take advantage of it before Steve could. V was my highest scoring letter totaling 4 points, so I had to use that letter for sure. I rearranged them a couple times coming up with different words. Vets. Vents. Vests. And then I saw it. I couldn't believe my luck.

"Invests. Nine points, times three because of the triple word score, plus fourteen points for Woodcuts, plus FIFTY bonus points for using all seven tiles, totaling ninety-one points. HA! TAKE THAT, STEVE!"

This is typically how our game nights went. We evolved into more civilized game players, but we still take jabs at each other.

If I wasn't playing board games with my family, then I was practicing the piano. The piano always served as my escape from most things in life. I started at an early age and had become quite accomplished. I enjoyed playing the piano because people paid attention to me. It was difficult to get noticed in a family of four kids. My mom's time was sucked up taking care of my sister who had mental disabilities and my youngest brother who was a caboose. I was pretty much on my own during my teenage years. But I got noticed when I played the piano. I impressed people and beamed when someone paid me a compliment. My piano teacher was a Juilliard graduate, and I was eager to please her. She was the epitome of perfection. She was skinny, elegant, graceful, and a master at playing the piano. I held her in the highest regard.

My mom created endless sources of entertainment which didn't cost very much money. We hiked many of the mountain ridges along the West Coast and spent weeks in the woods with only a pack on our backs. She always found the least populated trails and would push us hard. "Just two more miles," followed by, "just three more switchbacks," followed by, "just over the next ridge," and then finally we could stop and take a break. She wanted to make sure we grew up to be resilient and self-sufficient.

I graduated high school at sixteen years old. This meant I was smart enough to skip a grade but socially inept. I had become a moderately deviant teenager and didn't put much effort into applying for college, so I went to the only school I applied to, Occidental College. I focused my efforts on learning film scoring, determined to be the next John Williams, a prolific American film composer. I loved writing music and was quite good at improvisation.

The first month into college, my parents entered into a bitter divorce. My dad drained the bank account and hid all the money. We stopped talking. Since I didn't have a scholarship, I needed to find a way to pay for school. I found scrappy jobs to fill any available time slot in my day. I worked at the Los Angeles Times as an account clerk during the summer and on weekends, and I landed a job processing grants for a tumor virology lab at USC for a couple of years. I worked on the breakfast line in the cafeteria at 6:00 AM every weekday, taught guitar lessons to pay for my piano lessons, taught music classes at the local church, and worked in the school administrative office during lunch. When I wasn't at work, I was either falling asleep in economics from not getting enough sleep or practicing the piano inside a drab school practice room. I played for six hours at a time, and it served as a retreat from the real world, a place I didn't have to interact with anyone.

In total contrast, my freshman roommate hailed from Chicago where her parents drove matching Rolls Royces and owned four banks. Her name was Bitsy, and she drove a Datsun 260Z. And she had a pony, obviously. My sophomore year roommate was from Beverly Hills and drove a Mercedes Benz with the license plate EXPNSV. She wore Gucci by day and pretended to be into punk rock at night. It never bothered me that I hustled hard to get by. I even felt smug when I bought my own car with the money I made. It was an old, beat up Toyota Corona with a trunk that wouldn't open. The AC didn't work either, which was brutal during summer.

For me, money is a means. Money makes anything possible. My junior year, I had saved up enough to move off campus. I rented the top floor of a house that had its own entrance and patio. I relished my independence in my ultimate new pad.

During my senior year, I got my first taste of making investment decisions. An anonymous donor set up a fund at my college to allow students to make investment decisions. Twelve students served on the board, and we met once a week to discuss the markets. I figured I was eminently qualified from my years of working different jobs, but the truth was I knew little about the markets. The father of one of the students was the largest specialist on the floor of the American

Stock Exchange. That student knew more than all of us combined. He took the helm in a quiet, unassuming manner.

The markets were weak during this period. The great recession of 1979 intensified when oil embargoes took hold and interest rates went through the roof. Gas lines and whether you had an even number or odd number license plate were the topics *du jour*. It wasn't any fun investing in stocks that year, but we managed to keep our heads above water. My experience with the Charles R. Blyth Fund was my main credential from college, and I hoped to parlay it into something more significant in San Francisco. My dad may have deserted me during my first year of college, but I was determined to show him that I did not need him. I was going to figure out how to be successful and make lots of money, and it was partly out of spite.

I may not have found initial success on the Pacific Exchange, but that was only the first chapter in my book. Literally.

5

LAND OF CHEESESTEAKS

I flew out to New York to finally meet Morris face to face. I had no idea what to expect because, for the last 18 months, he had resembled a beige phone with a long curlicue cord attached. Morris turned out to be handsomely rugged with a shaggy beard, deep brown eyes, and thick wavy hair that had not been cut for awhile. Khaki Bermuda shorts and Sperry Topsiders were set off by a wide grin. His walls were lined with pictures of himself sailing solo on his sixty-foot sailboat, windsurfing boards, and an ergonomic toilet seat he had designed. Credentials included not only architecture and engineering degrees, but also an MBA from Harvard. The cherry on top was the fact he drove around in a red Porsche. I was happy I hadn't previously met Morris before we started working together. We usually spent the day yelling at each other over the phone and this picture would have ruined those calls. Morris and I ended up having a long friendship. He was one of my first investors when I became a Commodity Trading Advisor.

I took a day trip to Philadelphia to meet another one of Morris's traders. He had traded on the Philadelphia Exchange (PHLX) for two years, so we commiserated about working for Morris. My initial impression of Philadelphia was that it was a compact, well laid out city where every alley smelled of trash and urine. There was a ton of brick, decay, and cheese-steaks. It had not gone through its revival phase yet.

A good percentage of the traders on the PHLX were Irish, Italian, or Jewish. There was a noticeable absence of California surfer chicks. The female clerks on the floor were Italian. Black, bouffant hair framed their makeup-caked faces. Their long, sharp, red fingernails click-clacked as they typed up the filled orders. On breaks, cigarettes hung from their full lips, creating a thick fog outside the entrance to the floor. This place was the complete opposite of where I came from. I was Alice jumping feet first through the looking glass.

Morris's trader was super busy that day, so I did not get to spend any time with him. Instead, I spent the majority of my time sitting upstairs at the office of my clearing firm, First Options of Chicago. While hanging out killing time, I ran into another trader I had met back in San Francisco.

"You ever think about moving to the East Coast?"

"I don't know. I never thought about it before. I've only lived in California."

"Well, if you're serious about trading, you should consider moving to Philadelphia. There's a lot more action on the floor here than in San Francisco. You gotta go where the volumes are." He took a bite of an apple, winked at me and walked out of the room. At that moment, I decided to move to Philadelphia. Knowing a couple of familiar faces made a move seem possible, and I was determined to make it as a great trader.

Nobody ever understood how I could give up the land of sunshine and beaches for a city marked by decaying warehouses and gloomy skies. But, California held nothing but bad memories, and I was ready for a change of scenery. I went back home to pack up my life and move to Philadelphia. On my last night, my mom and I went to a bar to listen to some music. In the corner of the room, there was a sign which read "Palm Readings $5." Whenever we're in a transition period in our lives, we turn anywhere to find answers. What does it all mean? Am I making the right choice? I don't want to know exactly what my future holds, but I'd feel an enormous sense of relief if someone could give me a sign it was all going to be okay.

Philadelphia…here I come.

Usually, psychics are portrayed as haggard women with long, curly gray hair staring intensely into a crystal ball. My psychic came to me in another form. His name was Lance, and he was fabulous. Lance looked like he was ready to hit an underground rave in a warehouse outside the city. He spoke with a slight lisp and took my palm into his.

"Ohhh, ye *th*, honey! You are about to *th*tart a new chapter in your life and by the look of it, you are going to be wildly *th*-uc-*th*-e-*th*-ful."

I stared at him incredulously. "I'm going to be wildly what?"

"*Th*-uc-*th*-e-*th*-ful, honey! You're going to be *th*-uc-*th*-e-*th*-ful!"

Lance desperately wanted me to understand the impact of his words. It took me a second to register what he said. "Oh! Successful! I'm going to be wildly successful!"

"Ye*th*!"

The gay psychic told me I was going to make it big and I believed him.

6

LESSONS FROM PHILLY

I settled into my new apartment in Philadelphia. The modest brick loft-style barely accommodated a roommate. My one contribution to the furniture was a futon which served as my bed and a couch when needed. I unpacked my suitcase, filled to the brim with variations of my preferred uniform: J. Crew shirt, Eddy Bauer vest, and sturdy Rockport shoes. The classic style centered around comfort and efficiency. I wasn't trying to win any beauty contests on the floor.

Morris didn't need another trader in Philadelphia, so I set out to find a new backer.

My ad read like the dating section of the newspaper:

"Looking for financing: Blond, female trader with Twiggy haircut and preppy style. Can hold her own in an aggressive crowd, has strong vocal cords, and is quick with numbers. Already blown out once and promises not to do it again."

A group of three backers decided to take a chance on me. This proved to be an interesting dynamic since each trader had their own distinct style. Jerry headed up the gang. He rarely talked and had been a Master Bridge player who worked as a physicist during the day. He resembled a stereotypical scientist—ruddy complexion, dark-rimmed glasses, and Poindexter hair with a deep part on the side. I learned a great deal from watching Jerry and considered him to be my silent mentor. If it were not for the routines and rituals I observed him following, I probably would not be in the business today.

Jerry led by example. You could find him deep in concentration in the clearing firm's office two hours before the market opened. He looked like a monk meditating on the markets. His eyes focused on a different world far, far away. He always had an uncanny ability to think three steps ahead of everyone else in the room. His daily preparation was meticulous, and it paid off.

Before the days of electronic execution platforms, our stock orders went to a clerk on the sidelines who phoned them over to the brokers on the NYSE or AMEX. As pit traders in Philadelphia filled the order flow from the brokers, they had to run over to the side of the floor to place stock orders to hedge their options positions. But Jerry had the system figured out. He wrote out his tickets ahead of time for different stocks so they would be resting in the market when he was in the options pit. This way, he never had to leave the crowd and risk missing a trade.

Jerry was always the last person to leave at the end of the day. At night, he scoured the order books on individual stocks. In those days, you could see the resting orders parked on the books on the trading floor. He looked for the low priced "teeny" options that nobody wanted because it was unlikely they would ever be worth anything. A "teeny" was 1/16 of a point during an era when stocks traded in 1/8ths instead of pennies. Jerry did not expect these options to be worth much, but he explained how these low-priced, out-of-the-money options were used to sell the high-priced fat options safely if a stock ever came to life from a rumor on the street. It was like a kind of insurance policy.

It is the time spent on preparation outside the regular trading hours that makes a trader successful.

Jerry's partner, Nate, was the total opposite in character—short and talkative. A real people person. He quipped tidbits of Jewish wisdom to me, "Buy wholesale, sell retail, and if they don't come for your inventory, mark it down and move it out the door." Options were treated like inventory from a luggage store. We watched the SPs together on the upstairs Quotron. He pointed out the psychology of placing offers one or two ticks below and bids one or two ticks above the big, round numbers. The SPs traded in nickels, and a full-size contract was $500 a point. If the SPs were trading at 520.45, I would place a bid at 520.05 to buy and offer at 520.95 to sell. This was the start of learning the psychology of where to place orders to get the best fills.

Wisdom from Nate: Be pragmatic in how you run your business. Set emotions aside and do what you need to do.

My backers' lectures were usually about things I did not want to hear. One Saturday morning, Jerry and Nate told me to meet them in the office of the clearing firm. This was never a good sign. Earlier that week, I was on the receiving end of a lecture on the dangers of getting too big of a position on in any one options series.

It was a given that the traders in a particular pit were going to have similar positions. The order flow tended to be one way, unlike the futures markets. For example, if a customer was selling option premiums against a long-term stock position, the traders were the ones who had to buy the options. Holding excess long inventory was a problem because there was nobody to sell it to other than the trader standing next to you. He was just as anxious to get rid of his long inventory. If you were long call options, you had no choice but to short stock against them to hedge your position. It forced you to become adept at trading stock against your position to make up for the time decay. Otherwise, you might as well hang up a noose.

Jerry and Nate went through every single order which traded in my pit on Friday. They wanted to know why I had not participated in certain transactions to reduce my position size. *I was in the bathroom? No, that isn't going to fly.* I had not made enough of an effort to take part in the smaller transactions. Jerry looked disappointed. Even though he was a man of few words, I always knew when he disapproved of something. He would purse his lips and furrow his eyebrows. Jerry sighed and said, "It is never a problem getting into a market. It is always a problem getting out when you *need* to."

This was one of the most important lessons of my career. I encountered this issue in many markets over the next three decades.

Never get so big that you can't get out when you need to.

Liquidity is one of the fundamentals of trading. Traders think the game is about the conditions to get into a market, but you can get into most markets at any time. Always make sure there is an exit. You don't want to get stuck trying to get the last high price, so leave the last 5% for someone else. Once a market turns, liquidity vanishes. You need to have a market to sell into. And you don't want to be that person selling Beanie Babies in 2018.

Disappearing liquidity has been many smart traders' undoing. One of the most famous examples is Long-Term Capital Management. It was a hedge fund with two well-known Nobel Prize-winning economists on the board of directors. LTCM used extreme leverage to engage in arbitrage strategies. When the Russian government defaulted on bonds in 1998, LTCM got squeezed. There was no market to reduce the size of their arbitrage position and ultimately, the FED organized a bailout. But it was too late to save the investors who saw their equity drop from $4.7 billion at the start of the year to $400 million.

* * *

I made markets in a stock called Amerada Hess and the company's CEO, Leon Hess, was always supposedly on the verge of dying. Rumors of President Reagan getting shot were rampant. Scuttlebutt created short-lived fervor and caused speculators to overpay. The public was overly optimistic about a stock's prospects for the day. They wanted options at any price immediately at the opening bell. The enthusiasm was strongest at the opening as the public bid the price way above fair market value. We called this period "The Opening Bulge." The specialist in my pit used to smile and say, "Take the cookies when they pass the plate around." The cookies were the profits from retail customers overpaying.

The cookie plate isn't passed around every day, so when the trading is good, keep going. You don't want to stop because you have made a specified amount of money. A trader also has to know when to "tee it up, trade extra heavy, and use a full line." Most of the time trading opportunities are marginal, but it's important to maintain some level of activity on modest size, keeping risk low. By engaging in a nominal amount of trades, a trader gets information from the market. How weak is the decline? Where does support come in? Are the reactions shallow or deep? What is the volume and overall interest in the market? Then when a rare window of opportunity presents itself, you are in a position to trade aggressively.

When traders think about money management, they think about stops and trade management. But a big part of the equation is knowing when to go all in, increase the leverage and press your trading to the hilt. *Load the boat.* These opportunities have an increase in volume and volatility. There is no point in actively trading in a dull market. Let the market tip its hand and come to life first. And then if you are fortunate to be in the groove and know you've got a tiger by the tail, milk it for all it is worth. This is where the real money is made. A trader only needs a few great days a month, so "Take those cookies when they come your way."

When the market gives you an opening, capitalize on it.

Everyone got along well on the floor in Philadelphia. During lunch, someone would bring a copy of the New York Times crossword puzzle and we would all give it a try. I sucked at it and was utterly mystified how the usually crass traders had such eloquent vocabularies. I mostly only heard four-letter words come out of their mouths.

The one thing which separated the West Coast from the East Coast was the pranks. Mischief makers taped paper tails made from order tickets onto the back of trading jackets. Baby powder was sprinkled on an unsuspecting trader's shoes. A clerk's phone handle was covered with Vaseline. When trade volumes were low and traders were bored, anything went.

The worst thing I ever witnessed on the floor involved a giant, flying cockroach. The Exchange wasn't the cleanest place to work. Occasionally you saw one of these creepy-crawlers scuttle across the ground. One slow-moving morning, a trader named Mike caught a cockroach in a jar and dared a clerk named Harry to eat it. Harry took one look at the critter and said, "For enough money, I'll eat it." Lifeless traders jumped to their feet. Finally, something interesting to throw money at. We passed a hat around collecting loose bills to entice Harry to choke the sucker down. The excitement was built half on intrigue and half on disgust. Mike took the hat and began counting the cash. "$900! Harry, will you eat the cockroach for $900?" Harry looked at the money, grabbed the jar, and chomped down. The crowd roared. A couple traders bent over like they were going heave. Mike called out, "That was the best thing I bid on all day! I'm going home."

On the other end of the spectrum, tensions ran high when markets were swinging. Fines for bad behavior did little to curb fighting. Quarrels broke out when there were disagreements on who should get the trade

"Fuck you," said the slighted trader.

"No, fuck you, mother fucker," said the offending trader.

"No. Fuck you!"

Then one trader grabs the other guy by his tie and lifts him up as if to hang him. The crowd makes the noise a gathering of people does when drama unfolds. A few rows back, a wizened older trader sighs.

"Floor official, please!"

Trading halts for two minutes as the official trots over to the pit. It was like a hockey game where referees tried to keep high sticking and tripping to a minimum.

It seems like all traders use the F word in a million different contexts, just as someone would pepper their speech with "umm" or "like." Other words were considered uncouth, but fuck was part of the *lingua franca.*

Floor traders were a funny breed. The ones who whined about their bad trades were usually the ones who made the most money. The way they spoke made it sound as if they were losing tons of money every day. It was a contest; who got screwed the most on their stock fills? Who lost the most amount of money on options decay while they were away on vacation? It was unspoken bad juju to mention winning trades. If a trader was making great money, they kept a perfect poker face. If someone did happen to mention a winning trade, it was usually because they had so few wins. Their ego wanted the world to know they managed to make at least one. To this day I remain skeptical of anyone who brags about their trades or profits.

One of the best brokers on the floor was a massively tall fellow by the dubious nickname of "Bogsy." Everyone liked Bogsy, despite his picking the traders off. One day he walked back into the pit with his jaw hanging down to his knees and a long face that was chalk white.

"Guys—um um um…." Awkward pause. "I made an error. Can you let me out?" Oops. 500 options contracts had changed hands with 15 traders in the pit." This was a large trade and an expensive mistake. When a broker makes an error, he is responsible for making up the loss to his client. The broker has all the downside risk and none of the upside profit opportunity. He only makes commissions. The traders in the pit had already hedged the trade with stock, making it complicated to unwind the error. A trader known for adding a bit of levity to the situation turned and stared him down. "BARK LIKE A DOG." The crowd turned and nodded in agreement. This was the last thing Bogsy would ever do—he was an in your face type of broker. He was squirming. The sweat was dripping down his brow. His eyes darted left and then right. There was no escape. He sucked in his breath and let out a long, slow deep "WOOOOOOOOOOF." The crowd let him out of his error even though I am sure it cost each of them to do so. It was worth hearing Bogsy give a big Woof.

Humor keeps your spirits up even when your account is going down.

The PHLX floor proved to be yet another chapter in my continuing education about outliers. An outlier is something which comes as a surprise or is outside of our normal expectations. Statistically, it is a data point which is outside the expected range for value. Outliers are "rare events," which Nassim Taleb has christened *black swans*.

There is a quote from the movie *Guys and Dolls*, "One of these days in your travels, a guy is going to show you a brand-new deck of cards on which the seal is not yet broken. Then this guy is going to offer to bet you that he can make the Jack of Spades jump out of this brand-new deck of cards and squirt cider in your ear. But, son, do not accept this bet, because as sure as you stand there, you're going to end up with an ear full of cider."

In the eighties, there was an arbitrage strategy that proved too good to be true.

"Boxes" are an arbitrage strategy that involves buying a call spread along with the corresponding bear spread, or in the case of shorting the box, selling both spreads. This was a popular strategy when interest rates were high. The trader who sold the box collected the interest on the amount that was credited to his account. At the time, boxes were considered to be as low risk on the totem pole of strategies as one could get.

There were a few traders on the floor who made their entire living putting on boxes and locking in an eighth of an edge. One day in Conoco, the 5 point boxes were sellable at 5.25. It was like free money. The next day they started trading at 5.75. Excited traders seeing a slam dunk sale hollered, "Sold!" (Thinking they would be worth 5 at expiration). They put on their maximum positions. But the buyers came back the following day and were willing to pay 7.5 for more–all day long. This was totally contrary to a mathematical understanding of option arbitrage. I know of one trader who ended up covering all his boxes when they started trading at 9. A few days later Conoco was taken over in a two-part deal, mainly with cash, but with a backend "stub" stock that still used the puts. The boxes that would have been worth 5 points at expiration went to 12. Many traders got blown out on that because they then had to buy their positions back at the obscenely higher price.

The math was clear but did not include all the information in the system. Quant traders who rely on math continually get killed if they overleverage their expertise in math.

This two-tier tender deal was a new phenomenon. An offer is made to buy a controlling interest in the stock at a higher price, and the balance of shares is purchased later at a lower price. Nobody was thinking outside the box—literally.

There is no such thing as a risk-free arb. Straight-line thinking often proves to be a trap.

This was a striking reminder of how the theoretical world and the real world differ.

One of the great benefits of being on the floor in the early eighties was that you received your Ph.D. in trading at warp speed. Right off the bat, you learned who would and would not survive. Traders who had been in the business for at least three years were likely to stay in business. The others fell by the wayside through the revolving door of Darwinism. I was lucky enough to observe the common denominator of those who survived.

I learned from watching one of the savvier traders, Jeff Yass. Jeff had a towering presence in every room he walked into. He was tall, stiff, and almost frighteningly smart; he was a tremendously successful trader and a skilled poker player. There was gossip that he would memorize the closing prices in over 100 stocks at the end of each day. I watched him on a day where there was a significant pickup in activity. The implied volatility (part of the premium) on the options started creeping higher. The crowd grew, and the boat people migrated over towards the action. The air thickened and the decibel level soared. Jeff was selling the options along with the other traders. The historical range of the implied volatility on the options was 18 – 24. The crowd was selling 24 implied volatility. The next day, the implied volatility jumped to 26. Jeff walked into the pit and aggressively bid for options. This didn't make any sense to me. He had sold the options at 24 "vol" the previous day. Now he was paying 26, a level that appeared to be theoretically overvalued. It took me a few years to understand what Jeff was doing. When there is an established historical range for prices or relationships, it's natural to want to buy the lower end of the range and sell at the upper end of the range. "Buy wholesale, sell retail." But if something starts pushing outside its historical range, there is a good reason why. The market is imparting powerful information.

Most people don't know how to interpret the information the market shares with them. Markets are all about supply and demand. Stay positioned in the direction of the supply or demand imbalance, especially if it is pushing outside its historical range. This is the same thing as buyers paying above fair value for the boxes. There was a reason why but the traders did not know what it was at the time. It is more comfortable to hold on to what makes sense instead of accepting the seemingly irrational price action.

Aberrations are seen as something that falls outside of the norm or what is expected. Since it is usually an atypical event, most people think that it should be ignored or discounted. This might be true with certain types of modeling. For example, the Chernobyl explosion in 1986 led to extreme gaps in the agriculture markets that would have distorted the results in many systematic strategies. It was an outlier event that generated a one-time price shock.

However, the types of aberrations that generate profits for savvy traders are the ones that reflect a change in a relationship. In 1999, PE ratios were thought to be too high for many of the newly formed tech companies. The levels were well above the historical norm. But, in this case, it was not a sign of overvaluation. The rising trend of the PE ratios was the market placing a value on their future business. The early high readings led to a 1 ½ year parabolic rise in their stock prices.

When the 10-year treasury yields dropped below 3% for the first time in over 60 years, most traders had never seen this before. It was widely regarded as an aberration. Rates were well below their historical norm. Government debt levels were rising, and this was seen as a shorting opportunity in bonds and notes. But instead, yields went lower and stayed low for the next 9 years, frustrating bond bears. The reasons as to why this happened came out later after the fact.

If positive economic news is released and the market sells off on that news, this could also be perceived as an aberration. It is a divergence from what would normally be expected. But this, too, is the market's way of imparting powerful information. In this case, it may be that there are no buyers left, or that the news has long been discounted.

Trade in the direction of the aberration. The market is never too high to buy nor too low to sell.

7

PIPELINE TO GOD

I loved trading the SP futures. Each pit had a Quotron off to the side where a trader could stand at the edge of the crowd and call up quotes on other markets. It had a button called "Fast Quote." Every time I punched it, an updated reading of the Ticks flashed. Ticks are the net number of NYSE stocks which last traded on an up or down tick. They updated 2-3 times a minute back in the early eighties, but now I could update them every few seconds. When the market was falling and getting oversold, I hit the key repeatedly until I saw the ticks stop going down. At that point, I bought the SPs "at the market," and they bounced back up a few points. Stocks traded in 1/8s. Even if a small percentage of shares up-ticked one tick, it was enough to bounce the SPs a few points.

I learned how to trade the OEX index options by watching another astute trader, Ron. He was one of those traders you swore had a pipeline to God. He was a phenomenal tape reader. The funny thing about Ron was that he only liked to trade the market from the short side. I watched him trade from the short side for the next 10 years, making good money even when stocks were in an extended bull run. His secret was he was very selective about his entry spots, and he did not fight the tape when there was momentum.

With the OEX options, a trader still needed to time the entry and the exit well. Ron put on his position before the market turned and took them off before the swing ended. If you did not do this, then once the market turned, the option market makers "leaned" in the new direction. This meant you had to pay an extra 1/8th, hit the bid to sell, or buy the offer to cover or go long. A trader ended up paying too much "vig." "Vigorish" is the name for the spread plus commissions.

Ron liked to short the morning rallies. He followed the price action up until it stopped rising. Then he put his shorts out, often holding until the end of the day. There was always a protective stop resting in the market.

"How do you know where to put in a stop?" I asked.

"How much money do you want to lose?" he answered.

Never risk more than you want to lose. This sounds obvious, but traders have an infinite capacity to surprise. There is no one magic level. Ron's generic but practical response remains the best answer for discretionary traders.

For a short period, I made markets in the options on the Value Line index. The OEX is an index of 100 stocks, but the Value Line index had 1700 stocks. It is weighted differently as well. The OEXs had become such a popular product on the Chicago Board of Options Exchange (CBOE). We were excited when the PHLX (Philadelphia Stock Exchange) got approval to list the Value Line Options. I had been trading the OEX options and the SP futures for quite a while. I liked to tape read and make directional day trades in the market. I was looking forward to trading index options on our exchange. But I learned the hard way the Value Line options did not trade anything like the OEXs.

On one expiration, the call options were trading around 50 cents a minute before the closing bell. It looked like they were going to go out worthless. The index was still a full point lower than the strike price. A big order came in on the close to buy two thousand. Our job, of course, was to fill this order and I sold them along with the rest of the traders. After all, the market was now closed. But options continue to trade for another 15 minutes after the underlying index or stock has closed. I watched in horror as the closing bell rang. The expiration settlement price on the Value Line Index crept up... and up... and up... FIVE FULL POINTS! The options I sold at 50 cents were now worth $4.50 on expiration! OUCH. A sale of 100 options led to a $40,000 loss in just a few minutes, and there was nothing one could do about it. They were exercised into cash, so it was a double ouch.

The reason the Value Line index behaved like this was due to the fact there were 1700 small stocks equally weighted. All someone had to do to manipulate the index was place a large number of market orders for 100 shares each in several hundred of the stocks. If enough of them jumped an eighth of a point, it goosed the index by a significant amount. As a stock index settles, the final marking of the prices is called the expiration "runoff." It was not long before the regulatory agencies staggered the time of day for expiration on different products. That type of manipulation could no longer take place, but not before it had extracted a bit of my blood.

My initial reaction in these instances tended to be total disbelief. I'd stand in the pit after it closed, mouth open, jaw down to my knees. What can one do? The damage was done. If I had looked at my bottom line, I might have been too depressed to trade the next day. So instead I put my nose to the grindstone and concentrated extra hard. A few days later when I thought I had recouped the losses, I decided it was safe to peek to see what the actual damage had been. Opening my account statements in a sheltered corner where nobody could see,

I breathed a sigh of relief knowing that the account balance was back up. The detour had cost me an extra three days of trading efforts.

All lessons were learned the hard way.

One weekend when I was 14, my parents left for the weekend, leaving me in charge of my three younger siblings. To keep us from getting into trouble, they assigned a long list of yard work. We lived on a corner lot surrounded on three sides by streets. On the other side of the main road was the Arroyo Seco canyon. It was a kid's paradise for building tree forts and rope swings and catching pollywogs in the wash below. My mom had an affinity for roses and a knack for growing them; she would pick gorgeous roses for the house, but I can't think of a plant I hated more. My brother and I had to weed between the bushes and thorns. When she and my dad turned into maniacs with the electric hedge clippers, we picked up the branches. More chores included pulling crabgrass out of the ivy which surrounded three sides of the house—a two-day job. Picking up poisonous oleander branches and raking up the clippings from the miles of hedges were on the list as well.

This weekend, I got to be the hedge clipper queen. My job was to prune the trellis and vines running up the side of the house. It was a typical Los Angeles sunny day and I was working barefoot in my bikini. You can't ever pass up a chance to work on your tan when you're a teenager! I could not quite reach the top of this trellis and was too lazy to go into the garage and retrieve the ladder. I blithely pulled over the patio chair and stepped out onto the patio table against the side of the house, right into the middle so I could reach those top vines with my lethal weapon in hand. The patio table was made of tempered glass, all the rage in Southern California in the seventies. BAM! The gunshot sound of glass shattering echoed around the neighborhood.

"Steeeeeeeeeeeve!" I was sitting nearly naked on the concrete patio, surrounded by glass, and thinking it best not to move. My brother was on the far side of the property, and it took a few hollers before he came running. "Run down the street and get Dr. Matthias," our neighbor who was the Dean of USC medical school. Overkill, I know, but he was the only one around with a car since my parents were out of town. He gingerly lifted me out of the shattered glass and whisked me away to the emergency room. They stitched up the palm of my hand, a slice which was ½ an inch away from a major artery. All I remember was feeling a bit stunned I had been stupid enough to step onto the middle of a glass table.

Later in life, bad trades gave me a feeling of *déjà vu* that invoked that day on the patio: stupefied, surrounded by shattered glass, wondering, "How did that happen?"

* * *

The SMR (Security Market Research) charts for stocks and futures arrived on Saturday mornings. There was a particular pattern I was keen on—a divergence in the oscillator on a chart which fell within a specific period. This pattern had been lucrative for me on many of the stocks I traded. I was very particular about this formation. The divergence had to be 8-12 bars apart. Someone had told me 21 days made up a market cycle and half of a period set up the best divergences. I bought call or put spreads and exited 3-4 days later when the stock or market had a reaction.

One day this pattern unfolded in the Palladium market. I had never traded Palladium. I told Rick, the clerk who called in our futures orders to the other exchanges, to buy ten Palladium futures for my account.

Conversation with myself: "Hey, do you like bungee jumping? Hmm, haven't tried it before. I'll give it a go!"

My unbridled enthusiasm for trying new things often got me into trouble.

The next day, Palladium opened down limit. There was wicked overnight news about catalytic converters. "Down Limit" means the future market is down the maximum amount allowed on the day. Trading is halted at the limit down price. This was my first trade in the Palladium market. Could I not have waited one more day to jump?

Down limit is a bad scenario for any traders who are long. There is nobody to sell to, and the market is usually going lower the following day. Losing trades seemed to happen to me 99% of the time I made a trade in a new market or a new system. All the research in the world can't make up for real-life learning experiences. In this particular case, I scrambled to hedge in the cash market, for an extra price of course.

It's never a problem getting into a market; it's always a problem getting out when you need to. Rinse, repeat.

With all the funny goings-on in the 1980's—rumors and takeovers, Pac Man and Game Boys, I never got lucky and caught a windfall from a stock. It was not until 12 years of trading that the market finally delivered a gift. I was still updating my SMR charts by hand (except Palladium, which I permanently took off my trading list). It was June of 1993 and soybeans had my favorite 3/10 oscillator buy divergence. Nobody told me you are not supposed to buy Soybeans at the end of June. The seasonal trend is down due to harvest pressures. Nor did I know anything about how bad the fundamentals were. I did not know any better. I bought call option spreads, then outright calls, and eventually the futures as well. It was my version of the Texas hedge: long in the field and long in the futures market.

The next few days, rains began in earnest and the Mississippi River flooded. It was impossible to move the crop down the river where buyers waited at the other end. The product is sent on barges to be exported. With no supply available at the bottom of the Mississippi, beans proceeded to trade limit up for several days. It was pure luck. For the first time in my life, I was on the right side of an outlier. A benefactor of randomness in a cruel and unpredictable world. Profiting from a horrible flood on the Mississippi River! After holding positions in hundreds of stocks, I had never been on the right side of a takeover or gift. My windfall in the soybeans felt like pulling the handle on a casino slot machine and watching coins spray out faster than I could grab them. *Ka-ching!*

After that, I adopted the philosophy that trading has little to do with brains because overthinking mucks things up. Instead, it was about positioning yourself so that, once in a while, you might get lucky.

At the end of the day, it all comes down to staying in the game.

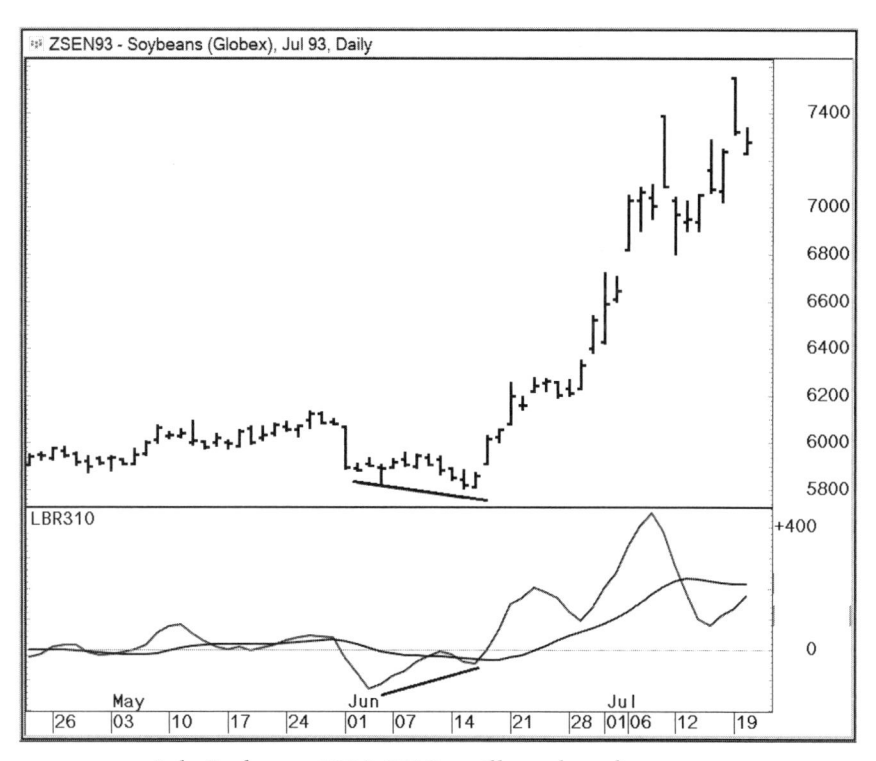

July Soybeans-1993 3/10 oscillator buy divergence.

8

UPSTAIRS TRADER

Independence was top of my value list, probably why not many guys came up to me outside of a business or platonic relationship. No guy wants a girlfriend who does not need him. It takes a pretty strong guy to be around that type of person. But, everyone wants to lend a helping hand to a kid sister! No complications or baggage. Ideal.

However, I did eventually end up getting hitched to another trader on the floor. He was the resident floor prankster, organizer of the fantasy football leagues, and comrade to everyone. His popularity was due to his endless storytelling, especially about when he pitched for the Yankees in the minor leagues and his love of sports. I fell into the pack and loved to be included as one of the good old boys.

We bought a fixer-upper townhouse on a lake in South Jersey. Cornfields and old cow barns peppered our daily commute to the train. How much did it cost to keep a horse at one of these old barns? Surely it could not be much! 1986 had been an excellent year. I had made the last payment to my clearing firm to clear my City Service debt. I made enough money to go out on my own and trade for myself. A ten-ton weight had been lifted off my shoulders and, to celebrate, I decided to buy a horse. It was my dream as a little girl to own a pony. Growing up in Los Angeles, horses only existed in the gray area between fantasy unicorns and summer camp hacks. Guys might take delight in riding dirt bikes, but girls can fly on a horse with wings.

Fate would have it that I had an accident on the first horse I tried when the bit broke in its mouth. This is like having the brakes go out on the Ferrari you are test driving on a track. Idyllic visions of me cantering through wildlife preserves were replaced by sterile blue curtains drawn around a bed in the emergency room. The sound of racing hoof beats was drowned out by the unearthly screams of a little boy with severe body burns from playing with matches. My muffled moans from fractured ribs and a punctured lung did not capture the same attention, so I laid there waiting.

This was a crash course introduction to my lifestyle for my good-natured new husband. He was also a floor trader on the PHLX, whom I had bumped into while still in San Francisco.

"Hi."

"Hello."

"How are you?"

"Good, and you?"

"Good, good."

"Well, good to see you! Good-bye."

That was the extent of our first conversation. He moved to Philadelphia from the sunshine state, another unexplainable migration from California. The first day I traded on the PHLX, the guys in his pit held up score cards rating me. Of course, I did not find this out until years later. On the floor, I kept my name Bradford, and he was Raschke. It could have been confusing otherwise.

He didn't mind that I went into the country to ride every few weeks, but this accident made my nontraditional pursuits a lot more real.

Husband: "What? Did you say my wife is in the emergency room? I thought she was out riding a horse."

Husband: "Which hospital did you say this was?"

Husband: "Really? This is not a joke?"

Husband: "Alright, well I can't come out there until after the markets close."

No amount of morphine was going to help the poor little boy. His screams persisted, and I closed my eyes, knowing I could not rewind this tape. I sometimes wonder—if we could have *one* day to start over again, which day would it be? Would we save that get out of jail free card for when we make a terrible trade? Or would we keep it for when there was a case of physical harm? Or, would we use it for someone else? I decided I would not waste it on this accident.

As my husband left the trading floor that afternoon, the rumor mill on the floor started whirring. "Did you hear, she fell off a horse!"

I separated my right shoulder too, so there went trading on the floor for a while. It seemed ridiculous: a newly-successful female trader could no longer trade on the floor because, instead of buying a Porsche, she tried to buy a horse. And promptly fell off.

I started trading from upstairs, but nothing was going to keep me from getting a horse now. I was more determined than ever.

Two months later with a foot of snow on the ground, a three-year-old thoroughbred packed me around with my shoulder still in a sling. "Yup, she seems safe enough, I'll take her." Who hops up on an unknown young racehorse in February with their arm still in a sling? My decision-making process was always "leap and then look." This bit me in the butt more than a few times later in life.

Leaving the trading floor turned out to be a blessing in disguise. I had to adapt to trading "upstairs" in my clearing firm's offices. Years later when electronic trading replaced the pits with screens, floor traders were unable to make the transition off the floor. Trading from upstairs meant keeping my eyes glued to the corner of the wall in the office. There hung a Quotron monitor peppered with 300 quotes. We did not have charts. I kept everything by hand, usually a chicken scratch line chart of the intra-day SPs along with periodic readings of the market internals. This proved to be time-consuming. But it was a fabulous exercise in tape reading and keeping mental roadmaps in one's head. Every five minutes I jotted down the SP and bond prices, the Ticks and Trin (Arms index), the advancing and declining issues (breadth), and the QCHA (the unweighted average percentage gain of NYSE stocks). This, along with my line chart, helped me to capture 2-3 intraday swings each day. I believe a trader develops a better feel after doing these types of exercises by hand.

I also traded the bonds around the early morning economic numbers. In the eighties, they set up a "fade the news trade" more often than not. As the markets have evolved and become more efficient, a trader must be careful about when to fade news spikes and when not to. I learned a lot from being upstairs because I could hear the order fill reports over the loudspeaker in my clearing firm's office. "*Trader X, you sold ten bonds at xyz price.*" Of course, I did not know if they were initiating or exiting a position. But it was enlightening to observe the timing of orders executed at the extreme of a swing, that moment of pause before the prices react in the opposite direction.

The markets entered "creeper mode" in the summer of 1987. The DOW finally took out 2400 and was grinding higher. A low volatility trend is the worst type of environment for a trader. There is always the temptation to pick a top. These types of moves don't let anyone in. At the same time, the market never gets so overbought that a reaction down unfolds. A rising market with low volatility is usually a sign of a super strong trend, so I try to avoid these markets. Newer traders get frustrated by the lack of opportunity and dips and short into these types of rallies too soon. But the last 10% of the move can go parabolic as people begin to chase for fear of being left out. Eventually, the market ends in a buying climax which squeezes out any premature shorts. I did not want to be around in this type of environment, so, I took two months off to train with my horse.

I was having a great time—it was the best year of my life. I got married, I bought a house and a horse, I was debt-free, and trading was good. I began an internship with a horse trainer. The horse I purchased after my accident was a race track reject, a three-year-old thoroughbred. Neither of us had any idea what we were doing. In Los Angeles, I had never known anyone who owned a horse.

I was galloping around the cornfields, my fingers tightly wound around the silky black mane. The evening wind was whipping at my neck and all memories of the trading day were gone. Racing hooves and pounding hearts and my horse's heavy breathing were all that filled the air.

Dusk was approaching, and I urged my horse on, trying to squeeze in an extra two laps around the hills. I hated to see the sun slip down on the horizon.

Proudly posing with my scrawny 3-year old racetrack reject.

My mind was blank other than hoping my horse did not stumble at our breakneck pace. Growing up in Los Angeles, I never would have guessed that I would one day be racing around New Jersey fields on my own horse.

Naiveté can open you up to a whole world of opportunities because you are too ignorant to know that something is not supposed to be possible.

9

OOPS!

I kept an eye on the market enough to catch some of the short side in September but had no idea of what was yet to come. The market had entered nebulous territory. Each morning from the barn, I called into the exchange to stay in touch with the markets.

One morning, my husband called me from the exchange, "You better get home. The market is gapping down big time."

"How big?"

"I don't know what is going on, but you might want to get home ASAP."

It was about a 15-minute drive back to my house, assuming no traffic and me breaking the speed limit.

Up to this point, the market had rallied 44% since the beginning of the year. There was not much cash left on the sidelines and the previous month displayed the classic deterioration typical of an overbought market. A new phenomenon was introduced the prior year—portfolio insurance. This was a dynamic hedging strategy designed to sell futures as prices dropped. It hedged an investor's portfolio against losses (in theory, of course). What it did instead was to create a "positive feedback loop," forcing prices lower and then selling more futures. It did not start the fire, but it sure poured gasoline on the flames.

Traders flock to volatility like moths to artificial light. I rushed home to where I now had my home trading setup: one Quotron screen and a phone line. Friday had closed weak. Typically, if the margin calls that were sent had not been met, an extra bit of liquidation occurred mid-morning. Then once this was out of the way, a reaction back up would unfold. The SPs hit a point where they were at a 20-handle discount. They had undone one year of gains in a few hours. "Buy Wholesale, Sell Retail," right? But, this was not a normal day.

For weeks I was patient, waiting for a market selloff to provide a buying opportunity. After a few hours, I started buying. Soon, my trading profits for the year were coming undone as well. I managed to lose five months of earnings in five hours. My eyes could not believe the prices in the stocks. My primary stock, Salomon Brothers, used to trade in the 34 – 38 range and it was now selling at 21. Yikes! Even in a drama-ridden world, this was unheard of.

It felt like a bomb had gone off flattening the landscape around it. Haunting stories about the crash of 1929 with stocks thrown away at fire-sale prices flashed through my mind. When the SPs ended the day at a significant discount, I bought more on the close. The basis for the trade was still there—the considerable discount to the underlying index. Accounts that turned debit during the day were forced to liquidate providing additional selling pressure on the close. This drove the futures down even more.

Nobody had any idea of the magnitude of the situation. There was no internet, no Tweets, only a television—not the most timely in its reporting. The floor was swirling with rumors.

I did not want to look at how much money I had lost on the day. I knew if I did, it would affect my ability to function the next day. Averaging a loser is the worst strategy a trader can adopt, especially if one gets away with it. This time I got away with it because the futures gapped up and traded up 25 points on Tuesday. It ended up being a $500,000 swing down and up in less than 18 hours.

The next day was a classic. Every conversation started the same way.

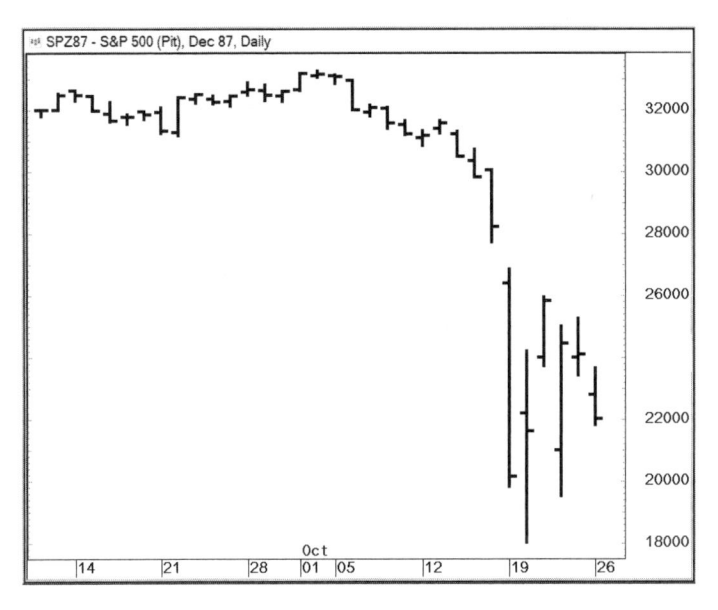

"Do you want the good news or the bad news?"

A large trader, known for selling premium (a bad thing when the market moves big), crawled into the office wearing a hockey mask. A hush fell over the office as they cautiously peeked around the corner.

"Ooohh."

"Ahhh."

"Did you see Manny?" He had lost $40 million. I hear he never traded again.

First Option's total loss was $112 million. This meant that the traders' capital, mine included, should have been long gone. Exchange members' accounts are not protected by SIPC (unlike an investor's account at a bank). Every penny I made was in my trading account. That was the bad news. The good news was that Continental Illinois Bank bought First Options less than a year earlier, so they ended up being the ones who ate the loss. All my capital would have disappeared overnight if Continental Illinois had not made that purchase.

That day became known as Black Monday, the crash of 1987.

Look out below. MSFT down 28% in one day.

I was young and resilient, but more importantly, after seven years of trading, I was still green and unjaded. Life was an adventure. My movies all had happy endings. This was just another incident where I had to make one more stagecoach escape. I was idealistic, not yet cynical. The flamboyant psychic promised I was going to be successful and I still believed him.

There was a study done on price behavior when the field of behavioral finance was just coming on the scene. It simulated trading with groups of individuals who were not traders. The price of the market would always rise first. It kept inching higher until everyone had bid and there was nobody left to buy. At that point, it broke sharply with no support underneath.

To this day, that is one of the main reasons markets sell off—there is nobody left to buy.

10

INSIGHT

At the beginning of 1987, I set up a home office. Why spend an hour commuting into Philadelphia each morning when I could trade from home? For a mere $1200 a month I leased my own Quotron. Add in another $1000 for the particular data line required, and I was set. Costs were much higher for everything in the eighties, including commissions. Most traders have no idea how good they have it these days.

Things got interesting at the clearing firm after the crash. The dust settled, and there was an increase in trader camaraderie.

"You alive?"

"Yup, still kicking."

"You survived?"

"What doesn't kill you makes you stronger!"

I was still an exchange member, so I occasionally commuted into Philadelphia and traded from my clearing firm's office. I wanted to be around other people and show that I had indeed survived.

One day a fellow named Barry came into the office with a marvelous software program called "Insight." Barry's partner had written software called Window on Wall Street which provided quotes and a ticker, but Insight was one of the first charting programs for a home PC. It also was the first filtering software. It was written in DOS using Pascal and was super clean and fast. This new frontier of home computing was exciting. I was one of the first buyers of Insight and ran it on a 386 PC with data from a Signal box, which came over FM radio. The average smartphone in 2018 is at least 1500 times faster. Right before midnight, I had to shut off the computer and then reboot it after midnight. If I did not do this, the data would merge into the next day. This meant that any time I traveled, a neighbor had to come to the house, shut down the computer and turn it back on the next morning. It was one notch easier than taking care of a dog, but a lot more awkward. Computer maintenance continues to be a big part of this business and my least favorite one.

Before I purchased Insight, I paid an extra $200 a month to get bar charts on my Quotron. They were 15-minute orange bar charts with no indicators. With Insight's software, I now had color (!) and lots of built-in indicators. I was a kid in a candy store and proceeded to lose money for the next three months trying to figure out the squiggly lines. It was a good thing my husband liked to do all the grocery shopping and cooking because we would have starved otherwise.

I was friends with another trader from the Philadelphia floor. I told him how lousy I felt because my strategy had not worked out. It was a horrible quarter of trading. And then he said he had lost ten times that amount—perspective. I felt a lot better. Someone else had made some of the same mistakes, but here they were, carrying away on the phone with me as if nothing had happened. So even if you are mildly depressed and down in the dumps, strike up a conversation with someone. If not a fellow trader, then the next-door neighbor or the check-out clerk at the supermarket. Talking leads to a notable physical change in your biochemistry that shows a lowering of stress hormones.

Insight had a quirky indicator called "Cyclic." It was a fast, sensitive version of a stochastic. A stochastic is a momentum indicator that measures overbought and oversold as well as momentum divergences. It is a good technical analysis tool for pattern recognition. Cyclic had been a programming mistake when the developer was trying to write a stochastic. I was trying to figure out how to use something which was like that oscillator on the SMR charts. I did not want to keep updating these by hand.

George Lane popularized the first stochastic oscillator known as %K and %D in the mid-eighties through a series of articles and pamphlets. The indicator was developed between 1954 and 1957 by a group of seven traders at the Chicago Board of Trade. George was one of those traders. They traded during the day and put in grueling hours of research at night, calculating over 60 different versions by hand before settling on one. It has been one of the most widely used tools in technical analysis, belonging to a class of indicators known as momentum oscillators. The guiding principle is: momentum precedes price. In a trending environment, it will reach its extreme in the direction of the trend well before price does.

I had figured out how to put the value of the cyclic next to the price quote and net change for each market, so I did not have to watch charts. I was used to watching the quote board on the trading floor. It was the easiest way to follow many markets at once. For tape reading purposes I watch the "net change" quotes instead of charts.

It took me two more years to figure out how to program the SMR Chart's oscillator that I updated by hand for a decade. I figured out that it was the difference between a 3 and 10-period simple moving average which was rescaled. A 16-period moving average of the 3/10 was overlaid on top of this. The 3/10 oscillator is quite similar to a slow stochastic with a %K = 7 and %D = 12. Indicators help to highlight the chart formations and swings. They also aid pattern recognition. They don't function well in mechanical systems because derivatives of price are late. I had acquired a good "feel" by plotting the SMR oscillator and updating charts by hand for many years.

Insight's coding made it easy to create scans and tools for filtering markets. My favorite scan is a scrolling vertical ticker tape showing the stocks making new highs or new lows on the day. It gives a great sense of intra-day market momentum. Scans which show the top % up or down from the opening price are also a good momentum indicator. Relative Strength work is hard to beat. Even as stock traders have become increasingly momentum driven and the opening drive (move off the opening) is a ridiculous dogpile, it still shows what is in play for the day.

It takes a long time to learn to process lots of information. It would have been impossible for me to monitor so many markets the first few years in my career. It is like learning to read an orchestral score. Start off learning one instrument and learn to understand numerous notations. Then add more instruments, one by one. With lots of study over many years, you can learn to read Beethoven's 9th symphony, chorus and all.

After the '87 crash, liquidity dried up in the equity options, and my trading gravitated to the futures markets. Every market was a learning experience. For example, I found out the hard way I could not trade Cotton the same way I had been trading Bonds. It was relentless in its trends, and my first trade mowed me over. The meats had their own personality and were prone to V-type bottoms. The metals at the time were exceedingly dull. Some markets were more prone to the deathly creeper trending price movement than the financials were. I did best when there was good volatility. Most traders will agree that high volatility environments are ideal.

In November 1989, the Berlin Wall came down. Before this, the best of the best young emigrants had left East Germany. It was one of the reasons East Germany's economy suffered for the next two decades. Also, the country had become a polluted cesspool. I don't mind saying this because my great-grandmother was from Dresden. My great-great-grandfather laid the Dresden sewer lines.

When it became clear that East and West Germany were going to be unified again, the number one trade in my mind was shorting the Deutsch Mark. Germany was going to have to absorb all this polluted wasteland. I watched the market for a few days until it seemed like it had stopped going up. Then I initiated a short position in the currency. After sitting with the trade for less than three days, my P&L lectured me.

"The Deutsch Mark has not stopped going up!"

"I thought…"

Mr. P&L shook his head. He knew what I thought, but it didn't matter. I thought wrong.

Time to GTFO–Get The Fuck Out. Exit at the market. It was like sticking my fingers on a hot stove. Any longer and I would have lost my shirt, not to mention a few fingers. I shook my head in wonder. The trade had seemed so obvious to me, what had I missed? The rebuilding process for Germany was going to be in Deutsch Marks. It created a noticeable increase in demand for the currency.

A fellow trader once told me the age-old adage: "If you throw a frog in a boiling pot of water, it will quickly jump out. But if you put it in lukewarm water and slowly turn up the heat, it will cook to death." In this case, I was a frog jumping into a pot of boiling water.

"Funnymentals" is a jocular expression for the fact that there are always two sides to a coin. I learned to throw the "funnymentals" out the window. Scenario building does not work for me. I will manage to get it wrong and the real reasons for the move will emerge after the fact. I do best when I stick to technicals based on the price. Morris used to say, "A blond thinking is like pouring honey into the gears of a fine Swiss watch."

Scenario building falls into the camp of preconceived notions and cognitive biases. There are a lot of smoke and mirrors that can make a smart person think they are really smart and can "figure the market out." But as the old saying goes, the market is going to do whatever it takes to drive the most amount of people crazy. Smart people fall into that camp too.

In the early nineties, the SP futures which had been my bread and butter went through a low volatility period. For three months the average daily range was 3 points. This was when they were trading around the 450 handle as well. I always joke this was when I started trading corn. But, it was not a joke. The average daily dollar range in corn has exceeded that of the SPs many times in the past. This is why it is good for a trader to have a stable of markets to trade and to never rely too much on one market or style.

These years taught me a lesson in patience. There was no room for error since the ranges were so narrow. Also, the lack of volatility led to fewer opportunities.

For general market timing, I was still logging the indicators my first backer, Gerry had shown me. When they became overbought or oversold, I put positions on in the OEX and SP futures, looking for a reaction in the opposite direction. Sometimes I was a bit too early. More than once I woke up in the middle of the night unable to sleep. It was another instance of being unhappy with my lack of patience. My husband was no help. He made sarcastic comments like, "The pioneers are the ones with the arrows in their back," and "You know where you can find sympathy—between shit and syphilis in the dictionary."

If you don't have a thick skin, you are not going to last very long in this business.

11

DANISHES

Taking a break from trading is difficult. It consumes you and swallows you up like a tsunami. The markets dance their two-step in my head twenty-four-seven. The continual process and routine keep you in the game, waiting and waiting until there is one big opening. I spoiled many family vacations because I needed to be attached to a phone line like an umbilical cord while we were on an island or at a ski resort. I cringe when I think back to times of me hiding in my room, laptop hooked up, while everyone else was playing cards.

There were only two previous times in my career when I had no positions on. This was because managing many options, hedges, and spreads was complicated. There was not always the best liquidity in far-out contracts or options series. The first time I was "flat" with no positions was when I moved from California to Philadelphia to trade on the PHLX. The second time was when I took a week off to get married and go on a honeymoon.

Two years later I was riding a strong trend in the currencies while in the later stages of my pregnancy. There was no reason to close the positions down, even though my belly was ripe like a big fat watermelon. But nobody rings the bell with a warning when labor is about to start. The doctors gave a three-week window, and that was the level of sophistication in those days. We were decorating the Christmas tree when I went into labor at midnight. The next morning my broker called me at the hospital after my husband gave him the number. I had one day left to roll my currency futures to the new front month. Oh jeez… What were my positions? I tried to remember how many contracts I had in each currency market after two hours of sleep. It would have been much easier if there had been an internet and electronic trading. But in those days the daily statements went into my box at my clearing firm in Philadelphia.

My executing broker had no idea of my actual position. My foggy brain groped for a number that sounded the most logical. Let's just say I got lucky in remembering the correct position sizes.

After a year, we decided to get an au pair who could live with us so I could be with my new daughter and continue to trade. My husband was now Mr. Mom, so between the three of us, there were no disruptions to my market operations. Our au pair was due to arrive at the Philadelphia train station. We only knew what she looked like from a grainy black and white postage stamp photo. Forty young girls from different parts of the world debarked onto the platform. We stood and squinted at each of them as they paraded out of the train. Which one was ours? A plump dark-haired girl walked by with a warm smile. Next came a homely looking girl with cropped hair and a cardigan which masked any womanly shape. And then we saw her, the tallest and prettiest one with blond hair and blue eyes and not an ounce of body fat. She saw us, waved, and trotted over. My husband's eyes lit up. "Hallo! My name is Tina!" Denmark had sent us one of their finest. On the way home, my husband said, "You know, we have something in the United States called a Danish. We like to eat them for breakfast." I rolled my eyes and let that one slide.

From then on, when traders came to our house to hang out, which was every weekend, there would be Tina in the pool, Tina sunbathing on the lawn, Tina in the hot tub batting her innocent blue eyes. Even though my husband was a fantastic cook, he actually thought the traders flocked to our house to eat his food.

My office was in an upstairs room. I looked out over the lush green lawn and pool and could see Tina reading while Erika napped on a quilt. Something was rotten in the state of Denmark. I worked so hard to get to where I was, but at that moment I realized that it was all backward. I literally brought someone from the other side of the world and was paying them to play the part that I wanted. Why was it not me on the grass reading while my toddler played in the grass? Why was I upstairs behind the computer screen instead of experiencing that moment? I had taken over as the breadwinner for the family, and my husband took the position of chef while the 20-year old Danish version of me took the position that I wanted: the mom.

In a flash of irritation, I grabbed my paperweight clock and chucked it across the room in my office. Bam! It flew through the closet door, which I did not realize was hollow until it proved an unsuccessful barrier for my clock. "FUCK A DUCK!" I screamed into the void.

As quickly as I lost my composure, I regained it. I inhaled for four counts and collapsed into my chair. I stared at the remnants of the closet door. A big hole stared back at me, which became a daily reminder of my loss of self-control until we moved out of the house.

In all honesty, I absolutely loved working.

Erika and I at a cross-country event.

slammed on the brakes and jerked to the right. She refused the jump, which was out of character. I gathered my reins and circled back around. Again, she jolted to the side like a scared bunny, refusing to go any further. "One more time," I thought, but something did not feel right. My body felt heavy, and it was difficult to move. I felt as though I was riding in molasses. As Pegasus and I approached the jump a third time, I knew she was going to refuse again. She could feel my hesitation and was responding to it appropriately. She instinctively knew I didn't want to go over that jump any more than she did.

Discouraged, I dismounted and walked back to the starting line. With every step, my legs grew heavier and heavier. I felt weak, and it took all my effort to move my legs forward. I stared down at the grass to see if the mud was sucking me into the ground, but the field was bone dry. My brain stopped functioning. After I got Pegasus back to the barn, I headed home and collapsed on my bed. My body had given up on me.

It's only when you feel so sick and you think you're going to die that you realize you've been taking your health for granted. We've all been there—lying in bed in a feverish state with every joint aching, staring at the ceiling while accusing every person who came into your personal space in the past five days. Then a cartoon lightbulb appears overhead, and you realize you haven't been this deathly ill in years. Remember all those times you could breathe through your nose? When did being able to breathe become such a luxury? Once your anger subsides, the bargaining campaign begins. "Please God, please let me be able to breathe through my left nostril again. I'll do anything!" Five minutes pass by and nothing. "Alrighty then... Please, Satan, please make me feel better again!" I've heard so many Faustian stories over the years, but Satan never shows his red, horned head when you need him.

I spent the next couple months in and out of doctors' offices. No one could figure out what was wrong with me. You know you've got something particularly bad when one doctor calls his

12

TRYING TO KEEP THE BALL IN PLAY

*Trading is like tennis: Keep the ball in play,
don't make unforced errors, be patient and wait for your opening.*

A year and a half after I gave birth to my daughter, I competed with my horse in a cross-country event. Cross-country is the upper-class's equivalent of a Tough Mudder, but for horses. I didn't fit into the upper-class description of this sport. I bought my first horse as a racetrack reject before she was sent to the glue factory.

Despite our lack of blue blood, we made a great team. My mare, Pegasus, was the bravest, most athletic horse on the field. We soared over fences and raced through muddy puddles with ease. We usually competed early on weekend mornings. Some people went to church, I went to the barn. It was there I felt peace from the chaos which surrounded me on a regular basis. However, this particular Sunday morning was different. Pegasus and I started our round in the competition. We galloped across a big field and approached a zig-zag fence halfway around the course. Right before we left Earth, Pegasus doctor buddies into the room to hypothesize what's wrong with you. They ruled out everything from allergies to a brain tumor until they settled on a newly diagnosed condition called Chronic Fatigue Immune Dysfunction Syndrome. "Oh goody, a new disease just for me!" I sarcastically thought. One sarcastic thought a day was all the energy I could muster. The rest of the time I laid in bed like a zombie vegetable.

Chronic Fatigue Immune Dysfunction Syndrome, or CFIDS for short, is a central nervous system dysfunction. It affects the neurological, endocrine, and immune systems. No doubt my adrenaline-filled lifestyle had pushed me over the edge. That time in my life was a blur. It was as if time ceased to exist, but for only me. Everyone else could go forward and live their lives. I remember looking out my bedroom window one morning and watching our Danish au pair play with my daughter. The sun was shining, and they were laughing and running in circles. Here I was, trapped in a body too weak to move. "What had it been like to run in the grass? Would I ever be able to experience that again? How can I get my energy back?" I desperately wondered. I was so tired of being tired.

There was one thing that kept me hopeful throughout this time. A girlfriend's sister was diagnosed with CFIDS, and she managed to recover after three years. So, I believed recovery was possible, and I would not live like this forever. I had to figure out what to do. I joined a support group. Nothing like going to a group meeting of teachers, lawyers, and other white-collar folks afflicted with a similar illness and half of them are dressed in pajamas.

I heard about a wellness center which had float tanks and decided to give it a try. A float tank looks like a giant egg which you climb into and then float as if you were in the Dead Sea. The tank has 1,600 pounds of high-grade magnesium sulfate (Epsom salts). This mineral is absorbed through the skin. When floating, the sympathetic nervous system learns to recalibrate itself. This is the part of our brain which activates the fight or flight response. After ten weeks of floating in a Zen meditative mindset, I was hooked. I bought a float tank and put it in an upstairs bedroom. I spent many hours floating in nothingness.

When my daughter Erika turned five, the float tank became a centerpiece on home tours she conducted for new school friends. "This is our spaceship," said Erika, proudly pointing to the float tank. A collective "Woooaaah!" echoed amongst her friends. She carried on the tour to the trading room, where stacks of computer monitors lined the walls. "And this is mission control, just like NASA," she continued. The children could hardly believe their eyes. Tiny mouths hung agape until their attention spans gave up and they returned to their adventures on the playground in the backyard. Our house was anything but normal.

It took a few years to recover fully. I floated several times a week and started walking again. At my weakest point, I could hardly walk around the block. Eventually, I joined my daughter's Tae Kwon Do class. And when I say I joined the group, I mean I was doing karate with a bunch of five-year-olds. Yes, there I was, barely able to do five jumping jacks in the back of the studio. But I had no pride, and I slowly gained my strength back. My husband's role was crucial during this time, and he kept the household running.

Late one night, I was unable to sleep, so I turned on the TV. A larger than life figure appeared on an infomercial, talking about the power of positive thinking. It was my first introduction to Tony Robbins, the motivational speaker. I picked up the phone and ordered his set of cassette tapes. Somehow, I knew these tapes were going to help me beat this disease. I had an assistant at the time, although I'm not sure why since I was hardly trading. I told him we were going to listen to one 30-minute tape after the markets closed every day. I was so drawn into the power of these tapes that I took notes. I started a journal and wrote down the things I wanted to do. At the top of my journal

I wrote, "Make $3,000,000 in the next four years." I was confident I could accomplish this goal. I knew it in the very core of my body. I was going to make both a full recovery and millions of dollars.

I ended up reaching both goals within two years.

I know I may sound like a Tony Robbins infomercial myself. "You too can make millions of dollars and beat weird immune diseases by listening to some tapes!" But no matter who inspires you, I am a big believer in the power of the pictures we put in our heads. I believe in positive thinking and the power of visualization. My favorite images are from luxury home magazines, the type found at airport newsstands. I love flipping through the pages and seeing multi-million-dollar homes in Aspen, Florida, Wyoming, and the Caribbean. Any gorgeous and tranquil place to live. A beautiful environment has always been a big motivator for me. I placed power in tokens, magic talismans, colored light bulbs, and ambient music. I had rose quartz crystals and light therapy boxes. I surrounded myself with anything I thought would help me get better. Funny hippie stuff aside, it turned out the main ingredient was time.

There is nothing more maddening than to lose one's short-term memory and cognitive functions. This is what happened to me during this time. I learned to be grateful for every healthy day.

Gratitude is a key ingredient of success. It means that even when bad things are happening, you always have something to focus on. Just like pilots have a gauge to make sure they can still tell which way is up, gratitude keeps me from ever feeling upside down. When you are trading the markets, you have to have a separate source of happiness—to know that there are still wonderful things all around, most of which do not require money. It is easier to take risks when you remove your personal happiness and well-being from the equation.

Gratitude leads to optimism, and a positive attitude is 90% of the game.

13

MARKET TECHNICIANS

It was 1990, and I felt isolated trading out of my home digs. My trading office was now in my downstairs basement which lacked any natural light. Being subterranean for a majority of the day did not bother me because it was peaceful and quiet except the humming from the computers and the occasional mouse clicks. But I missed having other traders around to break up the day and was in desperate need of the camaraderie from a community.

I am not sure how I found out about the Market Technicians Association (MTA), but it was a welcomed reprieve from my solitary confinement. The MTA was a nifty old boys club located in the World Trade Center. Institutional traders came together to share their research. It was established by three technicians from the institutional side: Ralph Acampora, John Brooks, and John Greely. There were about fifty of us who met on a monthly basis to discuss markets and share ideas. Each month, a speaker would present to the group. Speakers included technicians such as Dick Arms, Arch Crawford, Bob Prechter, and Sherman McClellan.

Attending these meetings allowed me to emerge from my cocoon and socialize with other market professionals. I took the Greyhound bus which ran up the New Jersey Turnpike to New York. I'd spend a few hours discussing what people had been working on and then hop on the bus back home. After our meetings, a handful of us headed down to the same old bar and grill located in a basement on a dirty New York street. Veterans swapped engrossing market stories over hamburgers and beer.

Arch Crawford had a particularly colorful way of looking at the markets. He had done a presentation that evening which seemed more like a tarot card reading than an academic view on technical analysis. His commentary left you wondering where he was hiding his crystal ball and turban. I cornered him at dinner and questioned his rationale. Arch looked at me with ruby red cheeks (his normal coloring) and a twinkle in his eye.

"Do you know what happened before the crash of 1987?"

My wedding, I thought. Surely, that couldn't have caused the market to crash.

Arch continued. "Solar flares! These unusual events associated with the sun exert an odd effect on human behavior. It causes people to feel agitated and uneasy."

The idea of the sun being able to control my feelings left me agitated and uneasy. It's more comfortable to think of this as pseudo-science.

"Many studies show an increase in murders and suicides around solar flares and magnetic storms." Arch spoke quite matter-of-factly.

This could have been written off as the ramblings of an eccentric, but his track record was spot-on. We continued to talk, and he told me he used a 5-day moving average of the Trin for short-term timing. I used a 10-day moving average as shown to me by Gerry. It turned out that Arch was a secretive technical trader hiding behind astrology. I look at the 5-day moving average to this day, even though the

Trin is not as useful as it once was. Still, it seems a lot simpler than pondering the choreographed chaos of the cosmos.

Fun piece of trader trivia: it shouldn't be called the "Trin." Richard "Dick" Arms created it, and it should be called the "Arms" index. But none of the data feed services would change the name. God forbid it costs a few extra bucks for them to acknowledge the legitimate inventor of a popular indicator. Dick wrote a book I had checked out from the San Francisco library in 1982 on equivolume. It is where the width of the bar varies with the volume. A short fat bar represents an increase in volume with no range. This loss in momentum often marks a swing reversal. Back then, I charted 20 stocks plotting these equivolume bars. Charting this way was a lot of work. I finally dropped the project, but it was educational to see how volume interplayed with the price. I always learn the most when doing things by hand.

Dick sent me the last book he wrote called *The Tackle Box: Stories about People Who Fish* before he passed in 2018. He may have been a classic market technician, but he was also an avid fisherman and a consummate Renaissance Man.

* * *

I served on the MTA board for a few years in the capacity of "librarian" which was right up my alley. I could bury myself in books 24/7. Plus, librarians don't have to look chic. The MTA's library had every book on technical analysis as well as many papers from the 20th century. This was a hundred times better than the *Wall Street Wisdom* book I read when I was young. There were also rare and unusual old books which were tragically lost in 9/11 because the World Trade Center housed the library.

After the meetings, I sat in the library for a few hours and skimmed through as many books as I could. I had the key to the rare classics which were locked away in a special cabinet. I came across a well-worn, xeroxed manuscript. The title was, "The Taylor Trading

Technique." This book deals with the day to day price movements as opposed to long-term trend analysis.

George Douglass Taylor was a grain trader in the forties and fifties at the CBOT. He was a trader first and foremost, trading the daily movements both on and off the floor unlike most of the other authors I read. He applied his technique not only to the agricultural futures but stocks as well.

Over the next two decades, I bought many copies of this book and marked them up with a yellow highlighter. Taylor's pearly words of wisdom became my doctrine, and he influenced my trading style. It is a great tape reading book with practical guidelines on all aspects of trading.

Some of my favorite quotes:

- The trader who knows how to act when the expected happens is in a better position to act when the unexpected happens.
- A trader is ready to trade or not to trade—at the opening or shortly thereafter—unencumbered by comments or opinions.
- A trader does not worry because he did not get the extreme of either play. He needs to feel he is right when he makes his play and when it turns out just as he anticipates it will, he has an intangible that is far greater than the material gain.
- Never make a trade unless it favors your play.
- Forget about a trade after you have made it. Take what the market offers you at the time and don't hold on for what you think the market should do. Trade on what the market does, not what it might do.
- Never try and anticipate the market farther ahead than your signals. Cinch your profits as the market gives them to you. Your play is to take whatever the market offers you and at the exact time of this offering.

You can believe in the tape at all times. Learn to read it and believe in nothing else for short-term trading. Taylor's words gave me great peace of mind that all I had to do was to do the best job I could at the time and not be perfect.

* * *

In 1991, the MTA held their annual conference in Santa Barbara at a beautiful resort near the ocean. In the good old days, institutions paid for their technical analysts' trips. The locations were quite plush. At the Santa Barbara conference, I heard a lecture which made an impression on me for life. Hank Pruden was the speaker. The title was, 'Doing your own analysis in a closed room with no windows and no doors.' In other words, you will always do your best work when you are free from distractions and the influence of others.

Hank was a short, enthusiastic whirlwind of energy. My favorite saying of his was, "You are your own best client." In other words, do your work for yourself. I made it a point to keep TV's out of my trading office after I heard his lecture and never subscribed to others' newsletters or analysis. Hank and I became great friends for the next 26 years until his passing in 2017. He was the world's leading authority on Wyckoff and taught technical analysis at Golden Gate University. I flew out to San Francisco periodically to speak at the conferences he hosted. My mother lived in the Bay area, and it was an excellent way for me to visit her, too.

My Mom did not approve of my profession in the beginning. Nobody likes to see their kid in misery. In the early eighties, I griped about a particularly depressing trading period. She told me I could always go into Human Resources. Where did this come from? This is about as far away from my skill set as one could get. She was a high school counselor and was good at working with people. I was not. My dad was no longer in my life after I started college which was a real shame because we had similar ways of thinking.

At another MTA annual conference, I met Alan Shaw after he gave his keynote speech. He was one of the original founding fathers of the MTA (founded in 1973) and was the second president of the organization.

I heard him speak several other times as well–always at nonprofit events. Alan had one of the best historical databases in the industry at the time. He said there are only back-to-back 30% years in the market once every 50-100 years. This was looking back through financial data going back to the 1600's. The market had come close to having 2 back-to-back 30% years. So, the next logical question was, what is the most probable outcome following this occurrence? Does the market crash? Are further small gains seen? He said to expect 6-8 years of consolidation. And that is precisely what happened, though not without some good directional swings in the process.

Alan showed a Point and Figure chart of a stock which went back many years. He and his staff still kept all their original Point and Figure charts by hand. Point and Figure charts are a charting technique developed over 100 years ago to keep track of the price fluctuations when there were no computers. X's and O's are used instead of numbers or bars. In the eighties when they were plotting their charts, they noted the long bases which had been building. Multiyear bases. One of the strengths of P&F charts is you can get a "count." The longer the base, the broader the eventual move. Or, as Ralph Acampora likes to say, "The broader the base, the higher into space." So, there was a stock which was trading around 14. The name of the company was Marion Lab, named after the founder's wife. When Alan was giving his lecture, he asked his audience to get a count on the price projection indicated by the base. One member shouted out 111, another 114. Everyone was trying to figure it out now.

Keep in mind, this chart example was before the big bull market of 1982. If a stock went from 14 to 20, it was a huge deal. Well, not only did this 14 dollar stock break out of its base and go to 114, but it went to 620. And this was before the nineties. That was fantastic back in those days! In the new era of quantitative analysis, there is something to the old school technicals of the past.

Both a market technician and a trader must have a set of rules and assumptions in which they believe. Everything comes down to supply and demand and this is what creates the chart patterns. According to Alan Shaw, technical analysis is based on three main assumptions:

1) The market is a discounting mechanism.
2) The market tops out when things could not look any better and makes a bottom when things could not look any worse.
3) "In price there is knowledge." He said this last phrase over and over.

And then he gave one last story about a senator who was speaking on television about the Enron situation. In the senator's hand, he was holding one of the analysts' reports on Enron. At the top of the page, it said: STRONG BUY. But there was also a chart on the front of the report which showed the stock had been in a downtrend for over a year. This was before all the ugly news started coming out. Price was screaming that there was something wrong with this stock. Not too shortly after that, a ruling passed that all analysts must now include a chart on the front of their reports showing the date and price of their recommendations. Chalk one up for the technicians.

Alan's parting words were, "We are always students first, and analysts or traders second."

I crossed paths several times with Ned Davis since we both often spoke at the same events. The last time was at a technical conference held in Miami and he was the keynote speaker. Ned had over 1,100 institutional clients and one of the most respected research shops in the industry. The very first thing he said was, "DO NOT ASK ME FOR MY FORECAST. I DO NOT BELIEVE YOU CAN FORECAST THE MARKET."

He then displayed two charts. One was a survey for the past 20 years on the direction of interest rates. It was taken from the country's top 50 experts in the field. Each year, about 1/3 of them get the direction right. He showed several examples where respected technicians and analysts were unable to get better than 50% correct on their calls. Nobody knows what the market can or will do each year. Nobody has been able to predict the direction of interest rates either consistently.

Ned likes objective indicators. Charts are not, strictly speaking, objective since they can be subject to interpretation. According to Ned:
1) Successful traders have an objective indicator they use.
2) Successful traders follow a disciplined methodology. They do not allow large losses. This is the number one rule.
3) They are disciplined in following their method, yet they are flexible. "For example, a trader can be bearish and hammer the downside." Ned pounded the table for extra emphasis. "But he must also be able to turn on a dime and switch to being bullish if the market changes."

Ned likes looking at Sentiment indicators and feels they have the most value at extremes.

It is always important to ask, "Where am I going to go wrong? How am I going to cover if I am wrong?"

In closing, Ned put up a long-term chart which showed the sentiment extremes.

If one had bought at the extreme in optimism and sold the extreme in pessimism, every trade would have been wrong. And if you had done the opposite, you would have made 6000 SP points. This was in 2006 when the SPs were trading around 1500.

Unfortunately, this can't lead to a trading system because you do not know the extremes until at LEAST one day after the fact. You can only see them in hindsight. But, you do have to be flexible when there is too much optimism or pessimism. Ned trades for himself using hourly charts. This is interesting because the nature of his business is to provide long-term charts to institutional clients.

"I am in the business of making mistakes. It is my job, though, to make small mistakes, not big mistakes."

I would like to practice not making mistakes at all, myself.

At an MTA meeting up in New York, I met another member named Robert who ended up becoming a lifelong best friend. He had sold his machine shop and retired. His cousin was the largest trader in the gold pit at the time. Robert was well-versed in the nature of trading. He was on the ultimate quest to explore every method out there until he found one that suited his style. We became great buddies even though he lived two hours north of me. I considered him to be my surrogate father when I needed to ask for advice on down the road.

Robert spent two years evaluating different trading styles, from Steve Moore's Seasonal program to trading spreads to mechanical systems. He traded one technique or strategy for three months. Then, he assessed how well it worked with his temperament and comfort level. He ultimately settled on day trading the SPs, looking for three pushes up or down to fade on 5-minute charts. He was thoughtful in his approach to evaluating methodologies. I enjoyed his friendship immensely. He was one of the few people I met with an engineer's mind who did not try to fit the market into an algebraic equation or black box.

On Robert's trading journey, he shared with me every resource he investigated or purchased. He introduced me to many systems. One was a volatility breakout system published by Bob Buran. It was an epiphany moment. The goal of a volatility breakout system is to capture range expansion and stay with the trade when it works. It gave me the tools to develop a framework to be on the right side of trend days. This had been my nemesis in the trading pits.

It might sound like an obvious statement, but when you are on the trading floor in the equity options, it is your job to accommodate the order flow. Buy orders come in when the market is going up, and somebody has to sell. That somebody was us, the members. In a fast-moving market, you had to be quick to hedge your option orders by trading stock on the NYSE. Once or twice a month it would be easy to get too short or long against the trend. The temptation for many floor traders was to average up or down. 90% of the time there was a reaction in the opposite direction, providing a chance to adjust a position. But the 10% of the time there was no intra-day reaction could cost a few days' profits.

It happened to me more than I care to admit. Hit my head against a cinderblock wall one more time, please.

Switching gears from countertrend trading to breakouts and momentum trading is like trying to turn a train 180 degrees on the tracks. It takes a concerted effort. Years of habits have to be undone. The thing that made it easiest was I was no longer on the trading floor. A trader can be nimble getting in and out when trading a small position. But this is not possible when trading larger sizes. I wanted to trade size.

A few years later, after I had started my CTA, Bob Buran traded for me in the early nineties. I created a volatility breakout "profit center," where we executed in a dozen overseas markets such as the JGBs (Japanese bonds), the Italian bonds, and the FTSE. The system was profitable in the JGBs but gave it back in the FTSE. After a year, it was a lot of extra work to add 1% to the bottom line, so I stopped running the profit center. But I learned a lot from Buran about the mentality it takes to trade a system. Here are some of his more thoughtful comments:

- Even if he lost money on a particular day, he still had done a great job because he followed the system. It was the SYSTEM that lost money, not him.
- You must take every trade. If you don't like the trade, you can always exit once you are in, but you never get a second chance to enter the very best ones.

- It was essential to have a basket of markets since there would always be 1 or 2 that did not make money. Each year there were different markets which performed the best, but it was impossible to tell in advance.
- You never know which markets are going to produce the best trades.
- A high percentage of your profits come from a few trading days each year.

It was a classic system, a pure numbers game. Buran also had another nifty concept—profit per units of time. For example, $5000 made in 4 hours was a superior trade than $7000 made in 3 days. I have a world of respect for Buran because he still trades his system to this day. He is the only trader I've met who is transparent. He published all his trading statements in 1991 when he sold his system, and he still posts his daily stock trades and P&L on his blog.

NEVER believe any claim a trader makes about their profitability unless you see their statements or they are a registered entity with an audited record. This business is crawling with people waiting to sell you a bridge.

There is something about this industry that makes people feel compelled to brag, boast, fib, tell white lies, and outright untruths about their performance. If someone brags they made 70% returns for the year, they will fail to mention that it was on a $5,000 account size. Or the trader who boasts about making 35% on their last trade but neglects to say it was on a two dollar option.

"Yeah, right, you are such a badass trader, you must be so much smarter than everyone else."

A good trader does not need validation. Does it matter if your win-loss ratio is 35% or 90%? No. The only thing that matters is, can you pay your bills, send your kids to college, live debt free, and sock money away for vacations and retirement with your trading profits. Oh, and have some semblance of a life.

I was never a systems trader though I try to stay systematic. It is hard for me to give up the control I get with tape reading. I don't want to give up control, period. I would like to believe my experience gives me an edge. But some people will only be able to make money following a system. The problem is, it's hard to muster the necessary confidence in a system unless you develop it yourself. Systems, even ones that make 100 trades a month, can go through brutal draw-down periods. And if the system isn't your baby, you'll abandon it with a loss instead of adhering to it long enough to recover a drawdown. If it even does. It's not only about the drawdowns, but about how long it takes to make the drawdown back. This is a crucial piece of information system developers often fail to mention. If it were so easy to develop and trade a profitable system, everyone would be driving EXPNSV Mercedes convertibles and making millions. Still, it's fun to try…

Buran told me a great story about a group of German traders he had sold his system to in the mid-nineties. Three of them were trading 10 million dollars. Despite the fact it was a system, it took a tremendous amount of record keeping and order placing back in those days. Nothing was automated. If you know a bit about systems, the distribution of big wins is quite skewed. This means a significant percentage of the profits are made on just a few days. This holds true even when the trade frequency is high and the average holding time is less than 24 hours. On this particular day, these German traders took the day off to watch the World Cup finals. As Murphy's Law would have it, it happened to be one of the four days which made 85% of the profits for that year. O'Shaughnessy's law says Murphy was an optimist. If you miss a trade, that one will be the big one.

You can't predict in advance where the big wins are going to come from–just keep taking every system signal.

14

WORKING THE SYSTEM

While reading books at the MTA's library, I stumbled across a work by George Angell. He had attempted to make a more detailed system out of Taylor's work. This system did not test out, but his mention of a 2-period rate of change intrigued me. I plotted this on my Insight Software and started logging data by hand.

My best work came from testing by hand. I could see where a signal worked and why. I could also look at the conditions where signals failed. When testing with a computer, too much data gets lumped together. This often cancels things out and it is easy to miss the subtle nuances that lead to learning. I've learned more by notating signals on charts, studying when signals don't work, looking for secondary or confirming signs, and recording seas of data by hand. There is no way I could have created my numerous nuanced tactics by backtesting and doing computer runs.

One weekend after a marathon session of 30 straight hours, I developed the Golf System, my first 100% mechanical system. I did not play golf but called it this because one could leave resting orders with a broker and go play golf for the day (meaning, not having to watch the screens.) The trade was to enter long or short on the close depending on where the market closed. There were also 2 filters that dictated when not to take a trade. The exit was a small fixed target for the next day. The stop was three times as great as the target but the win rate was 85%. This was the best ever mechanical trade—I was so excited! I usually entered 200-300 big SP contracts on the close. This was before the introduction of the smaller e-mini futures and before there was a liquid Globex market. I am sure the broker initiating my orders thought this female trader in New Jersey was crazy. But we ended up getting married 19 years later so, obviously, I made an impression.

I was set for life with my Golf System. I shared the signals with my friend Robert from the MTA. Later, when Steve Moore and I published a daily research fax, I included the signals at the bottom of the fax. Soon enough there was a rash of initiating orders on the close. One subscriber from Hawaii was doing 50 lots and other brokers were doing it for their clients. After a few years, the Asian currency crisis hit in the summer of 1997. An adverse overnight gap in the SPs left the trade deeply in the red. Ouch! There was not enough liquidity in the Globex market for me to use overnight stops on the size I was doing. So, I abandoned the Golf system but not until it gave me a good parting spanking.

Any time you find the key, they eventually change the lock.

At the time, I was obsessed with 1-5 day patterns and the 2-period ROC even though there was only a marginal statistical edge. I tried using NAVA patterns, a now-defunct program for analyzing patterns, and comparing them to past occurrences. I printed off endless amounts of charts. I showed my work to others, but it was like talking in a foreign language. This was OK, because this is what makes this business great—everyone has their own way of seeing things. But, it's nice to get feedback.

One of the people I showed my work to was Larry Williams, an industry icon. I had not heard of him when I was a floor trader since he catered to a different segment of the trading industry. I initially met him at an MTA meeting in New York. Later, when I went to California to visit family in LA, Larry invited me to come to visit his office. At the time he was living in Rancho Santa Fe, and his office was a few blocks from the beach. I did not know what to expect, but when I walked in, all I saw were books. I guess I was expecting an array of monitors but they did not exist. Instead, books were piled high on tables, in cluttered stacks on the floor, pushed sideways on shelves, all in total disarray. He had just published a book on the discovery of Mount Sinai and handed me another book titled, "How to Outfox the Foxes." How to beat attorneys at their own game. A man of many interests.

In the corner was a juicer that Larry used for his Monday juice fasts. He also ran marathons. When do we trade? In the entire office, I only saw one small primitive CRT. This was in the days when TradeStation charting software was in its infancy. I was one of the first 100 users to have a security block that plugged into the back of the CPU. My block number was "100." Larry had me beat because he was an original System Writer user—a generation before me. I tried in vain to show him the work I had been doing with the 2-period ROC, but it was too awkward trying to program my patterns in just a few minutes. This was frustrating because I was not great at writing code. I had failed to communicate. We decided to pack it in and go get lunch at an ocean café.

"My car or yours?"

"Oh, yours, definitely," I said, thinking of my bland rental car. Larry brought around an aged dirty white minivan, the type with an awkward sliding door half the length of the van. My rental might have been cooler. Obviously, Larry had no need to impress clients. I was struck by how down to Earth he was. He made a sly comment as we pulled away from the curb, "So, I can see you are the one who wears the pants in the family." I was mortified, not quite sure how to take that. It sure broke any ice that was left to be broken, and we became fast friends after that.

After failing to find a colleague to help me with back-testing, I continued to work on developing an integrated methodology based on the foundation of Taylor, Golf, Trend days, and the 2-period rate-of-change. I wanted a consistent model to trade the 1 to 2-day patterns in addition to the SMR patterns and SP trading. Taylor had a model for every day, "We separate and designate each trading day for its own expected action."

Models are just that—they give a trader an initial game plan but have to be flexible enough to adapt as the price action progresses. For example, if a market has a large opening gap, a model might suggest the price is likely to trade into the gap area. However, if this does not occur during the next three trading hours, the model suggests the market has better odds to trade in the direction of the initial gap. Taylor said his initial game plan had to be right only 55% of the time. The rest of the time, he had to know how to work around the days where his plan was wrong.

One of those universal aphorisms rang especially true: "It's better to have some game plan than no game plan at all." And you realize quickly enough when you have the wrong game plan.

I have seen traders who engage in an obsessive, yet futile pursuit of developing a black and white system with hard and fast rules. If the system has a losing streak, the developer concludes another filter is needed or a variable needs tweaking.

Taylor says, "Even when the book method trader may have an advantage with his method of trading, he does not have a surefire way of operating in the market, and it is well that no such method has been devised."

15

MY TRADING PROGRAM

In case you flipped to this chapter first, here are the things you missed so far: I repeatedly got my ass kicked by the markets, I had a baby, and I put more money than I care to admit into my horse fetish. So there, you are caught up. Here are my secrets:

Program 1: This is my SP day trading, my bread and butter. I do 95% of my trading in the SPs as opposed to the other stock index futures. It was my original game and continues to be the contract I am most consistent with. "If it ain't broke, don't fix it." One would be hard-pressed not to find at least 2-3 decent trading opportunities each day for small but sure pieces. I use the Russell or the NASDAQ futures when I want to carry a position.

I used to use the market internals such as Ticks, Trin, the trend of the breadth, and VIX. Ticks and Trin are less critical than they were in the eighties and nineties. At one time, I faded the tick extremes. Now ticks work better as a momentum indicator. This changed when stocks went to decimalization in 2001. Also, market internals, as well as indicators or time of day functions, work best when there is heavier volume.

No matter what you look at in the markets, context is everything. I like "tic" charts that are similar in appearance to 5 and 15-minute bar charts. Each bar is comprised of the same number of transactions or fluctuations in the price. And I follow Taylor's rhythm—do the odds favor a low to high day or a high to low day? All you have to do is get the main idea right—sometimes easier said than done.

Lastly, I consider trend days and consolidation days to be part of the Taylor language. On the ideal trend day, get long, stay long, and scalp every continuation pattern. Exit on the close. It's like Christmas, one day a month. The consolidation days are completely the opposite. Fade the small spikes up and down after a big move. Fade the noise as the market awaits a big economic report or FOMC release the next day. Fade the tests on light volume days. The real money is made on trend days and heavy volume days, though.

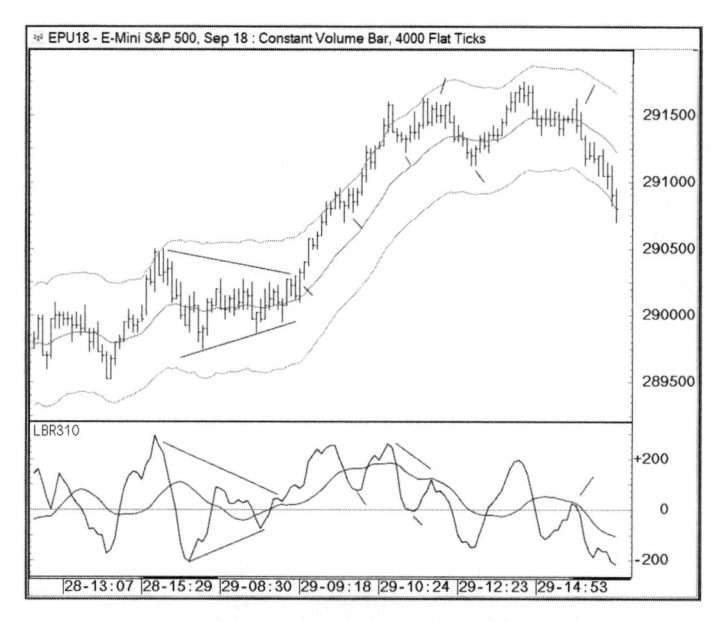

SP e-mini 4000 tic chart with technical entries (similar to 5 minute chart).

Program 2: This profit center is reserved for the top 24 domestic futures markets and the Bunds. The trades have a duration of 1-3 days. That is if it is a winning trade. It's not a great idea to hold a loser overnight. My rhythm is, "in one day, out the next." I learned this from the Taylor trades as well as the volatility breakout plays.

Over the years I have come up with kitschy names for the patterns. For example, pinballs, five fingers, Antis, and the black trade. I gave the 1-3-day patterns funny names for my own benefit. An unusual name is like a symbol in that it conveys a thousand words. I know precisely what that pattern looks like and how the market should behave if the trade kicks in. It is my own game board that I created in the absence of outside influences. It is, in a way, a "religion." Not everyone understands someone else's game board. That is why it is important to come up with your own.

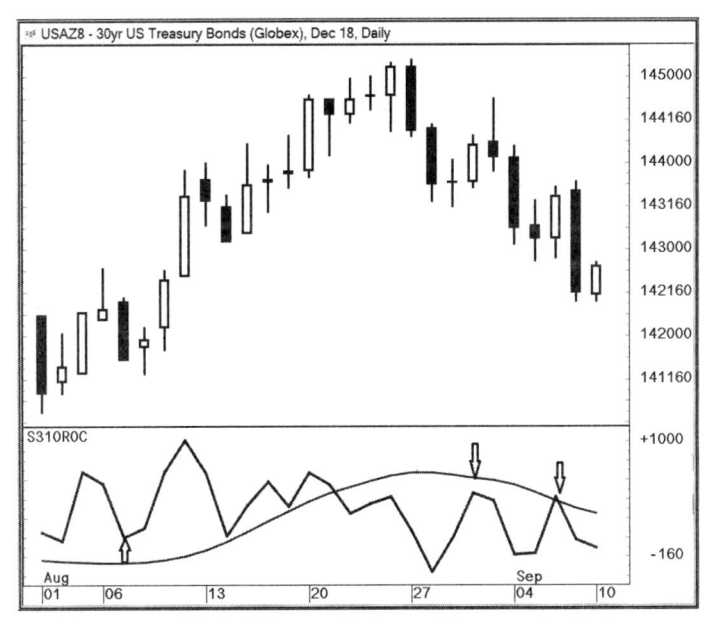

Two-period ROC (rate-of-change) buy and sell Antis.

For over 35 years I've written down the closing price and momentum readings for 24+ markets. This is the way I stay organized. Otherwise, the amount of data is overwhelming and it is too easy to miss something reviewing the patterns I have flagged on automated worksheets. I need to go through the process of seeing it in the data and the chart. Then the anticipation builds around the potential the next day might bring.

Program 3: These are trades made off the daily and weekly chart structure. Though they fall into the camp of classic technical analysis and pattern recognition, I try to quantify them. This is important because I will be the first to admit that I can see what I want to see. It's like looking at puffy cumulous clouds.

"Do you see that elephant in the sky?"

"No, I only see a bunny rabbit."

I use the 3/10 oscillator beneath all my charts because I am brainwashed from plotting the SMR charts by hand for decades. Even with a directional oscillator, a trader can still see what they want to see. So, I don't use oscillators to quantify anything—it is all done with ATRs and the pivots and patterns formed by swing highs and lows.

"Just basic technical analysis, sir."

Trail a stop on these patterns and "see what the market gives." An exit is also called for if there is a loss of momentum. Lastly, the market will let you know if you are wrong because the trade will show red. A good trade works right away and never looks back. More often than not my best trades come from the daily swings turning up or down rather than breakouts from chart formations. It's a matter of style.

A market might have 14-20 reasonable swing trades a year. With the benefit of hindsight, it is easy to imagine how simple it would be to accumulate vast fortunes swing trading. The reality is, I feel lucky if I capture one great swing trade a month in a market. The real trick is knowing when to stay OUT of a market—like when there are no swings and it is consolidating in an endless noisy line.

MY TRADING PROGRAM

Textbook technical swings. Everything works!

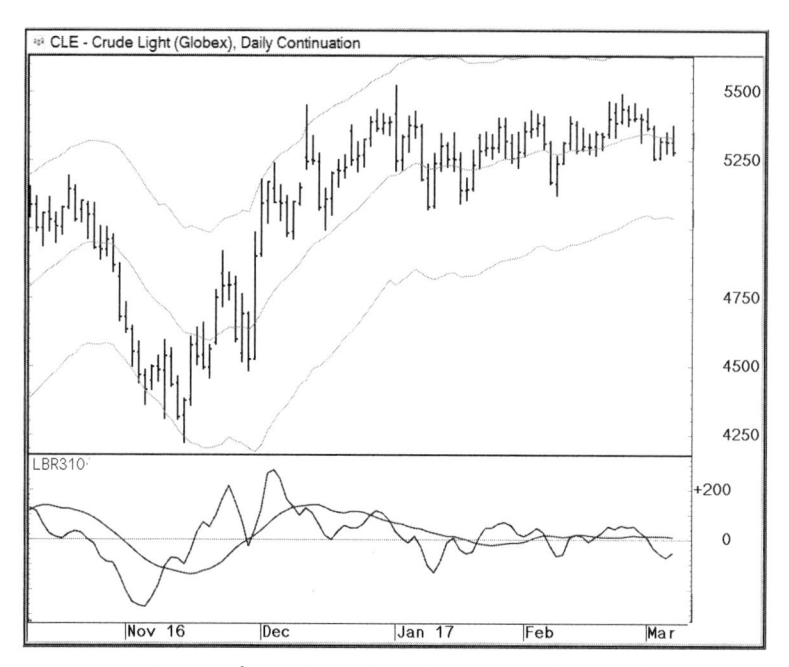

Low volume "noisy" environment. Stay out!

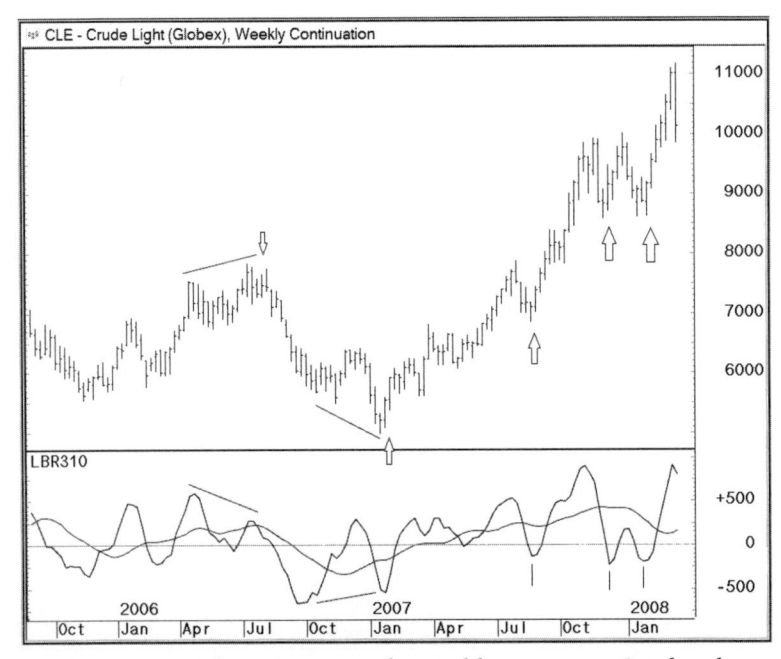

Momentum divergences on the weekly swings in Crude oil.

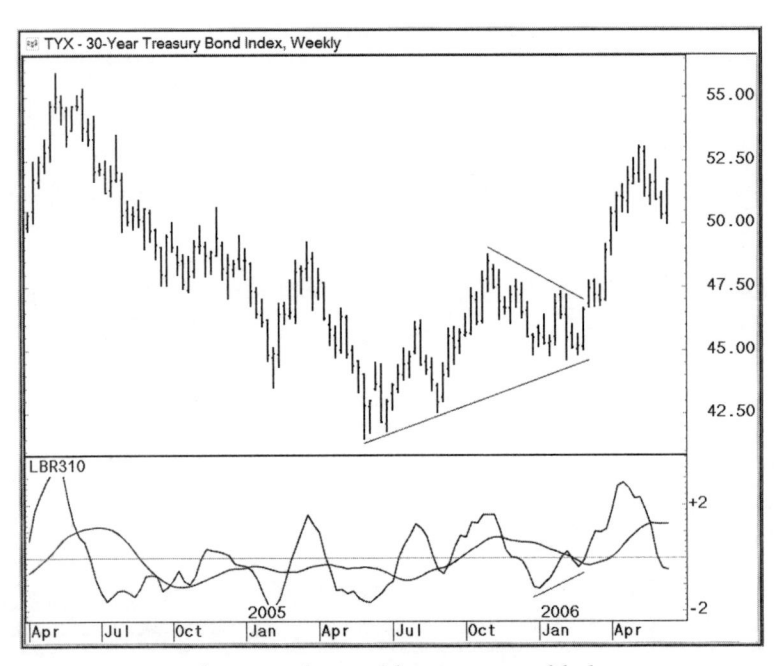

Breakout on the weekly 30-year yield chart.

Program 4: My fourth profit center is dubbed "everything else." These are the types of trades which might not happen very often. I purchase call or put spreads if the market reaches an extreme in sentiment, and sometimes I build an outright position in the futures. I establish a position if there is an interesting and unique stock opportunity. I put on positions if a seasonal trade looks interesting.

Program 4 involves opportunities that not easily modeled or quantified. These situations tend to be based off factors besides pure price data, unlike my other three programs.

I monitor how each profit center does on a quarterly basis. One quarter, the SP scalping might be the most profitable. The next quarter, Program 2 might produce the most profits. As the trade duration increases, the trade frequency drops and so does the win-loss ratio. For example, I can get a consistent 85% win rate scalping SPs, but this drops to 60-65% for profit center two. The third profit center has the lowest win/loss ratio. Sometimes it is less than 50% winners, much as a trend following system would show. However, it also produces the best gains each year. One year, the bonds were the best performing market and the next year the grains were rock stars. Another year, the yen put a 3-inch layer of frosting on the cake and in-between every layer, too.

Unfortunately, this is where the outliers have happened as well. The random unforeseen events which I was on the wrong side of.

The longer the holding time, the greater the risk.

I can tell when I am off track because the trade frequency goes way up or down for one of the profit centers. The problems are easily identifiable. Trying too hard to make something happen which is not going to happen, not getting rid of losers quickly enough, or trading when sleep deprived. We all know what we are doing wrong when our performance is suffering. At least, I do. I KNOW I fucked up. There

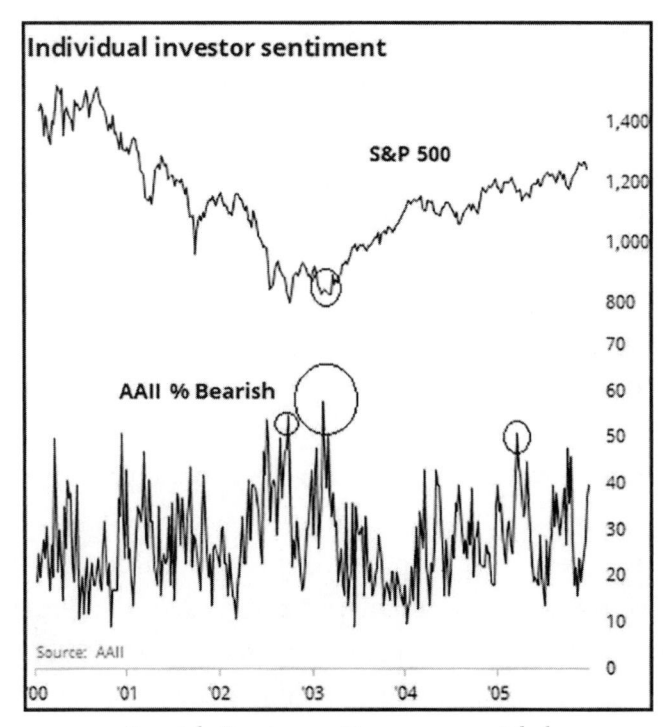

Bearish Sentiment Extremes provided an opportunity for bullish positions.

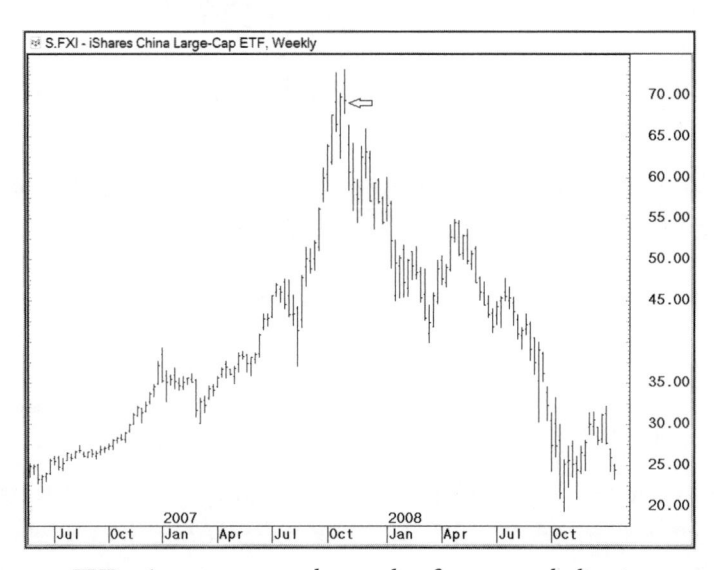

FXI - An opportune short sale after a parabolic rise.

is nothing like cold, hard statistics staring me in the face, though, to give me a sharp wake up call.

My program requires lots of time and organization, but who needs a life? I wouldn't do it if I didn't love it. It's all about eliminating outside distractions and influences. I have traded my same methodology for four decades. Nothing has changed except for me and my mailing address. I am older, smarter and slower.

16

JIGSAW PUZZLES

Every Christmas, my mom would give me a jigsaw puzzle as a present. This tradition started when I was a kid. And every year, my mother became more sadistic as she found what she thought were impossible-to-complete puzzles. There is one puzzle which will go down in infamy. It was hands down the most challenging puzzle ever created. This puzzle from hell was intimidating in that it was massive. There must have been 10,000 pieces. The box the puzzle came in displayed a map of the world. Upon further inspection, you could see the map was made from millions of itty bitty photographs. The state of Florida alone consisted of fifty photographs.

But never say never. The puzzle was finished sooner than later. It's an addiction for me which I only allow myself to indulge in once a year.

Puzzling is an art. It works best if you don't try too hard. Let your eyes glaze over the clumps of pieces. Different colors will seem to have different textures. Without looking too hard at the edges, the pieces jump into place, your hands guided by a magic sixth sense. There is an expression used in sports, "Have soft eyes." My riding instructor used this all the time. It means, relax the eyeballs so the head and neck stay soft. Then you can see out of the sides of your peripheral vision. When you over focus, you create tension in your body and it blocks the flow.

The same can be said about looking at the charts. Studying them too intensely would be "hard eyes." Think about keeping soft eyes and the markets then take on a more organic feel. It is easier to see the big holistic picture of the money flows. And this is how I feel on those rare occasions when all four of my profit centers are running smoothly. The markets seem effortless.

The ability to watch many markets on a discretionary basis does not happen overnight. It takes time to learn how to process lots of data consistently without getting the proverbial "brain-fry." Chunking data is one effective way to learn. Information is grouped into time of day segments, correlated markets and sectors, or specific patterns. Categorizing repetitive price behaviors are tricks for increasing one's capacity to process information. Always start out concentrating on just one thing at a time before building upon it.

It helped that I stood on a trading floor monitoring multiple options quotes in many stocks for years. A good part of the process is learning to discard everything that is not of value: too much data, outside sources, TV, and internet surfing. Kill the distractions until the day is nothing more than a series of observations. Stalk, be patient, and when you see your opening, act with decisiveness. Execute automatically and without hesitation.

And, play the cards you are dealt.

17

QUEEN OF SPADES

The tide was coming in, but we were sitting just out of reach on the pebbly beach in our wooden Adirondack chairs. It was almost lapping the now smoldering fire where we had roasted marshmallows and hot dogs earlier.

Roger was stuck with a mitt full of Hearts. We couldn't wait to lay a few more on him. My baby brother, who will still be the baby brother when we are all old and gray, turned out to be the best card player of all of us.

He played the ten of hearts. Steve played a five and Mom played a six.

"Ha! I'm getting rid of my nine of hearts!"

We were all happy to dump more hearts on Roger. Roger took the trick again, another 4 points against him. He next played the Ace of Clubs, taking that trick as well. None of us thought anything was amiss until he played the Jack of Hearts. I looked at Roger's face—he was giving away nothing. Hmmmm. You don't play the high card in hearts unless you WANT to take the trick. We all had to put down another heart.

"Don't tell me you have the Queen, King, and Ace of Hearts too?"

Yup, he sure did and he took the remaining hearts in the two rounds. Roger was making a not so desperate attempt to shoot the Moon, but there was still one card he needed—the Queen of Spades. A real nail-biter was building and my family members were wearing their best poker faces.

How was Roger going to get that Queen? Was he holding the Ace and King of Spades as well? They were the only cards that could smoke out the Queen. We darted furtive glances around the table. Roger was in control for now, but he had to stay in control. He played the Ace of Diamonds and took that hand. He then played the Queen of Diamonds, but when it came to Mom, she laid down the King. A chance for someone else to wrestle control. It was my turn next. It is moments like these when I try my hardest not to flash a grin. I did not have any diamonds left, meaning I could play any card I wanted. I pretended to study my cards with an added intensity. Then I slowly selected one and gently floated it on top of the pile so all could see the evil face of the Queen of Spades.

"Gee, Mom, I hate to do this to you!" It meant 13 points against her. Roger's face fell. He was stuck with 13 points in Hearts against him, but if he had been able to snag that Queen, we each would have had 26 points against us.

"I'll be the sacrificial lamb. Again." Mom said.

The tide had now dowsed our fire pit, so roasting more marshmallows was out. The beer supply was running low, too. But we were all in the best of spirits having foiled baby brother.

We all grew up losing. The games we played could only have one winner, so the majority of us were losers each round. The only thing that made losing tolerable was making snide comments and taking jabs at each other. We did not gloat if we won because the odds were that we were still going to lose more times than we won.

My brother Steve and I have many discussions on the analogies between poker and trading. I do not play poker and he does not trade. Yet every statement I make about trading can be applied to poker and vice versa. There is no right or wrong way to "trade." What is right for one person may be completely wrong for another. The biggest challenge is making decisions with incomplete information. We are going to be wrong a percentage of the time. What do you have to do to stay strong psychologically? How do you keep your ego out of the equation? Ego can be the undoing of traders and many different poker players. I have heard many stories about traders who blew out due to one big loss caused by an out of control ego.

I heard a story about Paul T. Jones when he did a stint trading in Tokyo back in the mid-eighties. The market was roaring. He was standing at a desk surrounded by Japanese traders, and he gets out of a losing trade. A few of the other traders were aghast and remarked, "Ahhh, you take losses?"

Every trading environment is unique, and the same goes for each poker game. The trading shifts from moment to moment just as poker shifts from hand to hand. My brother tells me that if you are acting early in the hand, enter only with a hand that's very likely to be the best hand. This is like initiating a trade too soon before there is an established trend. Take only the most compelling signals or the ripest trade location. Even so, the best hands may not play out to win the pot.

There is a Catch-22 that applies to cards and trading alike: "Know the rules and know when to break the rules." It might be even more important to know that you might not even know all the rules. Mike Epstein loved Maria Muldaur's music. He told me his favorite lyrics were, "Dem dat know, know that they know, and dem dat don't know, don't know dat they don't know." Think about that.

Everyone can agree on a few hard and fast rules in trading and poker, and they have to do with money management.

1) Protect your capital.
2) Protect open profits.
3) Set loss limits from your high point in equity. In other words, only give back so much.

This is the best advice to keep a discretionary trader from going on tilt. Nobody plays mistake-free poker forever—not even the best players in the world. No matter how good you are at something, you are going to go through losing streaks.

Tilt is a condition of poor decision making, a condition that usually results from some external force like losing a big hand or getting a bad phone call from your spouse. Anything that will affect you emotionally can cause you to make a lesser quality decision. Emotional control is paramount in trading and poker.

One would think that the solution to dealing with tilt, triggers, and emotions is to trade a 100% systematic model. If that were so easy, everyone would be doing it. The firms making a living trading 100% mechanically tend to have elaborate infrastructures to support running multiple models across multiple markets. Even then, there is the nagging question about a system's half life—at what point in time does the strategy deteriorate? Many strategies do as inefficiencies in the market are arbitraged out.

The market can go on "tilt" too. A market isn't an individual decision maker, so the clues when this is happening to the market are tricky to time. The most profitable times for a trader can be during huge emotional market extremes—the type of markets a professional is more likely to feel. A good example of this was when Reagan was shot, and the market had a very violent sell-off followed immediately by a comeback rally. That sell-off was poor decision making as a result of an emotional shock. Another example is a trap or false breakout followed by the anxiety of getting out of it. In 2016 the market made enormous gyrations after the election results, another case of the market going on tilt.

My brother Steve oversaw a team of PhDs who used Artificial Intelligence to map credit fraud. The driving premise is that aberrations gave information. But do all fat tails give information? Aberrations in long-term relationships can give information, but others are simply event driven. You might think a trader's skill is in finding the anomaly, but the real trick is finding a way to take advantage of it before the edge is gone. Perhaps this is becoming easier with machine learning because infinitely more dollars have been going into this area than into trend following.

Math models can't work all of the time in systems of imperfect information. No matter how on top of everything a trader might be, there are parts of the equation that will be hidden. A normal distribution works up to a point, but the gold is in finding where the distribution fails or is skewed. The math geeks have trouble seeing that. The problem is in taking math as a given and overweighting information.

Steve talks about the different poker styles: loose-passive, loose-aggressive, tight-passive, and tight aggressive. If you are a good player using a tight aggressive style you will possibly be a winner (providing the rake isn't too high). Your variance will be lower in the long run because you are entering a lesser number of hands but ones of higher quality. The most profitable players use a loose-aggressive style. Their variance is higher but their profit per year is also somewhat higher. You have to be willing to handle the style you choose. A loose aggressive player needs to be comfortable with large swings and the emotional components that come with that.

Let's talk about variance for a bit and how it factors into trading styles. Without getting bogged down in statistics, think of variance as the swings in the P and L. In poker, an aggressive style of play will play hands more frequently than other methods and will more often bet or raise than call. This leads to playing for bigger pots but bigger losses as well. Simply put, an aggressive style takes more risks. An aggressive trader trades with wider stops, takes more trades, or often enters where there is less confirmation, all leading to larger swings in the P and L. These traders need to be able to handle more significant losses and drawdowns emotionally.

I knew a poker player who was exceptionally good at handling the swings, not just the emotional components. He had great skill at ending his poker sessions when he had too much good variance or a big winning streak. I can remember more than a few times where I wished I walked away after a good run. It's only after I started to give some back that I took a break. Over time, we get to know ourselves and our patterns. Sometimes I wish that it didn't take so many years.

A player who can't handle a large loss appropriately is better suited to playing a tight aggressive style. For a trader, this means scalping or hitting singles with reasonable money management stops in place. Take fewer trades and pick your spots!

The Weakest Link is a television game show that debuted in the US in 2001. The eight contestants are asked questions one at a time, and if they answer correctly, they have the option of banking the money or opting to build it up. If the next player gets the answer correct, the money in the pot rises exponentially. However, the money is only safe and locked in once it has been banked. If a question is missed, the entire pot goes back to zero. There are 2 optimal betting strategies. Most contestants tend to bank after 2-3 correct answers or lose the pot that has been built up, precisely the wrong tactic to pursue. The strategy that maximizes the potential earnings is to never bank the small profits, but keep trying to score the entire pot by getting 8 correct answers in a row. The reward for one correct answer is $1000 but the payoff for 8 correct answers in a row is $125,000. The next best strategy is to bank after every correct answer. Each right answer earns money though not very much.

This last strategy parallels the trading style of the trader who scalps for a few ticks, locks it in, and has a high win-loss ratio. This is an example of low variance. The market might run much higher after he has booked his small profit, but on the other hand, his profits are locked in, and the market can't take them away. A trader who initiates on a breakout from a major chart formation will invariably have more losses due to false breakouts. And each breakout may not get too far, but the trader has to be willing to trail a stop and not bank profits too soon. All he needs is 1-2 huge moves a year, but it takes lots of patience, discipline, and fortitude. There is nothing like an open profit that starts to burn a hole in a novice trader's pocket.

Generally speaking, game players and traders find it easy to quit when they are winning but hard to quit when they are losing. A good reason as to why you should set loss limits. You never want to lose more in a single session than you can reasonably expect to win in a session of good poker, or for that matter, a period of trading. Don't get "stuck." How will you feel when you start the next trading day if you did not clean up your mess from the day before? You will be at a psychological disadvantage on the opening bell.

Stay in the process no matter what, and if you can't do this, then step away. The markets trade 24/7. There will always be trading opportunities.

What do you do when things aren't going well? Don't dig a deeper hole. I have to regroup first before making back a loss. The best trades I ever made were making back big losses. The worst trades I made were carrying over a bad position into the next morning and thinking I could get out at a better price. But after keeping track of the statistics, more often than not I was getting out at a worse price. The market is going to get worse because of the way it closed. It's hard to take advantage of the opportunities that the opening provides when you are still figuring out what to do with a losing position.

It's been said that to be a long-term winner in poker you need fire in your belly, a passion for the game and a passion for learning and growing. But you also need balance in your life. At the beginning of your poker career, you are thirsty for knowledge and experience because this is how you grow. But if you don't have other things in your life, you will get obsessed with the stimulation. Then it is not a career or a passion, it's an addiction. This is so true for newer traders.

To gain experience you need to play the game and learn the sophisticated depth of subtlety. Combining analytics and context takes experience. The math is the easy part. Isn't this true of most all games?

18

MY NAME IS IN THE PHONE BOOK

In the early nineties, I had set up my trading office in our downstairs basement. I had these clunky monitors that would look utterly primitive next to the flat screens we use today. My screens displayed my charts and quotes, pretty much what I use today but with a few more pixels. Every morning I would disappear into my cave and start my day. Once the markets were open, I was deaf to my surroundings. A bomb could have gone off, and I would not have noticed.

We lived in the middle of nowhere. We were surrounded by evergreen trees, and our house backed up to the clubhouse of the local golf course. It was a tranquil place to live.

One spring morning, as I was downstairs working and my husband was upstairs preparing lunch, our doorbell rang. Being completely oblivious to the world around me, I did not notice. However, it was hard for my husband to ignore. He paused for a moment, wondering who could be at our door in the middle of the trading day.

Fixing Erika's hair in my basement office.

My husband opened the door only to find three enthusiastic Japanese businessmen on our doorstep. After picking his jaw up off the floor, he asked, "Can I help you?" They took out a book, *The New Market Wizards,* and pointed at my name.

"Is this the home of Linda? We're here to see the wizard!"

My husband stared at them wondering what alternate dimension we were now inhabiting. "Uh, she's busy at the moment." They continued looking at my husband optimistically. "Maybe try later…" he said as he slowly closed the door. My husband raced down to the basement. "You will never guess what just happened."

The New Market Wizards is one of a series of books written by Jack Schwager. I am not sure how Jack came across my name in the early nineties, but he contacted me and wanted to have dinner. I did not know who he was and told him he would have to wait until I took another trip up to New York. My health was not 100%

yet and so I rode my favorite Greyhound bus which ran up the Jersey Turnpike.

Jack was skeptical that a trader could make such good profits trading on a short time horizon. But I told him it was impossible for me to predict much further than 2-3 days out. After some lengthy discussions, I showed him my work and methodology, as well as my profitability. We had dinner with a tape recorder running, and I had no idea I was to become a chapter in his *New Market Wizard* book. Weeks later, he called me up to ask for my address. In a few days, I found a package stuffed in my mailbox by the postal service. I was a chapter in the book.

That package invoked Steve Martin in *The Jerk*. "First, I get my name in the phone book, and now I'm on your ass. You know, I'll bet more people see that than the phone book."

The *Wizards* books turned out to be quite popular. I lived on the edge of the New Jersey Pinelands. It was woodsy and remote, at least 45 minutes from Philadelphia. The book turned out to be an open invitation for people from all walks of the industry to take it upon themselves to visit my office. I eventually begged the exchange to remove my address out of their listings since I was still a member.

Another individual showed up bearing an interesting gift. He was one of the original turtle traders. This was the name given to a group of traders whom Richard Dennis trained. He was not managing money at the time, but he wanted to meet me. He brought me a paper bag which had a copy of his notes in an 8 x 11 book format of Richard Dennis's program. I did not know much about trend following systems because it just wasn't my game. But when I read through it, I was surprised only 10% of the content had anything to do with a "system." The rest was a combination of psychology, game theory, and classic pattern recognition, allowing for discretion on add-ons.

Twenty-five years have passed since this visit, so it is OK to mention this now. Most of the pattern recognition was very simple bar chart formations. For example, let's say there was a big spike high, something that nowadays is called a hammer on a candlestick chart. If the market then took out this swing spike price, it was a point to add a unit and increase the leverage. When Rick came to work for me, he had been with a "Turtles" firm, Sjo, Inc., and he confirmed the use of these idiosyncrasies. He called them "structural points." The original Turtles System was more than a mechanical "system." But the nuances of discretion were something that stayed in the classroom between Dennis and his students. The biggest lesson was, you have to take the entries. You can't afford to miss the one trade which might make your year and you never know where it is going to come from. "Get the trade on," as Rick quipped.

* * *

Toby Crabel came to visit and stayed at my house with his family. I had met him earlier through a mutual broker and we had socialized in New York and Chicago together. He had signed a non-compete for 5 years after working for Victor Niederhoffer, which meant he had a head full of ideas and no outlet for them. Toby loves statistics the same way I do. And he loves tennis the way I love horses – he was actually a semi-pro for a while, and that seemed to be where he released all of his energy. That evening, I showed him much of my original modeling using short-term rates of change in conjunction with pattern recognition.

Toby got pensive while my husband cooked dinner. "I miss the industry. Five years is too long to sit around developing new models and not using them."

"Tell me about it! Five years is a long time to wait for anything. *Especially* the markets. What have you been working on?"

"I've been building a platform for automating multiple strategies. I still work with holding times of less than two to three days," he said.

"Ahhh…most of my work is with models only: 2 variables and one filter. There are subtle tweaks such as the number of look-back days to determine the ATR or time of day functions. I use large sample sizes, too, but I find that even 300 is not big enough." I was still looking for affirmation that I was on the right track.

Toby's wife was feeding her son a vegan gruel while we stood at the counter and contemplated the next great system. "So, do you plan on managing money?" I wanted to know.

"The day I hit the five-year mark," Toby smirked.

We had a great time that weekend, hanging out at Camp Raschke, staring at computer screens and talking strategies, even if we couldn't put them into effect.

Five years later, though, Toby did put them into effect and then some. He hit on a niche where there was a real need for a program delivering low drawdowns. His returns were quite small but extremely consistent. He exploited and scaled a time frame that nobody else had, which allowed firms to leverage his programs and allowed him to collect multiples of management fees. He moved to Beverly Hills and continues to run his firm as methodically as he plays tennis.

Professionals often develop concentration and consistency from other disciplines.

19

IT'S A PROFIT DEAL!

Over the years, the most unimaginable events have occurred. It would be impossible to make these things up. One morning, I got a call from the group of brokers who did my business up in Chicago.

"Hey Linda, we're sorry, but you can't do business with us today."

"What do you mean I can't place any orders? I have positions on!" I could not believe my ears.

"Sorry, Chicago is shut down." The brokers were curt, under the gun to make phone calls to dozens of clients.

"But, but, but? What about my positions? How am I supposed to trade?"

"Closed. Sorry. We will contact you tomorrow with an update." *click*

It was April 1992, and a tunnel beneath the Chicago River was breached. A contractor working on bridge pilings sought an easement from the city to preserve a historical component of the bridge, and the city approved the modifications to the plan. The contractor and its crews had no idea that somewhere deep beneath the river and sediment, an old decommissioned tunnel laid dormant—but still very much connected to other tunnels beneath the city. The construction led to a slight shift in the river bottom, which gradually grew to a slow-seeping leak of mud, which finally turned into a full-on breach, which was measured to be a 20-foot-wide hole. This allowed 250 million gallons of water to flood the basements and underground facilities in the Chicago financial area. Security crews at the Merchandise Mart reported fish swimming haplessly in the basement. The Loop and the Financial District were evacuated, and the CBOT and CME closed for a few days. My brokers set up shop in someone's house out in the suburbs, but the message was loud and clear: *Have backup accounts and backup brokers.*

One day in the middle of the afternoon, I received a cold call from a lady broker up in New York. She did not know who I was, so I decided to have some fun with her.

"Oh yeah, I do have a futures account, how did you get my name?" I asked.

"I'm with Vision up in New York. I want you to open an account with me." She spoke with an urgency only New Yorkers have mastered.

"Now why would I want to do that? I don't trade much. I live on a farm in southern New Jersey, and the most I do is buy an occasional corn contract to hedge my chicken feed."

"Like, *your* chicken feed? You raise chickens?" I could hear paper shuffling in the background as she frantically scoured her cold call list to figure out why I was on there.

"Yes, ma'am. I'm lookin' at the chickens in my backyard right now." I was actually looking at Tina's ass on the lawn below as she sunbathed with my daughter.

IT'S A PROFIT DEAL! 127

"Well, I think we could do some business together. I won't take no for an answer."

She was persistent and called many times. I already had great rates with my clearing firm but was trying to keep an open mind. I figured it wouldn't hurt to have accounts in several places, as I learned when the Chicago River flooded the Financial District. I told her we could meet for lunch when I was back in New York.

The next time I drove up to New York, I scoured the street corner where we were to meet. I did not see any broker, only a tiny speck of a person. And that speck was Liz—all 90 pounds of her, red hair piled up on her head and a colorful scarf flapping in the breeze. She had a deep throaty voice which made her sound like she weighed 200 pounds on the phone. I opened an account with her out of sheer respect at her gumption. When we got to know each other better, she told me she was raising money for a female CTA and that I should become one, too.

The institutional side of the business and managed money was an area I knew little about. Why would I want to trade money for someone else, give them 80% of the profits and keep only 20%? Over the previous years, I had backed quite a few traders. The deal was always 50-50. The trader kept at least 50% of the profits.

I funded 16 different traders over three decades, and only one ever made money—Bob Buran. So, I don't back traders anymore. One out of 16 makes for a bad win-loss ratio regarding trading traders; a true testament to how challenging the trading profession is. At any rate, I could not understand why I would go to someone else for money when I had my own.

Liz gave me the name of the trader she was raising money for so I could talk to her on the phone and learn more. The CTA was Liz Chevall, and she was as gracious and as helpful as could be. Liz was one of the original Turtle Traders taught by Richard Dennis and Bill Eckhardt. The Turtles were long-term trend followers and, in their heyday, managed a substantial amount of funds. Her firm, EMC Capital Advisors, was founded in 1988. It had respectable performance, modestly outperforming the SPs for 25 years.

Liz had a remarkably democratic view of trading. She once said, "Go for it. Today the physical advantage of men in the trading pits is inconsequential because trading is virtually 100% electronic. I give the same advice to both men and women seeking entry-level jobs in managed futures. Technical skills are mandatory. Great thinkers and idea creators need technical applications to test and execute trading strategies. Having those skills is a great way to gain entry or to build your own business." She believed that numbers were a meaningful way to combat discrimination—a profit sheet cannot tell the difference between a male or female trader.

And she believed that managing money would be worth my while—so much so that we often had phone conversations about it.

"You know, when you manage money, you don't have to get the same type of returns you do on your personal account. Yet indirectly you are using much greater leverage—just on other people's money.

"Oh, God, you have my attention."

"You already have a sound strategy and great experience. Just keep doing what you are doing except scale up the size."

She spoke with conviction, and it really planted a seed in my head. She stressed that the ability to adapt to change is the key to long-term success in trading. "It's relatively easy to develop a profitable trading strategy over a short time frame. It's far more challenging to develop a reliable method to continually adapt the strategy to future market conditions."

Go forth and prosper!

Liz passed in 2013 at age 56 of an aneurysm. I hope her name is remembered. She was the only original female 'Turtle' trader and one of the few to stay in business for so long. She was a force of nature, and I am so glad I knew her.

***

I educated myself as best I could about this new side of the business. I met with brokers in Chicago. I met with Richard Kovner, brother to the infamous Bruce Kovner. He had an unglamorous office in the garment district of New York. I went to Delaware and, courtesy of a friend met with folks who ran Delaware Pension money. I met contacts in everything from the seediest offices to the classiest digs. Everyone was willing to give me their two cents on the business and how to get started. I saw the low returns other managers were making and thought I could do better. It's doable to make a 100% return on a million dollars. It's nearly impossible to do that on a billion. Still, I appreciated Liz's advice. I wanted to build a business and not just trade for myself.

There is a great line in *The Jerk* when a light bulb goes off in Steve Martin's head: "Ah-ha! It's a profit deal!"

That is how I felt. There is a significant difference between generating returns on big money, meaning $100 to 300+ million, versus my personal account which was sizable by now. I was competitive, though, and thought it would be easy to produce the 200-300% returns I was used to doing. Wrong! I called up Morris, who had backed me on the Pacific Coast Exchange when I blew out. We had stayed in touch because I had convinced him to buy the Insight software I used. He loved it and used it every day to trade, so maybe he felt he owed me. But perhaps he liked talking to me now that he no longer had to chew me out for being too quick or slow in adjusting our positions. Somehow, we had remained good friends.

"Morris, I need to show a track record on a third-party account." Third party accounts were also known as OPMs—for "Other People's Money."

"What do you need?"

"I don't know, is $50,000 OK?"

"Sure!" He sounded unfazed.

This does not sound very impressive, but I figured if I traded 1 contract in a third-party account, it would be proof of the program I had been doing for myself. It could serve as a unit size—one contract per $50,000.

Just like that, I had my first OPM deal; thanks to Morris' undying optimism, I officially started managing money in 1992.

Some people can trade their own money but flop when under the pressure of trading OPM. Others can show impressive performance on OPM but are too lackadaisical when trading their own accounts. Thus, it is essential for investors to see a lengthy real-time record on OPM before committing funds to a trader.

I am not sure how word got out I was managing money because I never did any advertising. Nor did I have anyone raising money for me. The *Market Wizard* book had been published, and my name in print undoubtedly helped. I did well trading the Pritzkers' money which was placed with me through one of my Chicago contacts, and that was all the Street needed to know. The Pritzkers are one of the wealthiest families in America, having made a fortune from their stake in the Hyatt hotel chain. They were some of the first to be aggressive in allocating funds to alternative investments such as CTAs and hedge funds. If the Pritzkers had money with me, everyone had to have money with me. Soon I had to become a CTA because you are only allowed up to 15 accounts before the CFTC requires you to register. I delivered a 76% return after fees my first year, and I was up and running.

* * *

Shortly after that, I started running a copper hedging program courtesy of Morris. He sat on the board for a firm which produced copper widgets on razor thin margins. Periodically I bought a couple hundred copper futures 16 – 18 months out to hedge their commercial contracts. Then each month I liquidated a set number of contracts as the copper was used in production.

IT'S A PROFIT DEAL! 131

As traders, we look at futures as a speculative vehicle. But when futures were created in the mid-1800s, it was for the farmers to reduce the uncertainty in their business with their crops in the field. The actual users and producers are referred to as "commercials." My copper client could not afford to guarantee a fixed contract price and risk the raw material cost rising above his margins.

I relied on the brokers in the pit to shop around my orders. Who is going to sell me copper futures which don't expire until a year and a half later? Most of the trading is done in the "front month" which is the contract closest to the actual delivery date.

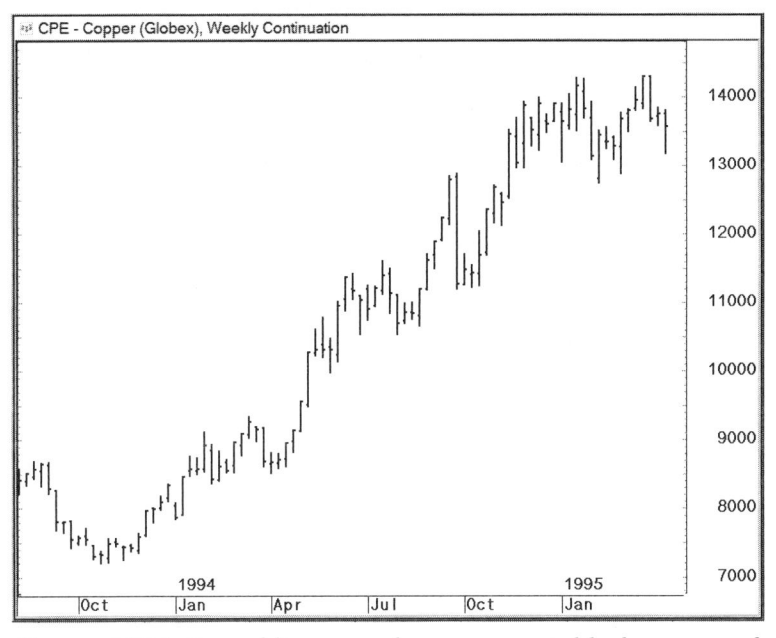

Copper-1994: Scrambling to get long commercial hedges executed.

The different years are assigned colors. If I want to buy copper for the following year, it is the "red month," meaning red for the second year out. I became good friends with the New York copper brokers out of necessity. I may not have known much about their lives, but I relied on them to help me find customers to take the other side of the orders for my commercial client. We had slang names for the individual markets. Copper was "the wire." "Buy me 50 cars of the wire, market." Cars = contracts. Another funny name was "sweet stuff" for sugar. "Offer 50 sweet stuff at 8.85."

Copper has strong seasonal tendencies—the largest orders are placed in the fall. To this day, I look for a ripe buying opportunity in October when I have a high degree of confidence that copper has reached its seasonal low. Prices are ready to rise, and a long position can pay well.

My horizons were expanding beyond trading as a sole proprietor.

20

SYNCHRONICITY AND THE MORGUE FILE

Frank was a unique, brilliant individual who entered my life most randomly. He looked the part of a stereotypical engineer—short sleeve shirt (plaid flannel in the winter), pen in the pocket, wire-rim glasses and a crew cut. Frank had written software for Hewlett Packard which extended the shelf life of one of their products by two more years. He was one of the few, if not the only person, to negotiate a percentage of the profits into his contract. HP thought it impossible to complete a particular job under three months, let alone at all. But Frank's motto was, "It's not *if* it can be done, but how fast it can be done."

It goes without saying he proved them wrong and ended up financially set for life. With his new windfall, it became his mission to conquer the markets with his genius brain. But he was having a tough time. Unlike software, the markets cannot be reliably won with raw intelligence.

Frank had a long-time assistant whose husband was the local morgue director. One day, she was poking around the morgue and came across a stack of old newspapers piled up in the corner. They were used to stuff cadavers. On top of the pile, she noticed my picture and an article about me on the front page of one of the local newspapers. It was after I was mentioned in the *Market Wizards* book. There obviously was a shortage of content for papers in the New Jersey Pinelands where I was living. One afternoon, I got a call out of the blue from Frank. His assistant had told him I might have all the secrets after showing him the article. Naturally, he wanted to come to my office to see what I was doing and pick my brain.

Frank drove to my office which, in those days, was a massive cave in my basement—quiet, cool and dim lit. No TVs, no windows, no distractions. He immediately wanted to backtest my technical indicators to see if he could build a system. Engineers!

But he did not understand that it is difficult to get a consistent edge using indicators. They might be aids for pattern recognition but are unlikely to be of use in a mechanical system other than a filter. This is where the deviation between the people who build the trading software and the people who use it begins.

Frank was a genius with computers. In 1992, he tried to expand the scripting language for TradeStation to process more complex backtesting tasks. He ran into memory and processing limitations on even the best home PCs. He was ahead of his time. He then wrote the scripting language for Aspen Graphics. Scripting code is what allows a developer to write indicators, formulas, and strategies. He ended up writing his own software using object-oriented programming, which no one was using at the time. Frank was a project design guru, but I later found out he had a programmer, Tom, who wrote all the code. Tom had his Ph.D., lived in an attic. I never actually saw him, but I heard about his talents for years.

Frank was lots of fun to hang with because he had all the toys: helicopters, military Hummers, the latest and greatest jet skis, and a million-dollar motorhome. When you have no kids, you can end up with way too much time on your hands. Frank lived in a modest, non-descript rancher in the woods, but his basement looked like a top-secret mission control center. He had the fastest computers and data feeds, surrounded by industrial size ionizers. Every cable and wire was perfectly tied back and hidden out of sight. There was an extensive collection of rifles in a separate room, complete with a sophisticated piece of equipment used to recalibrate laser sights.

The first time he showed it to me, all I could say was, "Pretty dangerous to keep that type of arsenal next to a trading office."

"Don't worry, I have all my files backed up." He was always an engineer.

* * *

Frank took us out to an abandoned airport in his military Hummer, and we all took turns doing donuts in the sand. Erika was hanging on for dear life trying not to get thrown out the window. Frank also gave Erika rides on the back of his Honda Gold Wing motorcycle, an early nineties model all tricked out. She wore a helmet, and they only went around the block. Somehow, she did not grow up to be a thrill seeker.

And Frank's jet skis! He had a Yamaha, the biggest and baddest you could buy at the time. Erika and I rode on the back. We put in at the Rancocas Creek in New Jersey and would go all the way out to the Delaware River. Frank was always trying to toe the line at 60 mph. I could not walk the next day since my quads would be screaming. Erika got squished between us. We'd all go out for a Coke afterward—standard fare for Frank.

Frank and I had a silent pact: I taught him everything I knew about the markets, and he taught me everything he knew that I could understand, which was not much. I drove to his house every

Wednesday after the markets closed. We spent several hours on his computers and then we went roller skating.

Nobody would believe this surreal image unless they saw it for themselves: an airplane hangar in the middle of New Jersey filled with dozens of roller skaters between the ages of fifty and seventy. Women with skinny flamingo legs twirled around in teeny skirts as a live organist played. Men stood erect like ballroom dancers, but on roller skates. The arena swirled to the rhythm of waltzes and foxtrots in what appeared to be a forgotten world. Each week the paramedics showed up and wheeled out a senior who slipped and fell, spraining an ankle or breaking a bone. They might have been the only outsiders who knew about the hanger and the weekly soiree on wheels.

Frank bought me an expensive pair of ritzy roller skates. He needed someone to go with him to this weekly event and be his skate partner. I was the youngest there by at least 20 years, as well as the worst skater. After a vigorous hour of roller skating, Frank and I would get a Coke, continue to talk shop, and then talk more shop all the way home. Topics included: writing scripting languages, comparing data feeds, improving computer efficiency. Statistics, more statistics, and technical subjects for which I had a rudimentary knowledge of. "Durable and Robust" were the two words Frank brainwashed into my head.

I started using Aspen Graphics in addition to my Insight and TradeStation software. Aspen was written by two rogue partners who had left CQG, another charting software firm. Since Frank wrote the scripting language for Aspen, he taught me how to write anything imaginable. I am not a programmer, but with his guidance, I soon felt like a master computer hacker. Now I had a language to describe any pattern or concept under the sun. I could make things pop out on my charts in pretty colors. Jackson Pollocked graphs exploded with hues that actually meant something to me.

A few years earlier, I developed a model on my Insight. It was a volatility model I used for buying or selling straddles on the OEX (similar to buying or selling premium). It consisted of overlaying multiple rates of change on top of each other and using the max/min of all these squiggly lines as an indicator. So, for example, when the readings were all clustered together, and the max/min was low, I bought straddles on the OEXs. When the bands were spread far apart, as would happen after a large standard deviation move, I shorted straddles.

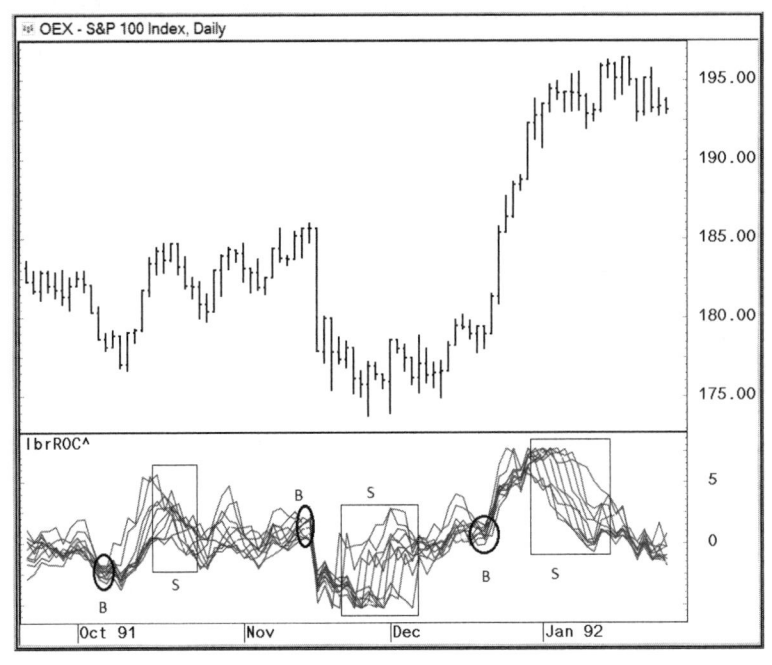

B=buy straddles, go long volatility. S=sell straddles, go short volatility.

I had the idea the first and second derivatives of these rates of changes could have value if programmed into a neural network. Frank had a fellow Hewlett Packard friend, Ernie, whose son worked for NASA. Nothing like getting help in training a neural net from a rocket scientist! We re-ran the data every three months to update its training. Neural networks might have sounded sexy at the time, but in the grand scheme, they are quite primitive. They cannot be used as a substitute for a system and are only as good as the questions you ask of them. As Frank explained, neural networks are best used as "pattern classifiers." They make a functional component in a more extensive, more complex system.

After running the data at the end of each day, I asked the network the question: what is the directional bias for the next day and how reliable is this bias? It spit out a reading from -5 to 5 with 0 representing no edge. I had lots of fun with this. It supported the work I was doing with my Taylor modeling and provided an added confidence factor.

Ah ha! This neural net was the key to everything. It was so good I was going to have to keep it in a vault! It was going to be better than my Golf system ever had been.

The market makers on the trading floor of the PHLX called each morning wanting to know what the net said for the day. I was popular and trusted because my complex and secret system was on a winning streak. A reading of +3 meant easy trading with a long side bias. But there was one exception. When it indicated a 5 or -5, there could be a huge move, but the direction might be completely wrong.

"Hey, what's the "Net" reading today?"

"Hmmm, -5. Gee…There's potential for a good trend day down."

When it turned out to be a massive trend day up instead, the traders were not so happy.

Here's what was happening: when the market wound down to a neutral equilibrium level, the net could not predict the directional outcome. It needed momentum to give a good reading. Instead, it indicated 5 or -5, implying the potential for a significant range day. Sometimes the market would jerk violently in one direction and

SYNCHRONICITY AND THE MORGUE FILE

then whipsaw in the opposite direction. My market maker buddies on the floor did not want to hear there was going to be a huge move, direction unknown. One does not need a neural net to model this. I learned to model anything linearly. Then it became too much work to keep it alive for amusement purposes.

There is no more glorious feeling in the world than capturing a huge trend day. My first seven-digit day came from a short position in the SPs. The market was overbought, the sentiment readings showed too much bullishness, the 2-period rate of change was poised to flip down and my models lined up like a rare planetary alignment. I had come into the day with a short side bias. When the market started selling off the opening, I added in a big way and held until the close. This is the ideal trend day—open on the high and close on the low with range expansion and volume. The market gives about 1-2 true trend days a month if it is feeling generous.

Million dollar trend day

After the markets closed, I went to taekwondo class with Erika or rode my horse. On this particular day, I will never forget driving down our two-lane country road to the karate studio. The sky could not have been any bluer, the trees were a deep lovely green, and the sun was a shining ball of yellow fire. My eyesight was razor sharp, and my senses heightened from my body drowning in endorphins. They say the first high is the best. I have never felt that intensity again, but I won't forget the feeling either. My game became hunting the big trend days. Lions and tigers and bears, oh my.

Technology offers the trader more resources than ever, but it is experience that has a greater edge.

21

MRCI

Living in the middle of nowhere, (the New Jersey Pinelands), had its benefits. For example, the barn was close. Besides that, it was a sandy wasteland with brackish cedar water in the streams. The running joke was that the state bird was the mosquito, though it was a close race between it and the greenhead horsefly.

To escape the Pinelands, I occasionally took a trip up to Chicago to have dinner with the brokers handling my business. My brokerage firm, Gerald which later became Rand Financial, arranged a dinner for ten clients at one of Chicago's amazing steakhouses. Chicago was the center of the meat-packing industry and it has some of the country's top steakhouses. Steve Moore sat at the opposite side of the table from me. Though we did not get a chance to talk much at dinner, we started sharing research over the phone shortly after.

Steve had been trading since the early seventies and set up a computer research facility in the mid-eighties. He founded Moore

Research Center, MRCI, in the early nineties. It was one of the finest computer research offices at the time. He lives on his ranch with his wife, assorted dogs, wild turkeys, and a goat on the side of a mountain outside of Eugene, Oregon. His monitor-lined office is next to his house in the woods. Steve is another can-do person. This is the theme amongst the traders I find myself working with. He single-handedly built a professional quality grass tennis court on the side of his mountain along with a 3-hole golf course and a putting green. How he made the time is a mystery because ever since I have known him, Steve has been in his office 24/7.

Playing tennis on Steve's grass court.

We formed a productive research partnership. I wrote a daily fax with trading signals and commentary to pay for the research. Nick was Steve's full-time programmer. He would take a day or two to program my ideas and then Steve set dozens of back-testing routines to run overnight. Two days later I received hundreds of pages by fax. Steve followed up by FedExing hard copies overnight. This was when the Internet was in its infancy. People would still pump page after page into a fax machine or even send a large envelope through the Pony Express.

My collaboration with Steve combined the best of the theoretical and real world. He was not only an ace statistician but a diehard trader as well. He was receptive to my ideas, and it turned out to be a tremendous learning experience for both of us. For example, in our early testing, the results seemed too good to be true. If both a buy and a sell signal were generated on the same day, the program was only counting the winning trade. It takes extra scrutiny to double check back-tested results, but the alternative is to find out the hard way by betting money and losing dollars. These initial overly-optimistic runs convinced me I was going to find a pot of gold at the end of the rainbow.

Steve had a massive database, well beyond the size found at most firms. He was known for his work on seasonals and produced different reports for the exchanges. He pioneered running correlation studies on everything from 5-minute charts to weekly data. He ran seasonals on individual stocks before it became popular elsewhere. One system he developed bought the three most overbought futures markets (based on a high stochastic reading). It then sold out one if it fell out of the top three. It was a clever relative strength system. Modeling and backtesting are like falling down a rabbit hole. Time melts away, and after many days, you may or may not end up with anything worthwhile. But if you do not try going down every possible path, you may miss something. And if you don't find anything new, at least you know you looked. It is an enjoyable, all-consuming process for me.

Steve taught me to think of modeling in terms of actuarial tables which is the basis for the seasonal trades. In other words, a seasonal trade might be "Buy Bonds—May 21, exit June 14." However, the trade is not necessarily timing sensitive. You might buy on May 21, but the market could sell off for a few days. It might not make its high on June 14, but perhaps a few days beforehand. Yet you will show a profit. This "window" has a positive expectation. If you make 20 trades each month capturing different windows of positive expectation and use a wide risk-stop to prevent disasters, over time the equity curve maintains a steady uptrend. And, once in a while, a trade will catch a windfall.

The sample size for each seasonal tends to be on the low side—typically it is the previous 20-25 years. If there is a seasonal window which has worked 85% of the time for the past 20 years, on a walk forward basis, it tends to work around 65% of the time. This is because the small sample size leads to a lower confidence factor. I took statistics in college for my economics degree. I learned just enough to feign a modest understanding when people with more expertise than I discuss confidence factors and regression analysis.

The most potent idea which Steve explained was that sometimes the best trade is a failed seasonal. If the market is doing something other than what it should be doing, there is a good reason why. Historically, crude oil had a strong downward bias at the start of January that lasted well into the next month. At the beginning of 1999, the crude market started creeping higher. It was up for the majority of days in January and proceeded to rally higher every month. It came close to doubling in price by year-end. It was the beginning of an uptrend which took the price from 16 to 145 over the next 9 years. The market's movement was imparting the powerful information that a fundamental change was happening in this market. The seasonal sell meant nothing in the face of this.

This harkens back to my days on the floor when I saw Jeff Yass switch from selling options to buying them back at higher implied volatility. When something moves beyond its historical boundaries, there is a strong reason why. A trader should be positioned in the direction of the aberration. This is difficult for most people to do. Aberrations do not happen often, and thus people do not know how to deal with them. These events are outside of our comfort zone, and the first reaction is to interpret the move as being wrong. It is more comfortable thinking that the market or relationship will revert back into its previous range.

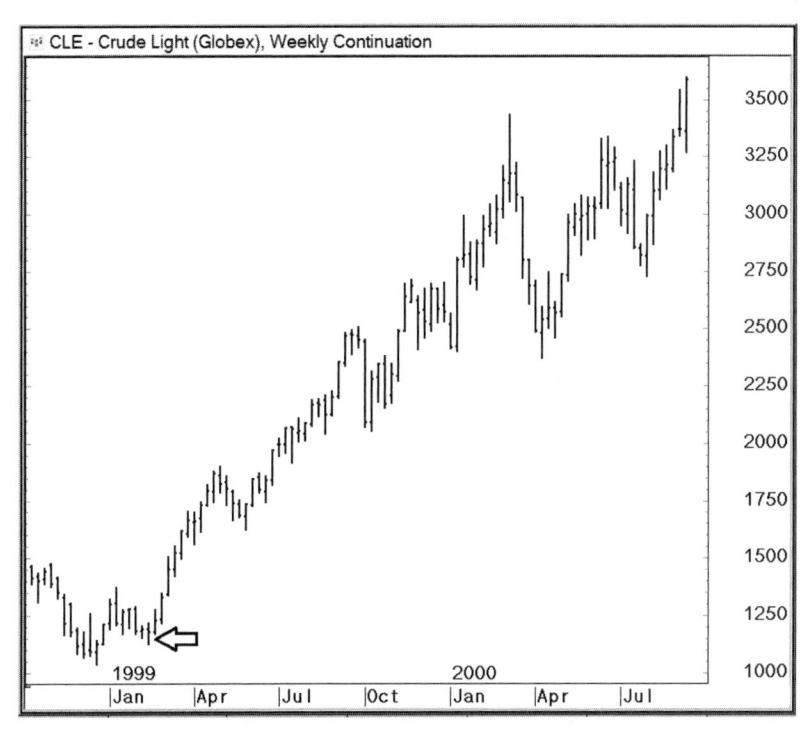

Crude-1999: January down seasonal fails, marking the start of a major uptrend.

But the market is NEVER wrong.

One day, Larry Connors stopped by my office with his partner from his latest book project. Why would they drive out to the Pinelands of New Jersey? They had written a book together and asked if I would write an endorsement. The name of the book was *Investment Secrets of a Hedge Fund Manager*—great title! I knew little about the publishing and marketing side of the business, but Connors was interested in doing more projects. We hit it off and for the next few months, talked on the phone. He mailed me a hilarious mockup making fun of all the hyped ads permeating the trading magazines.

"Look, I bought here and sold here and made $6000 off an initial investment of $100. You too can learn the secrets for only $29.99. But wait, there's more! Buy now and you will receive a $49 research report—FREE!" And it had my picture pasted on it. I still have it somewhere in my files along with articles, notebooks and test results spanning 35+ years.

We talked karate—Larry was a master in Muay Thai. By now I was a few months away from getting my black belt in Tae Kwon Do. Did we bond over searching for the most efficient way to destroy the enemy? He lived in Malibu and I had grown up on the beaches one hour south. We both had families and ferocious work ethics. Larry was keen on doing a book together and anyone who can make me laugh has my attention. I've never worked so hard in my life as I did on that project, which is why I never wrote another book until now. The year was 1996. I was getting up at 5 AM to write, trading from 8 AM – 4 PM, and then back to working on the book in the evening. Larry self-published it, which was even more work since we did the formatting. Steve Moore did the backtesting and tables for us which we printed in the back of the book. My husband, Skip, came up with the title, *Street Smarts*.

The principles in the book remain the same.

22

MOVING UP TO THE BIG LEAGUES

A few years earlier, I received a well-written letter from an individual named Mike. He professed an interest in working for me. My first assistant had moved on, and I needed another one, so Mike's timing was lucky for the both of us. Mike was the first on my team as I started to manage money, and thus LBRGroup was born. My office was still in the basement, and we both watched primitive CRT monitors in the semi-darkness. I appreciated how quiet Mike was. This is the number one most important trait I need in a work partner. He entered my orders because I hated telephones. Having someone place the orders with the floor brokers was a luxury at first, but soon became a necessity. I never had to break my concentration. We could sit next to each other on our computers and work an entire day speaking only a few words.

Mike was also adept in social situations. Once we took a trip to New York to meet with potential clients over dinner. He made sure to instruct me ahead of time where the clients should sit and where I should sit. It gave me confidence in an unfamiliar business environment.

LBRGroup was growing in AUM, or "Assets under Management." It was all word of mouth based on our performance. While LBRGroup grew, my husband was the ultimate Mr. Mom. He cooked, he baked his own sourdough bread, he made oyster stew. He did the dishes, he took Erika to school, he bought turkey decorations for the center of the table at Christmas time. He would run out and pick up a movie at Blockbuster Video each week. Just like the cliché how housewives watch soaps, he watched golf, baseball, basketball, football, and hockey all simultaneously, all taped, fast-forwarding from one to another. I did the yard work, which, in a twist of fate I now loved. The same roses that haunted me as a kid were now my afternoon therapy.

I had occasional panic attacks. As much as I prided myself on the way I could weasel through a trading floor crowd or weave through airports on the way to a meeting, crowded shopping malls did me in. One late afternoon on a weekend when the stores were not crowded, my husband and I went to the mall. He wandered off and I got lost. I froze and broke out in a cold sweat. There was no obvious destination, no trade to execute!

From then on, he bought my nylons, my suits, my earrings; everything except for shoes. There was no internet in those days and thus no online shopping. He did all the grocery shopping, too. It would take me two hours to get 10 items. Perhaps it was the number of decisions I had to make for my livelihood. I can deal with markets on a screen, but I can't decide which brand of dog food to buy. I bet I saved 3,000 hours over the years by not shopping.

* * *

After a successful year of trading, I built a new office on the side of the house. It had massive cathedral ceilings, high windows where we could watch the birds on the trees outside, and a cozy fireplace at our back. I was happy as a clam never having to leave my house other than to go to the barn or play tennis.

My husband still liked to go to visit the Exchange when my daughter was in preschool. One day he brought a new person back to the house. Rick had recently moved to Philadelphia. His wife was now the principal ballerina for the Philadelphia Ballet. She could not have weighed more than 85 pounds, and I remember her fine, petite features, colorful scarves, and vivacious personality.

Rick was a meticulous blue blood who looked like he had been born with a silver spoon in his mouth, but he was truly a hard worker. He was previously employed by Sjo, Inc., a managed futures firm run by Susan Sjo, Stig Ostgaard, and Irwin Berger. It was a well-known trend-following firm like the original Turtles. Rick knew how to place orders and he knew how to work size, so I invited him to be part of my team. We had everything in place to continue to grow.

* * *

My mom was always bringing people into our house when I was growing up. She used to joke that she was the Underground Railroad for Salvadorans. But it was no joke. A young lady named Rosa came to live with us, and my mom called her a pretend sister. She helped keep the household running because my sister took up considerable time with her disabilities. My mom learned Spanish, Rosa learned English, and before you knew it, my mom was helping bring Rosa's family and friends over. El Salvador was a mess in those days, and you really could claim political asylum, but it was a lengthy process. We had graduate students living with us who worked with special-ed children and one month, there was a friend from Montana who lived with us. I never knew who was going to be sitting at the dinner table. So, years later, when I was the one with the "cool house out in the country," I never thought it weird to invite random traders or colleagues in under my roof. It was one giant extended family with a few animals thrown in to make a full rounded zoo.

Our house was known as "Camp Raschke." Every weekend, traders from New York or Philadelphia came to hang around our pool in the summertime. My husband was the consummate host. He had an endless supply of people to tell his baseball stories—always about his pitching in the minor leagues for the Yankees. He repeated his story about ordering pizza in the dugout with Ron Guidry dozens of times. I knew the next line by heart, and then the lines after that, like someone who has seen the Rocky Horror Picture show a few too many times. I was thrilled because I never had to open my mouth. Me and the Art of Conversation? *Not.*

He bought stone crab claws, planned murder mystery dinners, and organized fantasy football leagues. It was a regular commune. My family and Mike went on ski vacations with Steve Moore. Frank took us on his luxury tour bus to Atlantic City for dinner. And we went into Philadelphia to see Rick's wife dance with the ballet. Best of all, the markets were well behaved, so all were happy at the commune. As always, there is a bit of the calm before the storm. Sometimes, it starts with tiny ripples.

Steve had introduced me to George, one of the best meat brokers on the floor. Everything is a lot more fun when you have a good broker. There is confidence that your orders are getting appropriately executed and the information passed back from the pit is legit. You feel you have a secret edge even though nobody knows any better than anyone else.

I never made great money in the meats, but they were one more market to offer a different flavor while waiting for trades to line up in other markets. The meats are prone to making V bottoms, unlike the grains which can take forever to base out. That and they have strong seasonal tendencies. I started trading the pork bellies a little bit at a time. And little bits plus little bits add up. I was still enamored with Steve's seasonal program.

One day George called Rick to talk meats. "Hey, you better be careful with these bellies."

"What's up?" Rick asked.

"Look, you guys have the largest position in bellies, and everyone in the pit knows who you are."

How could anyone know who we were and what my position was? But back in the early nineties, they did. Perhaps one of the clerks on the order desk let our name slip. It was easy to see which firm was creating the tickets.

This situation was not a good thing because if the market starts to weaken, the pit knows they have you by the proverbial balls. They are not going to make it easy for you to get out and the risk is a vicious one-way flush into first notice day. Our position was over 450 contracts which did not sound so big at the time but turned out to be a lot of pork bellies.

Each contract was 40,000 pounds of pork bellies. One hundred contracts represented 4,000,000 pounds or 80,000,000 pieces of bacon. Four hundred contracts made enough bacon to top 150,000,000 hamburgers. I was not ready to take delivery on a McDonald's franchise. Pork Belly futures stopped trading on the CME exchange in 2011 due to low volume. One could say they were eventually replaced by Bitcoin futures, a telling commentary on the evolution of the industry.

"Rick, we gotta lay low for a bit."

We did not call another order down to the meats for three weeks. We sat and waited for the pit to forget about us. Eventually they did, and by then the bellies were getting the seasonal lift we were playing for. After a month, we peeled out of some each day. I never traded the bellies again. Unfortunately, the pigs were to have the last laugh a decade later.

* * *

Rick took trips up to New York to meet with our brokers and schmooze them over spaghetti meals. Most of them were Italian. In return, our orders were taken care of in the opening rotations. A good relationship with the brokers on the New York floors was essential because they could choose to work for you or not. For example, if Rick gave an order to a broker to buy 300 Coffee futures over a 15-minute window, he didn't want the broker to tip off the order. We depended on him to judge the order flow for us and get the best average price possible.

The New York markets provided many harrowing trades, or "learning experiences." We got in early on a beautiful swing in the orange juice market in the mid-nineties. It was a breakout from a chart formation as well. We were pressing the long side for two weeks, and the price was ratcheting up like a roller coaster reaching its peak. Of course, once it finally creeps over the apex, the freefall begins. Arms either get thrown up in exultation or cling with a death grip to the restraining bars. It was a case of pressing our luck instead. The market had a radical reversal and broke sharply, starting with a limit gap down. It is no fun being long 400 contracts of Orange Juice with no bids to hit. Over a three-day period, the broker did the best job he could to get us out. But we gave back most of our profits by the time we were able to get flat again. That is a big part of trading—putting in a lot of work without much to show for it.

Another time we were long several hundred Cocoa futures. The basis for the trade was a technical chart formation. The 3/10 buy Divergence pattern was one of my staple trading patterns. But this time the market gapped out the downside and went into a two-day free fall. Ouch. What had I missed? It feels like losing your footing when trying to scale a rocky wall. A few stones fall, one foot slips, and you frantically grab with your hand to find something to hang onto, but the weight of your body is too much. The other foot slips. Before you know it, you slide back to the bottom in slow motion, unable to stop the freefall, knees and elbows losing skin along the way.

I vowed to figure out how to be on the right side of a move like this, not the wrong side. With this particular trade, I mistook the chart formation to be a bottoming formation instead of a consolidation pattern. Lesson learned. Momentum oscillators are useless in consolidations where there is too much price bar overlap. If there is a low ADX, which measure the amount of price bar overlap, toss the directional oscillators out the window because there are no swings to measure.

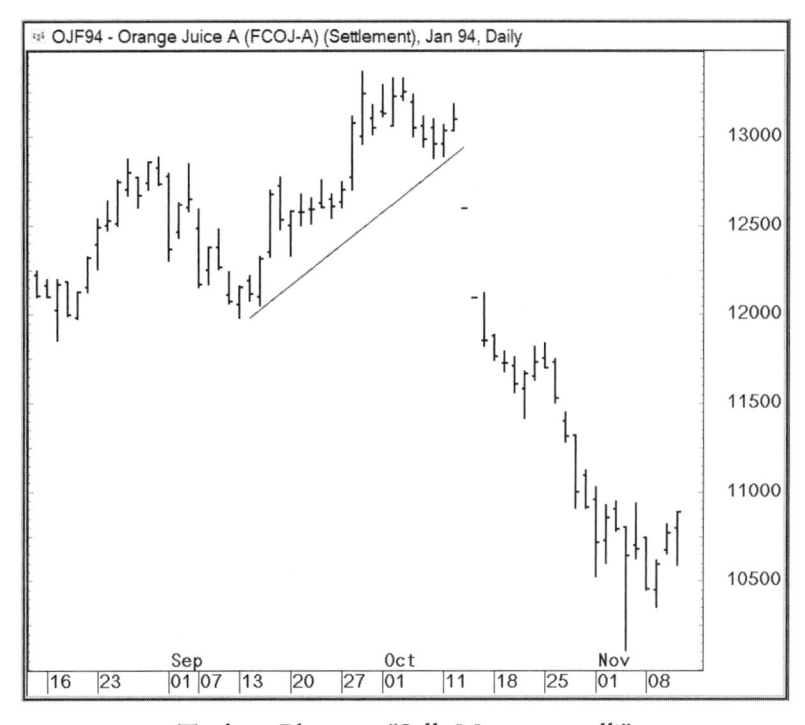

Trading Places – *"Sell, Mortimer, sell!"*

You know it hurt your feelings when you still remember the trade 25 years later. As always, much of my learning came from bad trades.

It might sound easy to initiate or exit a trade when there is a breakout from a chart formation. But try doing this on size in a New York futures pits through a broker when there is no liquidity in the early nineties. With electronic trading, orders are executed in microseconds with one mouse click. The worst-case scenario is nasty slippage, but at least you are filled immediately.

Order execution on the New York markets worked both ways. If you showed a size offer as the market was rallying it would most likely get taken and vice versa. An old expression from the floor was, "stock goes to size." The ticker tape for the individual transactions ran beneath the option quote board in the pit where we stood. For example, the bid for Amerada Hess, one of the stocks I traded, might be 24 1/8 x 24 1/4, 5,000 x 50,000. Pretty good odds that the 50,000 shares offered at 24 1/4 were going to get bought. Of course, this does not mean much anymore. Over the years, the average transaction size has gone from 1400 to 1000 to 100 shares. But, there still is something to this. We used this trick many times in the New York futures markets. If we offered out 8 sugar contracts 40 cents above where the market was trading, nobody cared. But if we offered 100 contracts and everyone knew they were there, it was likely the offer would be taken. And the market could drop right back down afterward.

Rick was instrumental in setting up our technique for position sizing. It allowed us to grow methodically without thinking about the number of contracts we were trading. It also is a super way to manage risk. Each quarter, we calculated the average daily dollar range per market. If gold had a 20-dollar average daily range over the previous 30 days, this translated into a $2000 average daily dollar range. If the SP e-minis had a 14-point average daily range, this is a $700 average daily dollar range. Gold sizing might be 4 contracts per million. If we had $100 million in AUM, it meant that 1 unit of gold equaled 400 contracts. In the SP e-minis, 1 unit might be 10 contracts per million or 1000 contracts.

I never thought about how many contracts I was trading. It was easier to say, "Buy one unit." As we grew in assets under management, it was simple to increase the unit size accordingly. We used 1/4 and 1/2 units too, to adjust for market correlation. For example, gold and silver are correlated, so we traded 1/2 unit of each if we had positions on in both. I used Steve Moore's site, MRCI, for its free correlation tables which he still publishes today.

Another benefit of trading with a predetermined unit size is that it is one less decision needed during the trading process. There are those who advocate adjusting the position size to the initial risk to never risk more than 1-3% of the capital. But who wants to take time in the heat of battle to do calculations? Always trade the same size but adjust the stop instead. For example, I am not going to risk more than 500 dollars per contract in the notes. If the volatility is greatly expanded, then my unit size might be halved, and the dollar stop doubled, but everything is determined ahead of time. I prefer very wide stops because it is essential to have something in place but then it is easy to adjust the risk point once the position is on.

The truth is that in many markets we did not keep resting stops in the market. That is an awkward thing to do when the position size is large. But we did know where and when we were wrong!

I had five people now in the office on the side of the house. When trading slowed, we watched the squirrels swing on the bird feeders hanging outside. The clunky CRT monitors were lined up in a row beneath the array of high windows facing the trees. The fireplace was always burning in the winter. Mike supplied an endless stack of CDs by female singers like Shawn Colvin, Sarah McLaughlin, and K.D. Lang.

LBRGroup was growing, and I added more profit centers. We had a seasonal spread program that used Steve Moore's research with a 2-period ROC to time entries. Bob Buran traded the volatility breakout system at night on the overseas markets. We made money in the JGBs and gave it back in the FTSE. There were two other assistants as well.

We were a team. We could do our respective tasks without saying many words. It's funny to spend so many hours close to someone without talking much.

The Jersey Boys - Mike, Rick, Jim, Brian Wolfe (RIP), and Ron from the PHLX floor.

There is no way I could have run the business without a talented business manager. I met Laura when she came to our office for a due diligence trip. Larger asset allocators make several trips to a CTA's office and monitor the real-time trading results for months before allocating capital. At the time, she was working for 6800 Capital, an alternative investment firm with a Fund of Funds. They ended up being one of my largest clients for many years.

When Laura came on board, she was working out of her own office in Memphis. The beautiful thing about having a separate business office location was that all the phone calls and mail went to her. The only interruptions we had in our office were the brokers calling back to report fills and us running outside to shake the squirrels off the bird feeders.

Laura took a trip to our office every three months to help me stay on top of things. There were so many moving parts to running the CTA. One night we went to see the *Team America* movie in theaters after a long day at the office. That movie is so vulgar and over-the-top, but hilarious. I remember looking over during one of the raunchiest, funniest bits and seeing my business manager, Laura, trying to act like she wasn't laughing. It was like a third grader who knows they can't laugh in class, which only makes whatever happened a million times funnier.

"Laura, you can laugh at the movie!" She looked so surprised and then bust out giggling.

Soon after, I flew down to Tennessee, but for a different reason than to visit Laura. A few months earlier, Steve Moore had introduced me to Robert Sparks. The Sparks were based out of Memphis and were huge in the cattle business and agricultural markets. I had the great pleasure of meeting Robert's father, Willard Sparks, who founded Sparks Commodities and was part owner of REFCO, one of the largest commodity trading firms at the time. Their division raised money for LBRGroup. We soon had multiple accounts and funds we traded, and so the Sparks invited me to their Memphis office.

The trip was memorable because I left with a bond position on that blew up while I was on the plane. There was a radical surprise economic report, and I had not left good instructions with my now overstaffed office back home. How does fate pick the timing of these outliers? It can't be random. Whatever the real reason, it keeps me eternally humble. I was about to meet my largest clients face-to-face for the first time with a two standard deviation move against us in the bonds. I think it was in May 1995, but my subconscious' tendency towards repressing bad memories makes it hard to be sure.

The opportunity to see the Sparks' operations was quite interesting so I had to collect myself and put on a poker face. Though my face was calm, my stomach was churning. Each morning, Willard conducted a meeting in which several economists, fundamental analysts, and two weathermen gave their forecasts for the day. It was an information orgy. One weather person presented the American model, and the other showed the European Model. The models offered conflicting views. What do fundamental traders do when there are contradictory weather models? Of course, my technical models were not so helpful either when that bond fat tail outlier hit.

The Sparks must have still been okay with my performance because they let me use their townhouse in the Cayman Islands, complete with data feeds and computers.

When I got back home, I had to do some serious rethinking in the light of the fiasco bond trade. I decided I did not like being a boss, only a trader. There was room for only one cook in my kitchen, and that was going to be me. Sometimes it is hard to draw the line. If four profit centers are good, why shouldn't five be even better? More trading strategies meant we could handle more money. But it does not work that way. More programs also leads to more exposure which translates to increased risk. And I did not want to track people or other systems, only my trading. It was too much to handle. Multitasking was taking the fun out of trading. So, I let everyone go except for Rick and figured the two of us could do okay.

The hardest thing to do is to say goodbye to someone, especially if you don't want to hurt their feelings. I wish everyone around me could make fabulous tons of money and be a big happy family that I missed growing up. It is difficult to separate business and pleasure, which is why I had to let them go but also why it was so awkward.

What do you do when you take a licking? Pick yourself up by the bootstraps yet again.

Step one: Take a few days off to clear the air and regain objectivity.
Step two: Be patient and wait for a 95% sure thing trade.
Step three: Make the trade on small size.
Step four: Convert! "Mortimer, we're back!"

I remember watching Andre Agassi in the French open in 1999. In the final, he was down the first two sets and came close to losing the third. But he managed to save the breakpoint and upon doing so, he pumped his fist high in the air. Convert! Seize the moment upon the first shift in momentum! He was still down, but the change in energy was palpable. Even he knew it. Agassi went on to win the third, fourth and fifth set to take the final. His determination and perseverance always stuck with me when I was in the situation of making back a loss.

This is the story of a trader's life. Keep putting one foot in front of the other.

"Don't look back, you can never look back." —Don Henley

23

ORANGE JUICE AND LEO

Our group at Camp Raschke included a hodge-podge of market enthusiasts whom Frank had collected. One of them was a young fellow who had worked for Louis Dreyfus trading cash commodities. He was in charge of juice concentrate and tomato paste. His specialties were pineapple, cranberry, and orange juice. He had an enlightening orange juice story that reflected my sentiments about fundamentals.

Once a year, the top orange juice executives from Dreyfus met in Brazil to assess the firm's hedges in front of an orange juice report. This release was the equivalent of all the unemployment reports for the year being crammed together in one day–a real "Trading Places" report. The talking heads took out a piece of paper and made a checklist. They put all the reasons why they should reduce the size of their hedges in one column and all the reasons why they should increase the size of their hedges in the other column (*Very* scientific!). These people had more information on the orange juice market than any other firm. They owned the crop, the processing plants, and the distribution systems. But even though they knew what the report was going to be, they could not predict how the market would react to the news.

It's never the news itself but always the market's reaction to the news that is most telling.

I managed multiple accounts at Sakura Dellsher, a clearing firm, and was trading a guaranteed fund for them as well. Guaranteed Funds came about in the mid-nineties. They were Japanese funds where the principle was supposed to be guaranteed. Futures are highly leveraged. So, the cash which is not used for margin can instead be used to purchase notes or zero-coupon securities. These then guarantee the principal at maturity. Several managers were selected to trade each fund with the theory that diversification smoothed volatility in the individual performances. Instead, one of the managers had a considerable drawdown and that in turn shut down the rest of the managers. The fund could not afford to lose anymore. We had only traded the fund for five months when it got axed due to another manager's losses. Investors then had their monies tied up for the three-year term. They had to count on the interest accrued to make them whole again. The popularity of this product did not last long, even in Japan where interest rates were close to zero.

Rick and I went to Chicago to visit Leo Melamed, the CEO of Sakura. Leo was a prominent figure in the Chicago landscape. He was one of the most important people in the evolution of the futures industry. Leo had started out as a runner at the CME (Chicago Mercantile Exchange) and worked his way up to the chairman of the CME in 1969 at age 37. Sakura Dellsher was founded by him in 1965. He was instrumental in creating the SP futures, currency futures, and Globex. Eventually, he led the exchange to go public in 2002. He probably held every title one could hold at the CME.

When we were in his office, the most notable thing besides the fine art was a set of hand-drawn charts lying on top of his desk. Leo excitedly called us over and showed us the trend lines he had drawn highlighting a significant chart formation. Despite his enormous responsibilities of running many businesses, he still found time to update his daily charts by hand. Wow! I was impressed. He graciously signed two of his books for us, and we were left standing there with a new burst of inspiration.

Trade location is essential when trading on a shorter time frame, and I traded on a tight time frame. On the flip side of the coin, the most important thing with a longer-term trend following approach was to get the trade on. This was Rick's motto—"get the trade on." You can't afford to miss the one move which might make your month if you were a trend follower. When evaluating trend following systems, we tested for decay. For example, what happens if we entered the order 24 hours later? The profit expectation should not be dependent on the initial trade location. But with shorter-term technical trading, it was more important to enter on reactions or right at the start of a breakout. I had a fantastic SP broker, one of the best in the business. He was exceptional at working a bid or offer since we still had to call our orders down to the pit. I only liked placing trades for the SPs. All other orders got passed off to Rick. Timely volume data was not transmitted to the screens in those days, so it was important to get a sense of volume and how deep the decks were.

When I told my broker at my clearing firm that I needed a good SP broker, he took me down to the floor and introduced me to Damon. Damon had not done any order execution for females before.

Right after I said my name, I said, "I do a minimum of a hundred contracts."

I think he was a bit surprised. It was 1991, and the range in the SPs was relatively small. It was the "big" SP contract before the e minis were created, so 100 big contracts were the equivalent of 10 million dollars' worth of stock. I could see him wavering between excitement at a new big client and a leery skepticism like he was talking to a fully crazy person.

"If you're going to trade that size, you're going to need a direct line to the floor. When you want to execute an order, call me and I will personally make it happen."

This meant I got my own private "bat phone." The phone did not ring; only a light would blink on Damon's end like the president calling some secret operative in the movies.

When I picked up my phone, Damon answered instantly. It was usually one of two responses:

I'd say, "Hi. How's it looking?"

"Pea-shooters only."

Or:

"How's it looking?"

"Size bid at double nickels," which was slick speak for 55.

Our conversations lasted only a few words, but this was all that was needed. I am not a gifted conversationalist. Pea-shooters were the small exchange member traders (locals) who traded 1-2 lots. Usually, it meant that it was quiet and the big traders were in the break room having lunch and playing cards. Any light volume day after that became a pea-shooter day.

The first day I had my direct line, I waited until the markets were about to close. Then I called and said, "Sell 100 SPs now." It was the opposite of what most people did, but at least he realized I was serious. In the pre-internet days, the trading floor was physical and unruly. Women in the pit were rare as hens' teeth, while women trading off-site were akin to flying pigs. So, coming in as an independent woman trader and immediately making trades unlike anything they'd ever seen put some people on alert.

After one of my early golf trades, Damon told my clerk, "Wow, she's got balls." Just like that, I was in.

Damon was the best. At one time he did execution for Tudor Jones, Monroe Trout, Toby Crabel, and Louis Bacon. Tudor asked to meet privately with Damon in Chicago. He said he was thinking of giving the majority of his SP business to him. Damon asked why he had picked him to do his execution, and Tudor told him he figured Damon got him a nickel better 50% of the time. It added up to an additional 2 million in profits throughout a year.

One time, Tudor gave him an order to buy 900 SPs to execute in a 10-minute period. Damon worked the order and got an exceptional fill.

Pause. All he heard on the other end of the line was, "Oh—oh."

"What's wrong?"

"You're a good broker, but anytime you buy that type of quantity, I expect to move the market in the direction you're buying and see the prices rally up quickly to the upside." This was not a good sign. Sure enough, the market broke sharply after that, and it was a sizable loss at the end of the day.

A trader learns a lot by watching how a market absorbs the buying or selling.

24

TAG

I was invited to speak at an annual "TAG" (Technical Analysis Group) conference, which showcased prominent technical analysts. Tim Slater started these conferences after he had founded Compu Trac, a charting program acquired by Telerate in 1985. Dow Jones then purchased Telerate in 1989. Tim organized the TAG seminars to promote technical analysis tools, and he had invited me to lecture. I did not feel confident in my speaking skills. I grew up as a pianist, sitting in front of the keyboard for up to six hours a day and letting the strings and hammers do all the talking. My conversation skills were abysmal. I still had my float tank in my house. Some people call float tanks 'sensory deprivation tanks,' others tout their benefits to the immune system, but they are perhaps even better for meditation.

I spent an hour at a time in my float tank repeating, "I am cool, calm, and collected" over and over, several times a week. When I delivered my presentation at that first conference, I was in the zone.

I have no idea of what I said, but it was well received. I repeat my mantra to this day whenever I feel a bit flustered. "I am cool, calm, and collected." The other mantra I learned from a hypnotist when I was in high school is, "I am loose, limp, and letting go." Just keep saying it over and over. "Loose and limp and letting go." And breathe.

Tim asked me if I would like to speak for the Dow Jones offices overseas on an annual tour. I never took vacations, so this was a grand opportunity to see the world yet be in touch with the markets, still working. My husband had no interest in traveling; this would be an excellent adventure for me.

The first trip was to Singapore and Kuala Lumpur, the capital of Malaysia. This was a fascinating trip for several reasons. The traders were a mix of Muslims, Buddhists, Christians, and Hindus, and half of them were women! After our morning talk, the organizers arranged a lunch for everyone, and I sat at a table where the majority of traders were women. How was it that so many women were able to be bank traders? If someone had visited the United States in the mid-nineties, they would have been hard-pressed to find any women on institutional trading desks. I doubt there were any at Goldman Sachs. They explained that in their culture, the men were the ones who brought home the paycheck but then turned the money over to the women who managed the household and finances. Women were considered to be far more responsible with the money than men. At least that was the story I was told by the female bank traders.

I found I could still log my daily numbers and fax the trading plan to Rick for the fund and so, for two to three weeks each year, I continued to travel to a different part of the world to work with bank traders and institutional clients.

On another tour, I traveled to Singapore, Perth, Melbourne, Sydney, and New Zealand with Perry Kaufman and his wife, Barbara. Perry has done some of the finest research in my opinion, and he made a lasting impression on me. He reminds me of a clean-cut version of Dr. Emmett Brown from *Back to the Future*—a brilliant academic professor who can explain things in plain English. This was a terrific opportunity to learn from him. His background was in engineering and finance with a strong quantitative bent which was right up my alley. He came up with the unique idea of modeling "Price Shocks," one of the more challenging things to model since they do not happen often and are unpredictable. For example, the Chernobyl disaster in 1986 led to price shocks—large gaps, in many futures markets, especially the agricultural commodities. Does a trader puke the position out at that point or do they double up? That is the trick in modeling these events since each case is unique.

One of Perry's main theses was that as markets mature, the noise level increases. As more market participants enter a market, each with different time horizons, trading ranges expand, stops need to be wider, and thus the initial risk is higher. This is bad for trend following systems. Perry spoke about this in the late nineties, and it is easy to see how this tendency has gone to extremes 20 years later. Though the noise is greater than ever, when a market does breakout, an efficient move tends to unfold. Dog-pile. Sometimes it is a straight-line markup or markdown which can last for days without any significant reactions. Once the move is over, the market often rotates in an endless consolidation period with numerous whipsaws. The ability to model these "state changes," from consolidation to trending, is a challenge for system developers. You can't lump all the data together when there are two diametrically opposed states at work. Suffice to say, Perry is number one in my book when it comes to system development.

Perry and I continued to cross paths in random ways. Once when in Florence with my daughter and husband, we turned down a little cobblestone street and surprise! We bumped into Perry and his wife, Barbara. Barbara was a member of the CME for 25 years and on the floor for 10 years. She still trades, another testimonial to how consuming this business is. Erika looked at all of us and without missing a beat, "Let's all go for a gelato!"

In Singapore, I went to a flea market and found the most marvelous ram's head adorned with decorative plates and metal studs. It had four huge curly horns. He was named Raffles, after the founder of Singapore. Raffles got a free berth on my ensuing flight to Australia and then to New Zealand. I doubt the airlines would let you schlep those bulky things in the overheads nowadays. But Raffles made it safely back to my office in New Jersey where I promptly hung him above the door. Nobody could come or go without the watchful eyes of Raffles staring at them. It was sort of creepy in retrospect. When I moved to Chicago, he was hung above the door of our office there—in fact, we moved multiple times, but Raffles always came with us.

Raffles was my good luck god, but years later I found out that Rams' heads are sacred in witchcraft and Satanism. Dear Lord! Had I unwittingly put a curse on my offices? To console myself, I visited Wikipedia which said the Egyptian ram-god was also identified with the Greek god Zeus. A ram is a non-castrated adult male sheep, so I took it that this essentially added an extra pair of balls in my office.

Raffles, named after the founder of Singapore.

* * *

Sue Herrera drove to my house in Southern Jersey to interview me for a book. She was a TV broadcaster for a financial news network and was writing a book on women in the industry called *Women of the Street*. Sue was famous and everyone knew her name. Okay, not *everyone*, but it was nice to see a female in a prominent position. We chatted like we were long lost friends while my husband cooked in the kitchen. Axle, the family Dalmatian, poked his head in the office. The only other female friends I had were either from the barn or from playing tennis. Horses and tennis—my girlfriend topics. It's easy to make conversation when you have a common subject, but I never knew any females in the markets. I wish Sue had lived closer.

I spoke on TV three times in my career. The first time was in Los Angeles for KWHY, one of the first stations to offer daily market news. It was in the early nineties, and I was speaking at an MTA conference in Orange County. One of the organizers had arranged it, and I thought it would be a novel experience. The studio was in a horrible, seedy part of town. I was wearing a silk suit, and it was a ridiculously hot day. Inside, there was a full array of makeup people, hair people, bright lights, and a cramped set. Everything designed to make one writhe in maximum discomfort. I was only on the air for 10 minutes, and the main thing I remember is the Dow was plunging the whole time I was talking. It was one of the biggest down days that year, and I was squirming in front of a camera with pancake slathered over my face. Why was I missing this fabulous trading day? I didn't even have anything to sell, no advisory services, no books, no nothing.

The second time I spoke was on the set where they filmed *Wall Street Week* in Bethesda, Maryland. I felt like a rock star when a big black limousine picked me up at the airport and drove me through rolling green hills to the studio. I did not care what the market was doing because this was a unique experience. The other guest speaking with me was Bernie Schaeffer. He specialized in stock options and market research for investors. We were asked what stocks we thought would do well over the next year. Are you kidding me? I have a hard time just getting the next day right. I have no idea what is going to happen over the next six months. I hope I said something smart, but I am sure nobody remembers anyway.

In the studio, I bumped into Jimmy Rogers who was rounding the corner. Jimmy was, well, classic Jimmy. Short and friendly, with a little bow tie which made me want to pinch his cheeks—the ones on his face—and say, "Jimmy, you are so cute." I refrained. Maybe if he had been 30 years younger than me, like two years old. Jimmy Rogers became a Wall Street legend when he co-founded the Quantum Fund. His impressive investing record allowed him to retire in 1980 at age 37. I had met him before at an annual Market Technicians Association where he was the keynote speaker. At the end of his talk, someone asked him how he handled big losses. "I puke them at the lows, like everyone else." And he was honest!

The last time I spoke on TV was on John Murphy's 30-minute technical segment for CNBC in Newark, New Jersey. This was a super impressive setup. One hour of makeup and hair in preparation for speaking for less than 15 minutes. I spoke on the gold market technicals, but the main thing I remember is that, once again, the Dow was plunging. I was missing a choice trading day. I vowed never to speak again during the day.

It's hard to keep your head in the game when you've got your head on TV.

25

FLORIDA

My husband was convinced that Florida was the place to move to because of the sunshine and no state income taxes. I knew nothing about Florida other than it was all reclaimed swampland and tattoo parlors. However, there were golf courses for him and horses for me. This year, I had surprised him with a trip to Florida for his birthday so he could visit the spring training camp he pitched at when he played for the Yankees.

The night before we left, it snowed a miserable, wet, heavy eight inches. We had to shovel our half-mile long driveway at 6 AM before we could drive to the airport. We landed in Palm Beach with the most fabulous weather conditions greeting us. The rental car agency had mixed up our reservation and to make up for it, gave us a brand-new red convertible. The hotel also managed to botch our reservations (everyone must have been in disarray after Christmas). To make it up to us, they gave us a room right on the beach. Big sliding glass doors led out onto the sand. It was as if the Chamber of Commerce had arranged everything in advance.

Saturday morning, I asked, "What would you like to do for your birthday today, Hon?" Thinking a leisurely drive up the coast to his old spring training fields might be nice.

"Well, I really want to take a drive out to see this town called Wellington." He had seen a reasonably priced house with a barn and tennis courts advertised on the back of my Dressage magazine. He was thinking he could entice me down to the land of golf courses with the lure of having my own barn.

Sure enough, we start driving down Southern Blvd, and it was nothing but pawn shops and tattoo parlors, exactly as I had suspected. In 1996, once you got past the cheesy strip malls, the roads were two lanes with cow pastures on both sides. When we drove through the grand entry with water fountains proclaiming "Wellington," it felt like we'd landed on a different planet.

The first thing we did was to drive to the stadium where they held the polo games. Wellington started out as the town where the Palm Beachers went to watch polo on the lone field where there was space and cheap land to build on. It is now home to over 45 polo fields. We got out of our red convertible sports car, it was still a notch down from the other cars parked there, and we walked across the grassy polo field. Someone must have come out at 5 AM and shaved every blade with a razor to get the perfect cut. It was a pristine blanket of lush, green velvet—the polar opposite of the sloppy, white stuff smothering our yard up north.

After that, we drove the short distance to the show grounds where the hunters and jumpers compete. We were hungry, so we stopped at the food court. No hamburgers and ordinary fare to be found here—it was all French crepes and seafood tacos. And there were baskets of geraniums hanging from wrought iron lamp posts in every direction. And then there were the horses! I felt like a dirty old man in South Beach watching topless models parade by in the sand. My jaw dropped to my knees. Million-dollar horses were everywhere, waltzing to and fro. Magnificent prancing athletic animals with glistening coats and sexy, lush, swinging tails. I was sold. Sign me up.

Wellington was going to be our new trading center of the universe. I bought two lots across the street from the showgrounds. A crew cleared the dense jungle of melaleuca trees. A friend who worked for me was the first to move there. He sent me a picture after it rained, and the entire five acres was a foot under water. Argh, I knew it. I bought proverbial Florida swampland. As it turned out, most of the lots were like that. All one had to do was pay for 1200 truckloads of dirt to build up the lot.

My dad was a builder for a few years when I was growing up, and I felt confident I could build too. I was still in my "the mind can do anything" phase of my life. I designed the house, found a draftsperson to draw up plans and a contractor to build it on a cost-

Draining the swamp

plus basis. Besides the house, there was a separate office, barn, groom's apartment, riding ring with night lights, and a courtyard fountain. One of Frank's friends had a Mooney, and we flew it back and forth from New Jersey to Florida. It should come as no surprise that the construction ended up taking a *lot* longer than planned. I am good about enthusiastically jumping into projects, but have unrealistic expectations about timelines. Laura found a townhouse to rent in Wellington and had already moved. My husband also rented a place so our daughter could start school. Rick bought a house and moved with his wife. I was the only person stuck in New Jersey holding down the fort and waiting for the new office completion.

Rick and I worked together over the phone. We had an ideal working relationship. He could read my mind half the time, though I could never read his. Rick is one of the most conscientious people in the world, which is a good thing since I am not. The small, capital block letters he used to document our trades sat perfectly atop straight ruled lines. His attention to detail was impeccable. One Friday afternoon when we had a sizable position in the grains, the market started to weaken. I do not like being long a market which starts to make new lows on the day in the afternoon, especially on a Friday. I told Rick to sell the beans and close out our positions.

He called me after the close that day. "Linda, we have a problem." From the tone of his voice, the first thing that came to mind was replacing my name with "Houston."

"Um, yes Rick?"

"Well, there was an error with the bean trade," he said.

"OK, umm, go on." Knowing him, I could hardly fathom what error could have occurred.

"Well. I told the brokers to sell 300 beans, but instead, they bought another 300 beans."

As Murphy's Law would have it, a crop report came out after the close on Friday, and it was an ugly one for the beans. I told Rick we should not have a problem because every broker on the floor has recorded lines. Right? I was wrong. This time there was a new group of grain brokers who had started clearing through Rand Financial the week before. Their head broker was out sick, and of course, they did not have recorded lines installed yet. The real problem was, we didn't either.

Rick was trading out of his house until I could move. Putting a recorded line on his phone was something I had not thought of at the time. Beans opened down on Sunday night and immediately hit limit down. They continued lower for the next few days. By the time we were able to peel out of our twice the normal size position under chaotic pit conditions, I had given back 80% of the year's profits. I could have fought and taken the bad trade to arbitration, but that would have taken many months.

Did I feel angry? Wronged? Sad? I felt nothing. A big black hole of nothingness. No feelings, just colors. Just one color—black. I was programmed growing up to keep putting one foot in front of the other. Don't look back. Only move forward. So, the feet keep marching onward and the feelings get left behind in the dust.

There is nothing more demoralizing than watching the majority of your hard-earned profits disappear in a few hours. And this was not the first time it had happened. Black Monday, the bond fiasco, and many other random outliers had done similar damage.

I had to clear my head, take my lumps and move on. If there is a time when I feel totally out of control, I flatten. Time to start with a clean slate. Forfeit a turn and exchange all your scrabble tiles for seven fresh ones. I had hit my max drawdown point and did not want to lose one more dime. This time I flattened the whole business.

"From the ashes arises the Phoenix." This Phoenix needed to get burnt to a crisp before being born again.

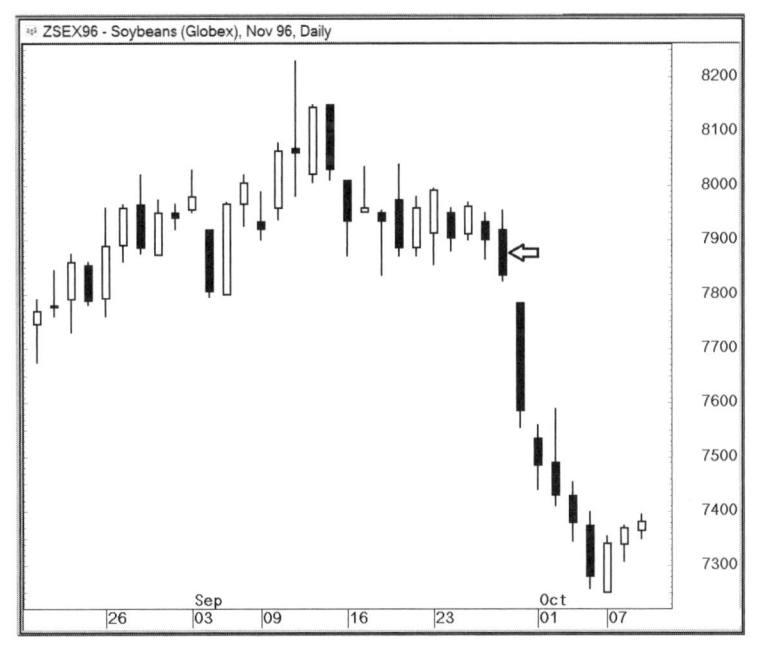

"Linda, we have an error…"

I called a good friend, Robert, and told him I was thinking of closing everything. I had worked hard to build a fabulous business with great people and wonderful clients. But I didn't think it was prudent to manage money when the house was still not finished. And I had to deal with an impending move. He told me he saw many people over the years make mid-life switches or career changes. Things worked out all the better for it. He gave me his blessing and said it was okay to shut down. My clients encouraged me to stay in business and said it was okay if I did not trade until I moved. It did not feel right, though. I needed to clear the air. I still wanted to end the year showing a profit. My only losing year in my career thus far had been in the beginning when I blew out in the City Service takeover deal.

Laura had enough pragmatism for both of us. She stayed focused and had confidence we would continue to manage money. Rick ended up taking another job with a hedge fund, then with Toby Crabel's office and later with Getco. I was sorry to lose him because he was a consummate professional.

"Profits are like eels, how easily they slip away." *Confusion de Confusiones,* **1688, one of the first books on trading.**

26

MAKING WAFFLES

Once the big move was over, Laura and I started another fund called "Watermark Fund." No more managed accounts—it was too much of a hassle back in those days. It was far more efficient to trade one pool of money. Watermark was an offshore fund as well since most of my previous clients had offshore operations. It was domiciled in the Caymans. We were back in the hedge fund business again. It was easier in those days to start these types of funds, but the process was still quite a bit of work. Laura had great contacts from working with sharp people she knew when she was at 6800 Capital.

The new property had a separate trading office with satellite dishes, generators, and built-in propane tanks for backup. But for all our doomsday preparations, we could not foresee the things which were to unfold around the corner.

One day in the middle of trading after I moved, the generators kicked in for no reason. At least we knew they worked. I was getting quotes from a giant satellite dish outside. It was a 4-foot silver saucer that looked like it could shoot laser beams. But when I went to place an order, the phone lines were out. Aside from the office chugging away on the generator, the electricity was out on the whole block. Unbeknownst to me, the next-door neighbor decided to plant a giant ficus tree without first checking with the city where the underground lines were. He was in commercial construction and sometimes certain people think they can get away with stuff—especially since we lived on a dirt road. I hopped on my bike and rode to the end of the driveway where I saw a giant claw poised high in the air, a black hole beneath it.

"Hey!" I called out. "What the heck do you think you're doing?" A bewildered construction worker just stared speechlessly. The neighborhood power and telephone lines were dangling from the claw, like tangled spaghetti. Cell phones were only just coming on the market, but I did not have one yet. I let out

"Anyone out there have a cell phone?"

a few more choice four-letter words before I took off on my bicycle to find a neighboring farm where someone had a cell phone. I needed to make a call and get out of my positions quickly.

It was the late nineties when tech stocks were on fire and nobody had seen PE ratios at these levels. Remember, when relationships push outside their historical ranges, it is a sign to be positioned in the direction of the move. Such was the case with valuation levels which were well above those seen in the past number of decades. Internet and technology stocks were going parabolic. Every day brought another 50-point gap up in a stock which was now in the triple digits. Traders either loved it and played the momentum game to the hilt or fought it and got taken out of the game. I had a savvy equestrian friend who told me about the trades she made on her

Blackberry at red lights while driving her kids to school. And she was making money! Another time, the TV was on in her house when I stopped by one morning. The financial network was on. Instead of talking about stocks, Joe Kernan was making waffles! The fat lady was singing, but we could not hear her over the TV.

* * *

How do you know when to short a market? When the price stops going up! I put on a sizable short position in the NASDAQ futures as the index started to roll over. The lure for traders on the short side was the markets went down a lot faster than they went up. One way to measure profits is how many dollars are made per unit of time. The more time you are in a market, the more risk you assume. The Internet and tech stocks broke hard, and I caught a 7-digit windfall in the NASDAQ futures. But it was bittersweet because my husband decided that would be the perfect time to serve me papers for a divorce. Talk about timing my trades.

"Laura, I'm sorry, but we are going to have to close our fund. I think we are going to be distracted for a bit. It does not look like it is going to be an amicable divorce."

"OK. Whatever you need me to do."

"Don't worry. We'll get back up and running when this is over with."

Every trader I knew from the trading floors who went through a divorce easily lost a million dollars in the process. I was not going to let that happen to me, and it was not right by my clients. My husband froze my personal accounts since he was sure I was hiding monies offshore. I was not, but it cost me a zillion hours to produce records proving I was not. God bless Laura because she did much of the work during this awful period.

Members of the technical community served as a lifeline. My friends consisted of my horse trainer, the people who worked for me, and ex-floor traders or market technicians. I did not have girlfriends to meet for coffee. I did not have anyone to bitch to when times were tough. But I always had other traders and technicians I could talk to about charts and technicals.

I spoke in Canada for the Canadian Technical Society, in New York for Bloomberg, for dozens of organizations just to hop on a plane and get out of town. Anything to stay busy and be in a different city from the divorce.

I loved speaking about the markets. It was the topic I knew best. I was invited to speak in Dallas for a technical society. A few years earlier I met Vic Sperandeo at an MTA meeting. A group of 10 of us had dinner in the traditional basement grill we took the speakers to after a talk. Vic is a trader I look up to—a direct, independent thinker with plenty of gumption. He had published his first book, *Methods of a Wall Street Master*, which is still one of my favorite books. It's all meat, coming from someone you know does not have to toot his own horn. I told Vic I was flying to Dallas for business and he got me a room at the Mansion, top digs to stay in at the time. I rode up the elevator with the band members from U2 who were in town for a concert. I did not even realize who they were—I was so focused on my own world in those days.

Vic was quite forward thinking. It was in the late nineties, and he told me he thought it would be a great idea to start a fund that only traded in products such as metals and energies. Commodities that had a finite supply. He was way ahead of the times.

I used this time to do more work on my positive feedback loop models. The majority of the time when price moves sharply, it has a reaction in the opposite direction—even if just a small check back. In system dynamics, this is referred to as negative feedback. Mean reverting strategies count on negative feedback. These corrections are self-regulating oscillations that serve as a stabilizing price factor. But there are also less frequent periods when the price movement triggers more movement in the same direction, amplifying or accelerating the move underway. For example, the crash of 1987 was one such case when portfolio insurance kicked in. As the price fell, it generated more selling and forced liquidation, thus accelerating the downside freefall.

My process is as follows: Identify the conditions that precede the positive feedback loops that are not generated by a news event, identify what characteristics mark the move as it is just starting, and then note what the expected range of outcomes look like from there. It is not so different than modeling any range expansion system except it uses momentum functions instead of price functions. It is easy to observe what the best trades look like after the fact. For example, there is an increase in volume, the market makes consecutive higher highs and higher lows or vice versa, and the hourly bars increase in range. It is a process of deductive logic.

I called the first model "PF3's". It measured the positive feedback in three separate ways. The first derivative of each indicator was in a position to be increasing. Another critical part of the process is to model what happens after the signal fails to deliver an expected outcome. For example, if a PF3 condition fails to lead to range expansion, this can be a powerful signal to trade in the opposite direction the next day.

It is easy to see how this is a Bayesian process of adding one new piece of information at a time into the system. If A happens, then expect B. If B does not happen, then expect C. If B does happen, then expect D. The decision tree is not as important as the process, but to start the process, you have to have the model.

There is a field in systems theory called "system dynamics" which tries to make sense of the nonlinear behavior of complex systems. You can Google it and see how nifty it would be if we could borrow concepts to model markets and price behavior. The main useful thing I extracted was this concept of positive feedback loops. And this was ten years later. So, take it for what it is worth–a grain of theory at the least.

Steve Moore did the early testing for me when we had our research partnership in the mid-nineties. There was a nominal statistical edge. I later tried to explain the concept at a conference. After viewing the sea of glazed eyes, I deleted all future references to this area of work. Sometimes something needs to incubate and crystallize for a few years. Then it can be worth revisiting with a second wind.

You have your brains in your head. You have your feet in your shoes. You can steer yourself any direction you choose. You're on your own. And you know what you know. And YOU are the one who'll decide where to go…" —Dr. Seuss

27

THE Y2K BUG

In the spirit of perfect timing, a computer proficient fellow by the name of James, contacted me. "Do you need any technical help with Y2K coming up? Are your computers ready to handle it?"

"I don't know, should I be concerned about Y2K?" People often contacted me out of the blue—no doubt from the chapter in the *Market Wizards* book.

Perry Kaufman later told me, "I must confess that I was one of the culprits that caused the problem. First, working for NASA and next writing compilers. If you don't remember, the problem was that we stored the date as 600215 for 2/15/1960. We never put the first two digits of the year for two good reasons: first, we didn't have the computer memory. Two extra digits for every date was a gigantic use of space when you have a 4K memory (that's 4,000 words or 8,000 bytes) when today's storage is measured in terabytes. I don't think anyone today can conceive of a 4K computer. You have 10x more in your toaster. The second reason is that, in 1960, the year 2000 was very, very, far away and we were all young. Who cares what will happen in 40 years? We'll worry about it then—or not. And, you see that we all got through it, so it never really mattered. Just a small software fix."

The fellow who contacted me about Y2K, James, was a savvy technical guy who had traded a volatility breakout system with his brother. He was quiet, handy, and the perfect assistant. My now-ex moved out, and James moved into a guest suite on the side of the house. Camp Raschke continued to live up to its reputation: "home and gathering place for random traders from all walks of life."

It was a blessing to have help on the property. We stuck to a routine. James and I woke at 5:30 AM, went to the gym, cooked eggs, and were ready to trade at 7:30 AM EST. If Erika was with her Dad, at the end of the day, I would ride the horses, cook fish and sweet potatoes and be back in the office until 11 PM. It was my ideal lifestyle after finalizing my divorce.

For Christmas, my daughter and I bought James a parrot. Looking back, I am not sure who wanted the parrot—James or Erika. We gave James a magnificent red-and-green macaw named Sara. This bird turned out to be one noisy sucker and had a vocabulary of 200 words. She was an exotic addition to our tropical paradise.

She sat in a seven-foot white cage next to the pool in front of our office doors. The pool was screened in, creating a 100-foot extended outdoor living area. In Florida, the screens are a protective measure to keep out Florida's state bird, the mosquito. Fearless of those nasty bloodsuckers, we kept the office doors wide open to enjoy the air. The only problem was that I had an aging Dalmatian with a bladder control problem who was no longer allowed in the office.

When Axle tried to come into the office, I yelled, "Axle, out!" Soon, Sara caught on to the daily routine and became the bouncer at the office door. Anytime she saw Axle approaching she would squawk, "AXLE, OUT! AXLE, OUT!" The whole neighborhood could hear her. She developed her vocabulary further by reciting our catchphrases for better or worse.

I also had a Pomeranian named Nazdoggie. At lunch we would play fetch with her, a game she could play forever. Sara would shriek, "GO GET IT, GO GET IT." Her most overused phrase was, "TRADE ALERT! TRADE ALERT!" She learned this from hearing our computers fire off in the middle of the day. Sara was a great source of amusement, but I was glad she left when James moved. No more distractions and sunflower seed shells crunching beneath our feet. Back to my place of Zen.

I was doing business through Sakura Dellsher. Victoria had been taking my orders for the previous three years on their trading desk. We never talked much because I was not a phone person, but one day I mentioned I had horses. She was enthralled, so I invited her to come to visit for a week. Victoria was one of the funniest people I ever met. I suggested starting a small chat room to have a business to pay Laura and James. My accounts were still frozen during the divorce. I dictated, Victoria typed, and we did this for a few years. She was a pro in the markets, having worked in Switzerland for a trading firm, and had moved to Chicago to work for Leo Melamed at Sakura. The main thing I remember about the next two years was laughing nonstop as she cracked jokes in the chat room. A friend opened an account for me so at least I could trade until my divorce settled and my accounts were unfrozen. We were rocking and rolling again.

Every few years when oats dropped below 120, I put on a sizable trade. Eventually, they always moved back up. This particular year I had to roll the position into the next series as the front month was approaching first notice day. This is the day that notices can be issued by the sellers to those holding long futures to take delivery of the physical commodity. I waited until the last minute and turned to Victoria. I dropped my chin and peered over my glasses. "We're going to take delivery of these oats."

Victoria jumped as though she had touched a hot stove. She swung her seat around and said, "What? What are you talking about?"

I didn't blink. My knee was rapidly bouncing up and down, which meant I was in a scheming mode. "I'm serious, we're taking delivery of these oats."

Victoria dropped her jaw. What I had proposed was legitimately fucking insane.

Maintaining my composure, I turned and pointed toward the patio. "And we're going to store it there." I jabbed my pointer finger as though I was in an air fencing match. "That pool can hold about 30,000 gallons of water. I reckon I can have someone come and drain the pool on Monday. Then we'll haul the oats down by truck and dump it out back. I figure we'll be able to feed the horses for the next year."

Victoria looked at me and then to the pool and then back at me. I could see her trying to figure out if I had lost my goddamn mind. To her credit, yes, I had, but that happened a long time ago.

"So, do you want me to call the exchange or something? I've never taken delivery of anything before."

I snorted through my nose and howled with laughter. "You city girls will believe ANYTHING!"

Victoria put her hand to her heart and let out a huge sigh. "You scared the shit out of me! I thought you were serious about your pool silo, you brat!"

We were crying while laughing. I rolled my position to the next front month, and the oat trade became a running joke. We caught one heck of a nice move to the upside, and the pool remained intact.

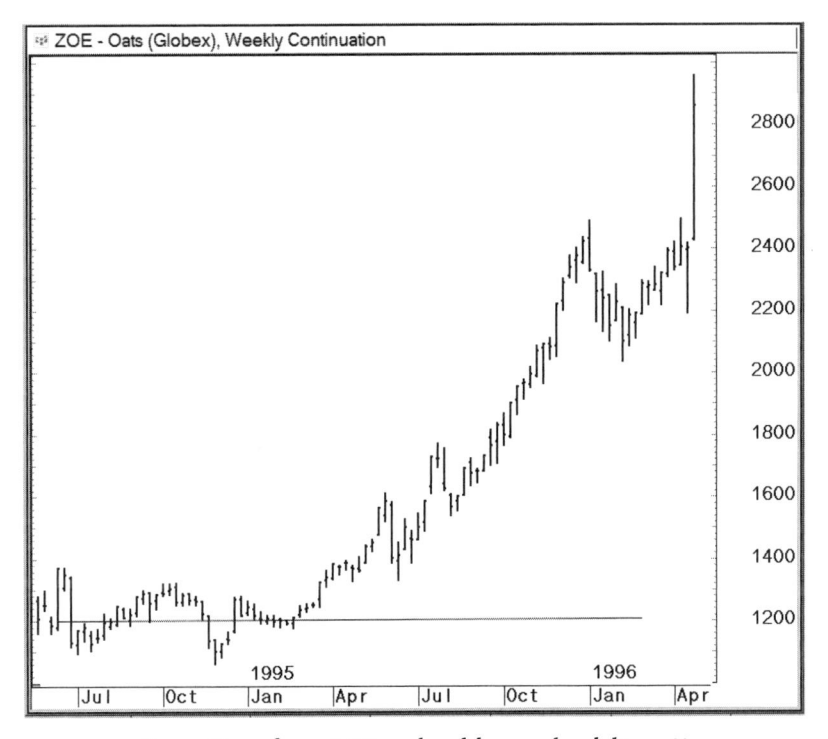

Long Oats from 120 – should we take delivery??

Here are some of the more hilarious sayings I credited to Victoria when she was working the chat room:

- *The Time Frame Justification System.* This is when you are in a trade which does not feel comfortable and scroll through different time frames until coming across one that seems to fit your bias. Yup, when you resort to engaging in the time frame justification system, it is a sure sign that you are in a bad trade.

- *The Short Skirt Trade.* Victoria was trying to explain to a newer client that small bull flags at the end of a swing are scalps only. Be quick to lock in profits. To quote her, "When you trade, you know, short skirt, no undies, quick in, quick out and don't get caught."
- *Bee's Butt Trade.* This is when a coil got so tight, it looks like the point of a bee's butt; if you're on the wrong side, you're going to get stung.

Before I moved to Florida, I rescued a handsome thoroughbred horse from an auction house. The barn owner called me up at 1 AM since she knew I was the only one who would answer, let alone take the horse. With snow on the ground in the middle of February, I made my husband drive out there to pick up this horse that was destined to be carted off for slaughter the next morning. $500. SOLD! He was another race track reject, the color of coffee. I named him Bucky, for Starbucks. It was my understanding that horses from the track labeled as "geldings" were certifiably castrated. This turned out to be not the case with Bucky. I brought him down to Florida along with the other horses I had accumulated.

Unbeknownst to me, Bucky was still intact on one side. Recessed *cajones*. I found this out the hard way. I had been invited to go foxhunting with an exclusive club in South Florida. If you are questioning whether there is foxhunting in Florida—you are right to do so. It was nothing like Pennsylvania or New Jersey where I had hunted before, but nonetheless, people dressed in full formal hunt attire.

We were in the flat scrub with makeshift fences to jump over. On this particular occasion, the hunt master was gone, and his daughter was leading the hunt. At the furthest point on the course, Bucky soared over the coop, refused to stop and immediately mounted the hunt master's daughter's horse from behind. With her on it. And me on Bucky. Not a pretty sight.

I was humiliated in front of everyone and was told to immediately dismount. I had to walk the entire way back home and it was hot. Another walk of shame. After that, I scheduled Bucky for some serious surgery. They put him flat out on his side and went searching for the mysterious recessed *cajones* that was driving his testosterone sky-high. The vet acknowledged he could not find what he was looking for. But the horse now had a huge incision that needed attending to which meant me giving him injections of antibiotics every few hours.

There was a little fridge on my office next to the door that led out to the barn. I had a collection of super long hypodermic needles on top and kept the meds inside the fridge. On this particular day, it was ridiculously hot and the AC was not keeping up. I had 28 monitors, 12 CPUs, assorted printers and routers, and then there was Victoria and me. The office was stuffy, and we opened the doors to let a cross breeze through which did not help. Meanwhile, we were running the chat room and trading as if everything was under control. Except, we stripped off our bras and tossed them into the middle of the floor, giggling.

As Victoria and I toiled away in the office, there was a revolving cast of characters outside the office we gave names to. Horseshoe Man, Feed Man, and Hay Man. Not very imaginative.

At that moment, Feed Man barged into the office, wondering if we needed extra bags of grain for the week. He had a habit of barging in. A short dude in a cowboy hat, boots, and a big belt buckle who drove a Ford F-350 pickup truck.

Victoria and I looked at each other. Then at the bras in the middle of the floor, then at the needles on top of the fridge, screens blinking the prices of corn and bonds in the background and proceeded to carry on as if nothing was happening. Moments like these made some of my more miserable years, divorce hassles and all, some of the funniest. Good thing traders have a sick sense of humor!

Sometime after, Bucky got donated to a wayward boys' home run by sheriffs. Of course, not before he tried mounting my daughter's pony.

28

MR. BILL

I surveyed the sea of assorted body shapes filling the local family gym at 6 AM. James was determined to shed 20 pounds after moving to Florida, and I was determined to get in top shape after my divorce. We had a pact to rise and shine and be at the gym five days a week at an hour I would much rather be sleeping.

My routine was getting old and stale. Sit-ups? Yawn. Bicep curls? Uninspiring. Who wants to break a sweat at that hour of the morning? I looked around for inspiration, and my eyes caught the white shirt of an elderly gentleman who looked like Mr. Miyagi from the Karate Kid. The gold nametag on his cotton trainer's shirt read "Mr. Bill." He had a body like Jack LaLanne.

I eyeballed him for the next hour watching him workout in a methodical fashion, before approaching him. "Will you train me?" I had worked with trainers in New Jersey, but none who were 35 years older than me. Everyone in the town of Wellington knew him as "Mr. Bill," and he had been a figure at the gym since 1980.

We met four times a week. Mr. Bill counted as I pushed out reps. Then he took the weights off the hack squat machine, tweaked the equipment, so it was facing perfectly straight, and meticulously wrote down in pencil the weight and reps in a workout booklet before we moved on to the next exercise. He planned each routine well ahead of time and was at the gym seven days a week.

"Concentrate on this spot here," he said as he touched the apple of my bicep. "Squeeze it up. Now hold it at the top." I loved working out with him because I hated cardio but enjoyed the weights. And his constant talking made an hour whiz past.

He never lectured me but led by example. What was his routine that day? What did he eat and which supplements did he take at which time? Did he work legs or chest that day and how many pull-ups did he do? Through gritted teeth and shared fitness secrets, we became best friends.

TVs ran in strategic corners of the gym, and Mr. Bill watched the market out of the corner of his eye. "You know, Linda, I think I am going to take my money out of the market." He had a very modest sum in a mutual fund and the year was 2007. "It has gone up enough, and I am happy with what I have now." His sole source of market information was from the TVs in the gym. He then moved it to a CD paying 5% for five years. One year later you would have been lucky to get 1 ½% on a CD. The universe paid back Mr. Bill for good karma.

"You know, Linda, I can't wait to get out of bed each morning. I get out of bed with a smile on my face because that is the proper way to greet the day. And if a negative thought pops into my head, I push it out and tell it that it does not belong there."

"Ahhh, I see." When I wake up each morning, the first thing I am thinking about is what the market did overnight.

"And then I can't wait to have my morning cup of coffee. MMMMMM." He closed his eyes and inhaled deeply through his nose, imagining the heavenly smell. "And I make that cup of coffee last half an hour while I meditate. It takes me 1 ½ hours to get ready each morning to go to the gym." Mr. Bill lives by routines and rituals.

A regular in the gym who ran Florida bodybuilding competitions and figure shows approached be after one of my sessions with Mr. Bill.

"Hey Linda, why don't you consider entering a bodybuilding competition?"

I was dubious. I knew nothing about this world. "When's the next one?" It was in 11 weeks.

"What do you think, Mr. Bill? Do you think 11 weeks is enough time?"

"I bet we can do it! I will email my good friend, John Defendis, and ask him about the proper diet and how to get prepared." John had been Mr. USA and met Mr. Bill through a gym in Del Ray.

"Diet" is a misleading word. Eating chicken, tuna, egg whites, and fish 6 or 7 times a day was lots of work. And, eating when you are not hungry is fun only if it is ice cream. The brain runs typically on carbs, but it can switch over to running on fats with a proper Keto diet. I was not eating enough carbs or fats, so my IQ slowly plummeted towards 90. Not exactly conducive to trading. On the other hand, my body fat fell below 17% which is low for a girl. I forgot how to carry on a conversation, but at least I could fit into my skinny jeans. I used to joke with my best friend that girls want three things in life: money, love, and to be thin. Somehow we seem to only end up with two at a time. We are in love and have money, but then we get fat and happy. Or, we are stressed because we don't have money, but then we lose weight and can fit into all our skinny clothes. Or, we are too busy working out and making money and don't have time to find love. I fell into the latter camp. I am still waiting to score three for three simultaneously before I die.

I entered the South Florida bodybuilding competition 11 weeks later and won the middleweight division. Frankly, it is not like there are dozens of female competitors in this event, but I will take my cheap accolades where I can get them. I had a friend take pictures of me because I knew it was unlikely I would ever be that lean again.

Mr. Bill never competed. But he did 200 pull-ups on his 82nd birthday. REAL pullups, not the fake half-up kind. He said he was never going to do that again because it was going to kill him the next time. His biggest love in life is his great-grandchild and family. He is the happiest person I know.

There are common threads among those who are successful in life and have reached a level of excellence in their chosen field.

Success is not defined by monetary standards but by levels of happiness, personal fulfillment, and mastery in their discipline. Mr. Bill has achieved this lofty plateau. If you substitute the word "trading" for "training," Mr. Bill's lessons are the perfect recipe for success in the markets.

Mr. Bill says a good foundation is a key to everything, whether it is bodybuilding or trading. How can you start on a journey towards reaching competency, let alone mastery, if you don't start from a base of solid principles? If you take shortcuts the cracks in the foundation will show up later and inevitably hold you back.

To start, there must be a robust methodology used to build a foundation, and this has to be applied CONSISTENTLY. For example, when working out, it is essential to work the muscle groups in a particular order because blood flows from one group to the next. There is a logical rationale behind everything, even if you can't see the results for a while. A good foundation is built on basics–core exercises for the major muscle groups. Proper technique is everything. Mr. Bill always says, "If you have the proper technique in what you do, you will be able to accomplish twice as much in half the time."

This certainly applies to the bottom line in trading. Keep a core group of markets and strategies that you trade. Don't try to do too many things at once. Follow your program consistently using proper technique when it comes to managing your trades. Proper technique is the equivalent of good habits. Even though a trader may not see immediate eye-popping results in the bottom line, it is the habits that will eventually enable the trader to climb to a higher level by using more leverage. It is the sound foundation and practices that give a trader confidence that their goals are achievable.

Rituals are the primary tool used to achieve consistency. They are not just a tool, but a lifestyle. Mr. Bill's routines start with how he wakes up. Shave first, then brush your teeth, the same way every day. Next, his cup of coffee with condensed milk, his one sweet luxury of the day. Check the computer for emails, walk outside and stick his feet in the dirt (for grounding), and leave plenty of time to get to the gym, so he never feels rushed. This methodical approach to everything offers the real luxury of freeing the mind—from stress, anxieties, and negative thoughts.

Record keeping is a critical part of building a good foundation. He keeps track of every exercise, weight, rep, and minute that goes by for each client and notes all details, soreness or aberrations. If a client has a unique problem, he thinks about it at night and lets his mind come up with a creative solution while he sleeps.

Monitoring your statistics is also a tool that can help you stay focused and gain control over areas that are prone to distractions. It is vital for tracking performance. Every top athlete keeps detailed records of their physical performance and progress.

Much of the wisdom I received from Mr. Bill came while I was looking at him upside down or trying to keep my core tight while swinging heavy objects around. One day, he delivered a sermon on goals while I was doing inverted chest presses.

"FIVE. It's good to have a goal!"

"Mmm."

"If your goals are not written down, they are worthless."

"Ahhh-ha."

"SEVEN. Once you write something down, that is the first step towards commitment. We wrote twenty presses in the book today."

"Ooooh."

"TEN. Writing something down implants it in the subconscious. I write down my goals for myself each week."

Mr. Bill suggests learning how to schedule things into your daily routine properly. Then they became integrated into your rituals. If you don't plan something, it is too easy to talk yourself out of it or procrastinate. Schedule your preparation time that is necessary for the next day's markets. You will welcome making rituals part of your routine when you find that it helps you start the trading day totally prepared and in control, ready to go.

Mr. Bill says that if you concentrate on a specific muscle you are working and give it your whole attention, it helps it grow faster. Concentration is the key to everything. Learn to concentrate specifically on the task that is at hand. When I put on a trade or am managing a position, I give whatever I am doing my full attention at the time. With practice, it gets easier to eliminate distracting thoughts.

Everything starts with positive thinking. Mr. Bill was not always that way. He used to be an alcoholic and smoke three packs a day up to until his late-40s. Then one day he said, "THAT IS IT! No more!" And he just quit. This six-foot-tall man weighed 135 pounds at the time. He substituted his vices for the gym and spiritual pursuits and packed on at least 40 pounds of pure muscle. He does not talk about it to most people but walks the walk.

Now he exudes more energy than people half his age. We regularly email each other links to positive thinking sites, PDFs of inspirational books, and of course, plenty of jokes and cartoons. Hardly a day has gone by in the past 20 years where we have not emailed each other.

So, praise for exercise in trading regimes! It is one of the easiest areas that you can quickly start to feel good about yourself. As you become fit, you gain strength and confidence. Everything branches out from there. You eat healthier as your body feels better. Organic food and vitamins become part of your daily life. Alcohol and sugar become less attractive. And you will find yourself making more time at night to get good sleep (in theory, of course).

This analogy applies to the business of trading. When you do proper homework and preparation at the end of each day, you are in a stronger position at the start of the new day. The first few successful trades give you a taste of the satisfaction gained in running a well thought out program. This, in turn, increases the incentive to continue to eliminate all the distractions and wasted time engaging in frivolous activities. The person who starts to follow a consistent trading program will set higher goals, such as one day running a successful money management business or striving for continuous new account highs.

To sum up Mr. Bill's lessons: Stick with the basics, follow a methodology, be consistent, use rituals to achieve consistency, concentrate on your form, keep records of your progress, and above all, practice positive thinking!

29

ANIMAL KINGDOM

When I was growing up, I lived in a converted storage room. It was originally used for tools and was attached to the garage which was later remodeled into a family room. Even though my living quarters were 6 by 9 feet—the size of a prison cell—this was every teenager's dream. My parents slept upstairs in the opposite side of the house, meaning nobody, and I mean nobody, could hear me coming or going when I was supposed to be sleeping. Except for the hamster in the family room. It turns out hamsters are nocturnal animals. This one had an over-sized plastic hamster wheel in its cage. A squeaky "exercise spinner." Nobody wants a fat hamster.

One night I couldn't take the noise any longer. It was 3 AM, and the household was deep in the REM stage of their snoozes. I went into the kitchen to look under the sink for anything in an aerosol can—preferable something toxic like ant spray. I was planning on fumigating that hamster. In a perfect world, I hoped to wake in the morning with him dead in his cage, no trace of any mysterious poison.

"Aww, the little guy must have had a heart attack exercising in his wheel last night." Snicker.

I would not have admitted to anything if he had died—a testimonial to my lack of teenage moral integrity that would make my mother wince. But come morning, the hamster was cozily curled up in his shavings, exhausted from his squeaky wheel exploits, but alive nonetheless.

God has mysterious ways of payback for my evil thoughts and deeds from 20 years earlier. The universe manifested a string of animal deaths over a four-month period, exquisitely timed for maximum trading interference.

I was now a single mom in a household with Erika, two dozen animals (26 to be exact, counting the gerbil babies), and two staff who worked in the office. Victoria had moved from Chicago and lived in the barn apartment. She was sure Erika needed a bird. Like a bird is going to make up for the absence of a father. We bought a beautiful white African lovebird that Erika named Dew Drop. Erika and I would kiss the bird goodnight, put him in his cage where he could watch over her while she slept, and then turn off the lights.

"Ayeeeeeee, Ayeeeeeee!"

Blood-curdling screams echoed down the stone hallways at 3 AM.

This sound was beyond raccoons making mischief in the attic above my bedroom. Someone had been MURDERED. I darted out of bed in the direction of the shriek which happened to be coming from my daughter's room. Dead, at the bottom of its cage, was the African lovebird. How did my daughter know it had died while she was sleeping? Hmm. She soon confessed in-between massive sobs that she took the bird to bed with her to cuddle. While sleeping, she rolled over on top of it, suffocating the innocent, pure white Dew Drop. Needless to say, I got no sleep that night, and she refused to go to school the next day.

Why do these things happen on nights when we have maximum exposure in the markets, and there are significant economic data reports or the ECB Monetary Policy release? ECB days can be my worst trading day or my best. They were my worst until I realized they were my worst and then I tried very hard to concentrate so they would no longer be my worst. Does that sound convoluted? That is what my brain felt like the next morning. I slogged down as much coffee as possible and prayed for the weekend to come without me making too many errors.

For the next two months, Erika slept in my bed at night. The ghost of the African lovebird was still lingering in her room.

Victoria was insistent that Erika needed more pets. I was convinced that she did this to punish me, in a sort of friendly, sadistic way. My role was to buy food for all of them. Food and horseshoes. I could have bought ten pairs of Manolos, Sara Jessica Parker specials, for what it cost to shoe 6 horses in Florida. I was happy to walk around barefoot because that is how I grew up in Southern California. Except we had fire ants in Florida, so you had to be very careful where you stepped.

I heard the funniest story when driving Erika to the bus stop on Howard Stern's radio show. It was a contest as to who had the most tragic love story. The winner was a guy who got hot and bothered over a girl he met at a bar. After a few drinks, they decided to get frisky and roll around in the bushes outside. Until one mother of all mothers sounded the alarm and a thousand fire ants bit him simultaneously. Nothing like having sex on top of a fire ant mound. He ended up in the hospital. You only need to hear a story like that once to look where you are stepping.

Victoria decided the next best thing would be to get Erika a pair of gerbils. Why? Every kid has gerbils. Besides, they don't need a noisy exercise wheel like hamsters do. The pet store assured us these were two female gerbils. How did I expect a store clerk getting paid minimum wage to determine the sex of a gerbil correctly?

One month later, one of the gerbils had grown much fatter than the other. It must be hogging all the food. No, it was about to give birth to ten babies. Victoria said if you don't remove the father from the cage, he will eat the babies. Why do daddy gerbils eat their young? No clue. All I know is we had to keep him in a separate cage, and both of those cages were in Erika's bathroom.

It was just after 2:30 PM, the last hour and a half of the trading day on a Wednesday. Not any Wednesday but FOMC meeting day. Historically, this is one of my best trading days. I have an elaborate ritual. Shut out all outside influences, close any unnecessary programs on the CPUs so there is no risk of latency, and lock all the doors so nobody can come in. The crazy FOMC gyrations had begun.

"Eeeeeee! Ay-eeeeeeee!"

Terrifying howls were reverberating through the house. Loud enough to shake the glass doors on my office building.

Danny Kay, the male gerbil, had made a swan dive from the top of his cage directly into the toilet below. He was floating belly-up in a state of rigor mortis when Erika found him. I had built a separate office specifically to insulate myself from the distractions of traumatized children. My contractor had failed to do his job like the store clerk who had failed to sex the gerbils correctly. When was this going to end? It turns out, we still went through a cat dying, a dog dying, and worst of all, a horse had to be put down over a four-month period.

If we do the math on the probabilities that two animals would die on two of the choicest trading days, you will see it is not that far-fetched. I had 26 creatures (including the ten baby gerbils). The average life expectancy of the assorted horses, ponies, cats, dogs, birds, and gerbils came out to 10 years. There were about six Big Event days a month if we count the high alert economic report days: FOMC, ECB, significant elections. The odds that an animal will die on one of these 72 days over the next year is around 1 out of 50. If we have 26 animals, this translates to 26/50 meaning around a 50% chance that one lands on our roulette wheel. Square the probability since the event of one animal dying is independent of the others and you got 25% odds that two animals die on a significant trend day in one year.

*　*　*

This is ballpark thinking. It is how the markets work. My brother likes to call it "pseudo-math." He is a genius and has an advanced degree in applied mathematics. It means everything is a fuzzy variable and you never have to give an exact answer to anything. If I did not keep so many animals around, the math would be no good. So, while we think the odds of any one thing going wrong and upsetting our plans are low when you consider all the assorted stuff which can go wrong and add up the individual probabilities, the odds are high that something comes along and screws up what was otherwise a great plan. Count on hitting some potholes, because they are there. The best you can do is to minimize the damage they do.

The main creature who refused to die was Axle, the Dalmatian. When I won the South Florida bodybuilding middleweight title, a client immediately mailed me three pounds of chocolates. Sadistic client. Maybe he thought I would trade better in a state of insulin shock instead of carbohydrate depletion. I ate half of the three-foot platter of chocolates and put the rest of the tray on the island in the kitchen. I stepped outside to go over to the barn and throw up. Axle snuck into the kitchen and ate the other half of the chocolates while I was gone. I thought chocolate was supposed to kill a dog, but he refused to die. He didn't even get sick. The dog would burp and move on to the next edible (or inedible) thing in the house.

Axle was the reincarnation of Rasputin. We named him this after a previous incident which happened in New Jersey. A client came to visit my office which, at the time, was still in the basement. A very dark, dank, and unglamorous space. We were talking about markets when I thought, "What's that horrid smell?" I looked around but could see nothing except Axle slinking out of the office with his tail between his legs. Then I spotted it. There on the mottled gray carpet sat a giant deposit of Milorganite, an organic fertilizer made from reprocessed sewage sludge. Axle had relieved himself right behind my client after feasting from the opened bag in my garage.

My ex-husband tried to give the dog away to a group of firemen who had tirelessly worked all night to extinguish a fire in our old neighborhood in New Jersey. The firemen took one look at the dog and replied, "No thanks, we tried that before. Dalmatians are just too stupid." He was incredulous. The firemen had already figured out that their stereotypical Dalmatians weren't all they were cracked up to be.

Knowing we were stuck with Axle, he became our resident vacuum. He followed me into the kitchen drooling in anticipation of his egg yolks, always optimistic, assuming I wouldn't burn them. I cooked six eggs at a time but only wanted one yolk. The dogs shared the rest. A good number of times I practiced burning the kitchen down by forgetting about them after I went into the office. Intense market focus dictated my every move until I walked out of the office and back into the kitchen around 10:30. Oh, crap. Black acrid smoke would be billowing from the stove. Burned another pan. It is not good for the earth's environment to waste so many frying pans. When I ran out of frying pans, I started making protein shakes. How much harm can you do blending powder and water with crushed ice?

Nazdoggie did not care. She trotted back and forth from building to building with a perpetual smile on her Pomeranian face. Oh, there was a lousy economic report? Look, the sky is blue, the sun is shining, and I am such a happy little doggie.

Interestingly, none of the people who worked in my office ever said anything about the animal farm. I might as well have posted a sign at the entrance to the driveway:

ENTER AT YOUR OWN RISK OF BEING SLOBBERED ON BY A DOG, SNORTED ON BY A HORSE, OR HAVING EARDRUMS RUPTURED BY A PARROT.

30

GENERIC AND BIG DADDY

Ron Shear was a good friend of mine. His brother had been the specialist in one of the pits I traded in at the PHLX. Ron founded Carlin Equities and owned one of the largest proprietary trading firms, Generic Trading. I was visiting Ron in his office on a trip to New York in the late nineties and happened to mention the chat room I started while waiting for my divorce to settle. He suggested he was interested in something like that for his traders. He had 800 prop traders who needed trade ideas. Ever since the *Market Wizards* book came out, I would get random calls out of the blue. One was from Chris, who would call me at 2 o'clock in the morning.

"Hey Linda, *Linda*! I faxed you a chart, can you take a look at it?"

I tried to get my tired mouth to make sounds. "Chris, do you *know* what time it is? You woke me up. I cannot take a look at your chart. Please don't call me at these hours."

This went on over several weeks. Chris emailed me that he had been studying Ticks while on vacation on some island, or that he came across a chart formation he wanted me to analyze. The dude was persistent with the craziest unlimited energy. The worst part was, he really did have an eye for the charts.

One day I saw on the caller I.D. that Chris was calling me, so I answered the phone and started talking before he could, "Chris, I have an idea. How would you like a job? But you must promise never to call me after midnight again, no matter what."

Ron wanted someone to make stock calls for his 800 traders. So, we did a three-year exclusive where we provided stock analysis for Ron's firm. I brought Chris on board to provide an endless stream of equity trade ideas. And we killed the markets. Chris was the master of being able to reverse on a dime. When the market was rallying, he would nail the bull flags in a dozen stocks.

"Chris, the market is looking a bit toppy here. I'm getting sell divergences and non-confirmations between the indexes."

"Ok!"

He told the traders in the room, "Sell out everything." And we would start working the short side. Chris did not trade during this period, so he remained objective and did not speak about his position. Before working for me, he was in the construction business finishing the inside of skyscrapers in New York. Working from blueprints demands a good sense of spatial relationships, and thus Chris had an excellent eye for the charts.

He did not have any college education, only sheer Italian chutzpah. I am not sure he even finished high school. He came with the nickname "Big Daddy" and is one of the hardest-working and funniest people I know. Nothing they teach in school prepares you for the stock market, so he was well-prepared.

Chris lived up in New York. I drove my car up there to meet him for a conference which was held at the Marriot on Times Square. Parking is a bitch in Manhattan and very expensive. My car was nothing fancy, an average black Jeep.

When we pulled up to the Marriot, Chris said to the doorman, "You know who I am?" The doorman's eyes scanned his inner mind, trying to figure out if he recognized Chris. The doorman was large and dignified, dressed as fancy as a character in costume at Disneyworld. Before he could muster a response, Chris continued.

"I am Big Daddy." The doorman stared at Chris and blinked. "Yup, I am Big Daddy. You do know who I am, don't you?" The doorman nodded his head, suddenly acting as if he realized Chris was famous, but he still couldn't quite place him.

"Of course, sir."

"I need for you to take care of this car for me, can you do that?"

"Yes, sir."

"Good. Now I am going to take my friend inside." We walked in and left the doorman with my Jeep running so he could valet it which he ended up doing for free.

In the late nineties, October 16, 1998, to be exact, the Fed made a surprise move to cut interest rates by a half-percentage point. This was going into the last hour and it caught Wall Street by surprise. The SPs rallied 50 points in five minutes while the Dow rallied 330 points. This was before electronic trading, too. Fifty points on the big SPs contract would be an expensive lesson if you did not have a stop in place especially since at the time they were trading just above 1000. Chris had a stop in place and only got slippage of 6 points. This is why I paid Chris not to trade after that incident so he could concentrate full time and remain unbiased for Ron's traders.

Damon, my SP broker, had quite a few other horror stories though. His partner had a protective buy stop on a short position at 1232. The futures were trading around 1226 when the news hit. But by the time it took out 30, there was such an influx of orders that almost every buy stop got filled at the high around 1325. His partner was filled there too, costing him $105,000. Slippage of 93 points was unheard of! It goes to show that even floor brokers standing next to the pit can get screwed along with everyone else.

This was one tape bomb I managed to miss.

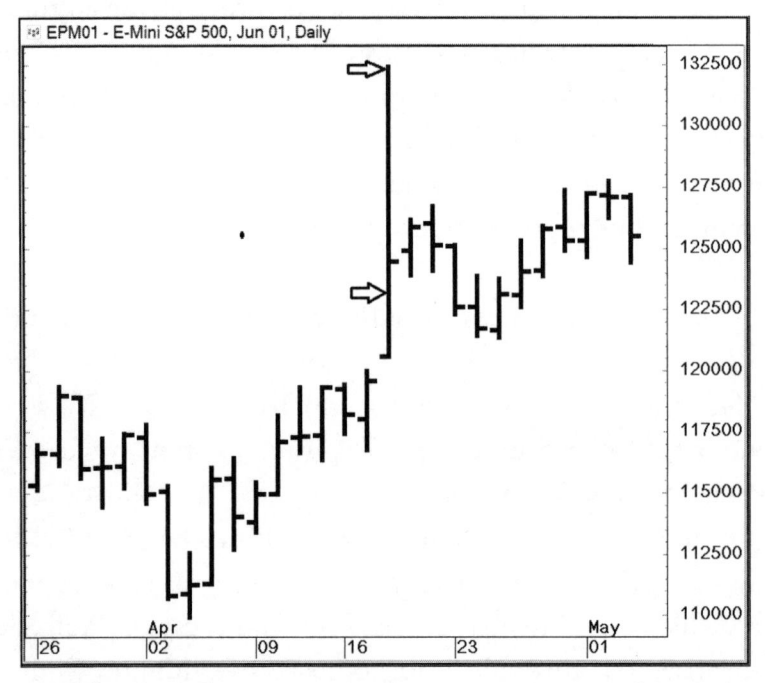

Wednesday afternoon…95 points up in 5 minutes. Surprise!

* * *

When the bear market hit in technology stocks in 2001, most traders could not trade from the short side. Over the next three years, it was a war of attrition for stock traders and the prop shops. That is the beauty of the futures markets. There is always something to trade from either the long or short side. Plus, there was no uptick rule at the time as there was for shorting stocks. Any time the index futures popped their heads up we played Whack-a-Mole (aka "hit the bid") until the SPs bottomed in late 2002.

The chat room kept me on my game during what was an otherwise unbearable period of my life. I was so happy when the divorce was finalized. The process was a depressing grind—three years of document production and bickering. All the stuff that 90% of divorces entail, designed to make one think twice about getting married again. But the chat room provided humor! We let our hair down and cracked jokes. We called the turning points of the intraday swings and stayed in the game.

We ran periodic research projects. I promised to share our research with anyone in the room who did their work. The room became the ultimate talent pool. Every individual who came to work for me when I ran the fund came from the chat room. It had some of the best, brightest and most talented traders as members. I still have monies invested in three funds started by traders who gained experience in the chat room. And, my best friends with whom I trade online with every day came from the room.

I never made a dime from the room because every bit of revenue it created went towards creating jobs for others. I had Laura, James, Victoria, Chris, two other moderators, someone to run the video, do research, run the trade sheet routines and handle customer support. It was an excellent way to pay it forward by creating jobs for aspiring traders. Most people need a transition period with some alternative income to make their way to full-time trading.

The room also provided me with a structure and kept me accountable during a period when I was not handling client monies. It placed a lot of demands on my time, but it was how I found Nigel, Judd, Roland, and other future trading colleagues. And I laughed my ass off at Victoria's jokes while watching every tick in the SPs.

Big Daddy seemed to know everyone. One of the people he met at a party in New York found her way down to Camp Raschke in Wellington where she stayed for a few nights. Flavia Cymbalista is one of the most delightful and authentic souls. She has a Ph.D. in cognitive psychology but prefers to be called an "uncertainty specialist." Her published paper, *How George Soros Knows What He Knows*, was a good source of raised eyebrows in an era where the trend was towards quantifying everything. Flavia took the opposite approach. What information can the experienced trader gain from listening to themselves? She was ahead of her time when it comes to mindfulness. She told me about her friendship with George Soros and how he listens to his back. If he had on a good position, his back did not bother him. He could ride out a bit of heat or noise and be patient. But if his back was bothering him, most likely his position was wrong.

I am not sure if this would fly as a legitimate tool these days for a multi-million dollar hedge fund manager, but there is a lot of truth to this. What does that Green Light GO feeling *feel* like? The one where the window of opportunity is thrown wide open and stays open a few minutes longer than usual? When you *know* you've got a tiger by the tail and the winds are filling your sails. Green light, go! Step on the gas, pedal full throttle, make a run for it. How many of those times do we get per year? Maybe two? Perhaps four, if a trader is lucky. These are the types of trades that newer traders imagine happening to experienced pros who pull down seven digits in trading profits year after year. But trading is a game of patience and grind. Weeks turn into months. Will the volatility ever come back? Will a market ever break from its narrowing weekly trading range? And right when we are close to forgetting what riding that big wave feels like, a tsunami hits.

I know myself and my patterns by now. There are days when I come in and my positions are against me from the day before. I mark my trades to the closing price of each day and use that as my baseline for the next day. It does not matter where the trade was initially established. I had confidence in my roadmap the day before, and that was why I held overnight. Now I am starting out my day underwater from the overnight activity. But I also know that in the past these situations have turned out to be some of my best days. So, I don't get discouraged by sloppy overnight activity. Instead, I get excited about the day. I know I have come back so many times before, and a down morning means nothing on any decent timeline.

Experience counts not just in knowing the markets, but in understanding your own personal trading patterns.

31

ENTER ENTER ENTER

I was trading my personal funds and rebuilding equity after the divorce chopped my net worth in half. I gave my ex most of the cash because I wanted to keep the house, barn, and horses. This was okay with me. I would not have been able to build the career I did without him taking care of the household and being Mr. Mom. After enough losses throughout a trading career, what is building up capital yet one more time? I was a real pro at making money back by now.

James was still my assistant, and I had two other traders sharing my office as well. One of them had a television, something I did not keep in the office. One morning we all saw what appeared to be a small plane flying into a big building. It looked like an accident, a little blip on a big TV screen.

Steve Moore called me on the phone, "Did we see that?" My initial thought was an airplane had gone off course, or the pilot had had a heart attack. And then we all watched in horror as the second plane hit the other World Trade Center.

A few months earlier, I had moved my main business to Refco's trading desk in New York which was one block from the World Trade Center. Have you ever experienced a nightmare where you can only move in slow motion? Like trying to jog in quicksand? My largest position happened to be short Eurodollars. It is the last position a trader wants to have when disaster hits. By the time I picked up the phone and called to close out my position, the phones were unmanned. Refco's office in New York had been evacuated.

The US Exchanges stopped trading and stayed closed for five days. Trading in the bond market screeched to a halt. I watched every tick in the DAX for five days. It was my way of reassuring myself that the world was still turning. When the German markets closed in the middle of the day, I wandered around the house holding Nazdoggie, my Pomeranian dog close for comfort. The Federal Reserve added $300 billion in liquidity over the next three days. Gold rallied $70. The US dollar plummeted, and when trading resumed in the Eurodollars, they were radically higher. Ouch. After watching them for no more than an hour or two, it became quickly apparent that they were not going to come back down, so I bit the bullet and closed out my position. I had recently made back the money I had paid out in my divorce. And now Mr. Market was taking it away yet again. Four steps forward, three steps back.

* * *

Electronic trading replaced my direct-line bat phones to the pits. New execution software was popping up every day. James and I tried many execution platforms over the next few years. We encountered latency issues and glitches in every one. Around this time, I was out in California at a convention in Orange County. I had flown out there to make peace with my Dad who was on his deathbed. It was a fluke that I stopped by this industry conference.

I wandered through the deserted convention center hallways. It was 7 PM on a Friday night. Everyone was gone. I heard piano music coming from around the corner. Damon, my old SP broker from the nineties, sat at the keyboard playing "Maybe I'm Amazed" by Paul McCartney. Who would have known he was an accomplished musician? We had done business together for over a decade, but I knew nothing personal about him. After I stopped placing orders in the pit and the markets went electronic, Damon and I had lost touch. But fate meant for our paths to cross one more time. It turns out he used to be the lead guitarist for a rock and roll band which toured the country for a year. I did not tell him I was a pianist but instead batted my eyelashes and enjoyed his playing.

Damon and his two partners built state-of-the-art, robust execution software. It was used by prop shops to trade the arb between the 10-year notes and the 30-year bonds, (also called the NOB and FIT spreads). He offered to set me up with their Photon Trader software and in one week shipped a new CPU with the trading platform already installed to my Florida office. I ended up doing all my business through his firm, FuturePath, after that.

One morning I was talking to Damon on the phone. I told him before the markets opened that I wanted to build a sizable long position. The stock indexes had a breakout formation, and my models showed potential for a glorious trend day. Damon took note of my market sentiment and agreed. I began buying on the opening and accumulated 600 long SP e-minis. I sold 100 to book profits, test the market and get a feel. I like doing a bit of trading at times to get additional feedback on how strong or weak a market is. I often put something out and then if I have to buy it back a bit higher to add to the original position, I will. Not too long after, Damon walked into the risk control center to talk to one of his employees. His risk guy said, "Wow, Linda is selling quite a bit!" Damon looked on the screen and noticed my account selling 100 contracts every 10 seconds. Remembering our conversation from the morning, he was confused after I had sold so much. I had reversed my position to 600 short as the market was screaming higher. He called to ask why I had changed my mind about the direction of the market.

"Why did you just sell 1200 cars?" (Cars was slang for contracts in our parlance).

"What are you talking about?"

I had been typing on the wrong keyboard and every time I hit "Enter," it sold another 100 contracts unbeknownst to me. I kept the execution monitor off to the side because the fluctuating P and L and ladders were distracting. I only wanted the main market quotes in front of my face. I was trying to hit "Enter" to change a chart and could not figure why it was not changing as I pounded away at "Enter" multiple times.

"Fuck! Fuck! Fuck!" The duck got left out on this one.

I immediately hung up on Damon. The SPs were five points higher now. I bought back the shorts "at the market" and doubled up on the long side. By the end of the day, the market was significantly higher.

For three decades, I have kept two sayings at the bottom of my daily trade sheet:

"Correct Mistakes Immediately" and "Winners Admit Errors"

"Correct Mistakes Immediately" has saved me millions of dollars—literally. I am not quite as fast to admit errors, but I learned that the market forces you to accept them sooner or later. It's cheaper to get it over with sooner than later.

32

MIKE EPSTEIN

Mike and I met through the MTA in the early nineties. He was one of my best friends in the industry, but then again, Mike was probably best friends to a lot of people. Born in Brooklyn, he attended Harvard Business School after leaving the Navy in the position of what is now the Navy SEALS. His career included 50 years on the floor of the NYSE.

Over the years, I heard hundreds of Mike's stories and quotes. He told me a story about when he was a broker on the exchange floor in an oil stock. This stock had traded in a 3/4 point range for the prior two weeks. Volatility was a bit different in those days. The brokers, including Mike, had instructions to notify their clients if the stock traded above 21. When it finally did, they all ran to the phones to contact their customers. During this time, an order came into the pit to sell 20,000 shares at 21. Since all the brokers were on the phone to their customers, the specialist took the shares. When the brokers returned to the pit bidding 21, the specialist sold out his

20,000 shares at 21 1/8. Mike was incredulous. "Why did you sell out all your stock for only 1/8 profit? Why didn't you hold out for a bit more or sell partial?"

The specialist had the only inventory, and now everyone wanted it. He reached into his pocket and pulled out a big fat 3-inch roll of $100 bills. He told Mike to hold his hand out and then placed the roll in his hand. "Now, slowly close your fingers around those bills and tell me what it feels like!" No profit is yours until it is locked in. Once you start extending your time frame, there are lower odds of that "sure trade." The specialist was content to quickly pocket a profit.

This next story was right after Mike had joined Bear Sterns in 1962. It was during the Cuban missile crisis when warships parked off the coast of Cuba and the Soviet Union. The United States and Russia had nuclear weapons pointed at each other in the highest possible state of alert. The market was falling and Mike was in the heat of the battle on the floor of the NYSE. Mike turns to his boss and asks what he should do. His boss tells him, "Take the offer and buy 'em." Mike questioned the sanity of his boss as the world was on the brink of ending in a nuclear holocaust. His boss told him to keep buying. "If they don't nuke us the market will bounce and if they do you won't have to worry about paying for them!"

My favorite Mike story is when he was a broker on the floor, and everyone left early for the Hamptons in the summertime. On this Friday afternoon, not much had been going on, so Mike left early and caught a mid-day train. When he got to his beach house, his wife mentioned she had been at the hairdresser's yacking with another lady under the hair dryers.

"Mike, didn't you mention XYZ stock last week? Well, Mrs. Schnitzel (wife of the CEO) said her husband was staying in town that night to finish a deal."

In two seconds flat, Mike did a 180-degree turnaround, caught the train back into New York and rebought all the stock of XYZ they had liquidated that day. He then bought more just before the closing bell. Sure enough, a deal was announced over the weekend! Mike did not believe in news or tips, but he said, "*This* is the type of tip which means something. Gossip from your wife at the hairdressers who has no idea about what was going on in the markets."

I visited Mike and his German wife, Erika, in Boston several times. The last trip I took, Mike was looking at his monitor through a giant magnifying glass. His eyesight was failing him. It was 2008, and he pointed out an upside breakout from a bond chart formation. Thirty-year yields were breaking below 4% for the first time in my lifetime. Mike turned to me and said, "I have no idea where bonds are going or why they are breaking out, but the charts say to stay long." So, long he was.

He was a pure technician and chuckled at the business school students who over-thought things. He wore an olive green pair of Crocs on his feet every day. I thought Crocs were the ugliest shoes until I saw Mike wearing them and then, of course, I had to get a pair. He spent the last seven years of his life as a visiting scholar and research affiliate at MIT's laboratory for financial engineering at the invitation of Professor Andrew Lo. But his mentality remained a consummate floor trader first and a classic technician second. At one point he had held seats on almost every major US exchange.

My favorite Mike expression: "Don't eat like a bird and shit like an elephant." In other words, don't take small wins and big losses.

Mike sent us a steady stream of interns from MIT. Camp Raschke's guest quarters were never vacant. It worked for me since I could stay on my property and still enjoy the company of others. One of the interns was working on his Ph.D. in finance. Anyone Mike tutored in his financial engineering lab at MIT was right there at the top in brain power. MIT and Ph.D.'s have nothing to do with being a trader though, and this guy's forte was cell phones and video games. He would disappear into his room in the late afternoon and re-emerge the next morning.

The intern was very proficient at gaming, so we created a trading game. It consisted of strategically placed Buy and Sell stops on 100 lots in the indexes. His job was to scalp out for 3-4 ticks once an order triggered. A crazy game but quite successful. If you take away the decision-making process which overwhelms many people and focus on one task, i.e., exit for a few ticks, you end up with a steady equity curve. The size, market, entry, and direction are determined ahead of time. All you have to do is manage the trade for a few minutes and exit. The problem for most is they get bored or think they can get cute and improve upon the game.

The SP game originated from a project I schemed up with Brett Steenbarger. What is the most effective way to train traders? I based the game on the OODA loop: Observe, Orient, Decide, and Act. It was as close to simulating my experience in the options pits as I could imagine. Brokers walked into the crowd, and the market makers did not know if they had buy or sell orders. Nobody knew the order size or what stock was going to do next. It was as if the broker was tossing a hot potato into the crowd in the form of an order to fill immediately. The traders had to think on their feet how they were going to hedge the trade. We did exercises to simulate this process with a group of 50 traders from the chat room for six weeks.

* * *

You can only help someone who would have made it on their own anyway. You cannot instill a knack, just hone it and accelerate its refinement. Another project I did with Andrew Lo's colleagues examined the emotional profile of successful traders. The main problem was that it was difficult to separate the survivorship bias. Are top professional traders successful because they are unflappable under pressure and thus less prone to being reactive? Or, did they develop a thicker skin over time? The conclusion was, the longer a trader had been trading, the less their emotional sensitivity.

However, it was not clear if top traders had those traits when they were starting out. Over time, we become desensitized to everything.

I had several more assistants over this period, none of whom had a college degree. They were smart and driven. The best thing about this business is you don't have to have a formal education unless you are going to engage in a quantitative discipline.

Chris referred a young trader from New York named Harry. Victoria had left, and I needed someone to type for me and execute orders. Harry was home-schooled by his French father, spoke several languages, and excelled in math. He was a scrawny kid with glasses and bad teeth. His dad died, leaving Harry with a small inheritance and a lack of motivation to pursue higher studies. I am sure Harry had an IQ well above 145. He was hysterically funny. An absolute riot to have around.

On Monday morning, Harry walked into the office and his glasses were gone. He had Lasik done over the weekend on his eyes. Then he went on a mission to gain weight and build muscle. I've never seen anyone pack on 20 pounds, none of them fat, in such a short period of time. I was trying to trade, and my assistant was binge eating Cheerios and chicken at his desk throughout the day. I put up with it because he was so entertaining and he and James had become great friends. He was also good at his job.

The next month, he had all his teeth capped. A gleaming white smile greeted me each morning. Packages arrived in my mailbox for Harry: designer clothes purchased on Amazon and eBay. One was a blue Versace pajama type of outfit. James and I nicknamed him "Harry the Smurf," and the name stuck. One day, I was trying to concentrate and I hear this noise coming from the desk next to me, *chhh chhh, chhh chhh*. I look over, and Harry was spraying his nipples with an aerosol antiseptic after getting them pierced the night before. I almost fell out of my chair. Soon the transformation of Harry was complete. He looked like the consummate professional gigolo. Sadly,

I had to fire him when he started coming in late after staying up all night in Miami. Not too long after, we saw Harry on TV. The first hurricane was about to hit in South Florida and there he was, swimming in the ocean and taunting the huge waves. The camera crews found him, and he found national notoriety.

Harry embarked on a six-year adventure of world travels, charming people around the globe. His incredible pictures on Facebook were viewed by thousands. He ate with the richest of the rich and slept with the poorest of the poor, explored every corner of the earth, and escaped countless brushes with death. One day his nine lives ran out, and he met his death tangling with drug lords on a motorcycle trip in Mexico. Harry Devert deserves a movie made of his life, though he is no longer here to charm anyone into making it.

* * *

Intern, Big Daddy, Damon, Harry, and a colleague, palling around in Florida

After Harry left, Chris sent down another referral from up north. She was already familiar with the Photon software since her mom used it, so she fit in perfectly doing my execution. Like Harry, she didn't have an Ivy League pedigree, but she was damn smart. She was a math wiz, which worked out well for Erika who was suffering through the performing arts satellite school of the Florida public school system and desperately in need of a tutor.

I am forever grateful that she held down the fort through the last hurricane while I was in Chicago. The winds shredded the 100-foot long screen enclosure over the pool, toppled numerous trees and blew the chimney off the roof. The electricity and water were out for eight days. But, our female intern was unperturbed.

Anyone can be anything in this business, and formal education has little to do with it.

33

BURNING DOG

There is a well-known expression: *the teacher learns more than the student.*

There was a brief period where I hosted a three-day conference every two or three years. I summarized the findings of my most recent research efforts and taught my approach to the markets. It forced me to update my previous research and put it in tables which I made into thick manuals for the attendees. I took pride in these conferences and strove to make them the crème de la crème for the industry. The most beautiful hotels, cocktail parties, first-class lunches and dinners, and even full audio tapes of the conference. Lots of planning went into these, much of which Laura handled. We stopped doing them after a few years when the Fund grew and it became too much work. But before it all ended, I booked the conference at the Saint Francis hotel in San Francisco.

The Saint Francis is a luxury hotel on Union Square. Built in 1904, it managed to survive the terrible earthquake of 1906.

Unfortunately, the fires which followed gutted the inside. The renovation elevated the elegance and luxury to the platinum standard. Reagan, Ford, Queen Elizabeth, and many celebrities stayed in the rich gold and red velvet suites. This chichi and snobby backdrop was an ironic setting for a trading conference.

Unfortunately, the weekend scheduled turned out to be less than two weeks after 9/11. This unfathomable event affected people in different ways, so airlines and hotels issued full refunds. The uncertainty in the air was thicker than a San Francisco fog. We called the clients and gave them the option for a full refund if they chose not to come. However, I would still be hopping on a plane and proceeding with the conference if they wished to attend. I figured anyone showing up had to be a hardcore trader. And, I was right.

There was one attendee who stood out in total contrast to the finery of the hotel. His muscle T-shirt revealed massive black tattoos covering his arms and shoulders. He had a gold earring in one ear and his shaved head gave off a Sinbad the Sailor vibe. He nicknamed himself Genghis. His slouch with his arms across his chest and legs stuck out in the middle of the aisle broadcast, "Okay, prove to me you are the best and that it was worth my money to come here."

Everyone has a story in this business.

Genghis jackhammered concrete for 20 years. Arthritis took his knees as prisoners, and his hearing was shot. It was no way to grow old. His cousin took a Ken Roberts course and dabbled in options. Genghis followed along branching out into futures. He borrowed 30,000 dollars on a credit card to open a trading account (yes, you could do that until 2007). No doubt the cost of the conference and hotel went on that credit card, too. He satisfied the three-G Rating: Guts, Gumption, and Grit.

At the end of the conference, Genghis made a resting offer. If I ever needed help in any way, even mucking the stalls, he'd be there. I did not need anyone until I had to ask Harry to leave after his lifestyle became too much of a distraction for professional operations. Genghis came out for a few weeks and stayed for six months. Harry continued to hang out with us on a social basis, and we were all fast friends.

I told Genghis he could continue to trade for his account, but I needed someone to type for me. He loved to trade the openings in the SPs.

"Genghis, what are you doing, blindly fading every opening gap?"

"It's a burning dog. I have to trade the burning dog."

"What the heck? What's that?"

"Well, have you ever met anyone who wants to pet a burning dog?"

Hmm, not a pleasant image, but definitely one Genghis would use. The main point he was trying to make was people feel uncomfortable with large opening gaps.

"OK, if you would like to turn this into a tradable strategy, let's model it. Let's create a structure we can quantify to trade around."

We hunkered down for the next two days. Ten-hour stretches, the tattoo man and me. We wrote down every data point for the previous three years which had a gap opening in the SPs of greater than 2 points. We then noted the maximum excursion on both sides of the opening price. It was not meant to be a mechanical trade, but I wanted to draw Genghis's attention to the values that might be significant regarding risks and targets. Sometimes doing things by hand reveals subtle nuances.

For this three-year period, if the SPs gapped by more than 4 points, the market retraced a minimum of 4 points 76% of the time. Not a bad start. The flaw in this type of modeling is that fixed variables such as 4 points do not account for periods of expanded volatility and range. For example, later in 2009, the SPs had gaps three times as big as the average gap we were modeling. But at the time, 4 points was significant, and we had a lot of fun around this concept. I loved it for the pure novelty of the name—"burning dog."

Genghis brought his girlfriend out from California, and they rented a townhouse. He remained part of our commune until Harry split for good. Harry was a magnet for fun, life, humor, and stress relief.

I was itching to get back to managing money after my divorce was finalized. My trading funds were freed. Everyone moved on. I ran into Genghis ten years later on an airplane when he was flying back from New York after attending his best friend's funeral. He no longer lived in Florida and was a single man. We did not talk about markets or business, but I assumed he was successful at whatever he was doing. He was the type of person who saw only the possibilities, never the limitations.

Later, I embarked upon building a "theory of everything and modeling the universe." Start off by asking, what is the distribution for the time of day this 4-point objective is hit? If the burning dog did not get its 4 points by noon, there were higher odds the market would make new highs or lows in the afternoon. The permutations of this type of modeling are endless.

Multiple models are like the limbs of a tree. You must have a large number of models, and they must be robust, lasting ideas. Build the tree in your mind with deep roots and strong branches and then hang the leaves of experience. This concept was from Charlie Munger, Vice Chairman of Berkshire Hathaway and one of the finest thinkers in the world.

Another essential step is to layer on top of our multiple model tree a form of Bayesian process. Start with prior models and probabilities and then continuously update them as new information unfolds. "One data point at a time." To go one step further, we can even weight these new pieces of information. And as the volume of information increases exponentially, you see how easy it is to fall down a rabbit hole.

The two most important takeaways in understanding these principles are:

1) We are limited in our ability to forecast the future.
2) Following a process systematically is essential.

One data point at a time.

Nigel

34

NIGEL

Nigel pulled into my driveway in a silver bullet of a sports car, leaving a cinematic trail of dust behind him as he roared down the dirt road that led to my entrance. He was dressed sharply, but subtly. It is always funny meeting someone from an online chat room for the first time—you never know what they'll look like, or sound like for that matter. I'm not sure what I expected Nigel to be like, but he made a dashing first impression.

The car was a silver Jaguar XKE convertible. He got a new one off lease once every three years. Once he bought one off lease before his old contract ran out, so I got to drive it for six months. You would think a convertible in Florida would be a blast, but in the summertime, it rains every afternoon, so I never put the top down. It still felt like driving a James Bond car.

"This is quite a place you have here." Even though he knew more about computers than I ever knew, he acted impressed by our whirring machines and blinking screens.

"Thank you, we're still figuring out how to streamline our network."

"I understand that all too well."

Nigel developed sophisticated distribution software and sold his company at the top of the 2000 Internet bubble. Unfortunately, he was unable to cash out his shares until a year after the bubble burst. Initial lockup periods are a bitch. He figured if you could lose that much in stock value you ought to be able to make that much too. So, he became involved in the markets. He moved to West Palm Beach to make it his full-time trading home. When he discovered his condo building had poor Internet connectivity he mentioned it in the chat room. I invited him to come and check out my office. James had since moved back west, and I welcomed a technically savvy colleague.

The day after he visited, I received a huge bouquet of flowers from him as a thank-you. He was classy and understated, and even though I thought of him as a computer guru and aspiring trader, I was not surprised at all when we found out he was an accomplished swing dancer. In all the years we did business, I don't think I ever saw him wearing jeans or sandals. Even in Florida, he never dressed like he was headed to Margaritaville.

Nigel was a genius at coding and back-testing. After talking to him, I realized that if he came on board, I could start up my fund again. Managing money brought me great satisfaction. I was the kid who wanted to bring an apple to the teacher, to please my piano teacher with my latest song, to have someone say, "Good job!" I loved making money for clients and being near the top of the performance board. I was one of the biggest clients in my fund. I preferred to keep my dollars in a formalized trading program. But, I knew better than to think I could manage running a fund with just Laura and myself. It's a lot of work.

Nigel was all-in; he knew my style from subscribing to the online group the previous year. I made him and Laura partners in the fund and was back in the hedge fund business. It is difficult to find a good name for a fund these days. The astrological constellations, precious metals, and Roman gods are all taken. I named it the Granat Fund after a famous dressage horse. He was big-boned, ugly, and blind in one eye but he went on to win the 1976 Olympics with Christine Stuckelberger. They stayed at the top of the world rankings for years. My core group of clients from the previous decade jumped back on board. I never had to advertise or pay someone to raise money nor did I make it a point to go to the industry conferences. I was fortunate.

In addition to Raffles, assorted other icons lined our office. A colleague gave me a chain link license plate that framed the words, "Coja un Pato." This is Spanish for my overused swear phrase, "fuck a duck." I think he was telling me to tone it down. Just before the downturn of 2008, Nigel found a dartboard with stocks on each tab. Half of the companies vanished in the economic downturn. We ceremoniously stuck a dart in each company on the dartboard as it went bankrupt. After we ran out of darts, we resorted to thumbtacks. When the board was half full, I came up with the idea of making dog bones with the symbols of the vanished companies stamped on the top.

"LEH for you, MER for you. Here, feed the dog a bone!" I found dog bone recipes and contacted a manufacturing company in Miami. It was a great idea, but I lacked follow-through.

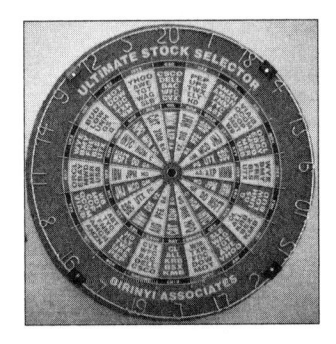

* * *

Mike Epstein was the one who originally introduced me to Andrew Lo at MIT. Andrew and his colleague, Jasmina, were writing a book titled *The Heretics of Finance: Conversations with Leading Practitioners of Technical Analysis.* Jasmina came to Florida to interview me and stayed at my house for a few days. It turns out she liked riding horses, too. We set up a video camera in my office and taped after the markets closed one day. I told her she could ride one of the horses in the barn and my groom would get the horse ready for her while she changed. Jasmina was a tall, thin blond with a Ph.D. She looked like a librarian, glasses, hair pulled back in a tight bun, and shirt buttoned up to the top. I will never forget when she came back into our office after changing into riding clothes. I asked her, "Jasmina, what is your favorite hobby?"

"I just love time series data."

And with that, she nonchalantly whipped off her glasses, pulled the pin out of her hair holding up her long blond locks, and marched out through the other office door to the barn in her slim riding pants. Nigel's jaw dropped to his knees. He could not speak for at least five minutes. It was something I will never forget. *I just love time series data.*

Nigel and I embarked on an 8-year journey modeling everything under the sun. With his help, I built upon the foundation created from years of modeling with Moore Research Center. A modeling process starts out by asking simple questions. For example, what happens if you enter on a breakout of the first 15-minute bar after the opening? What is the distribution of how many ticks you can get in the next 15-minute bar? What happens if you enter on a breakout of the 15-minute bar going into the last hour and exit MOC (market on close)? Is there a distribution pattern showing the most common time for highs or lows? The permutations are endless.

Much of my modeling uses time-based exits. Exit on the close or the next day's close, Exit after one hour. Exit when Europe closes. Time-based exits are not dependent on the range or volatility conditions, and they are robust. We also use ATR functions (average true range) to quantify the market's structure. It is similar to what Art Merrill did with *Filtered Waves,* which he wrote in the 1970s. He used percent functions to quantify the swings. The trick was to use wide enough parameters to stay above the noise level. Art's engineering background led him to be the ultimate market statistician. He was one of the first to quantify how prices tend to close higher the day before U.S. Holidays.

I modified a version of Welles Wilder's volatility stop and reverse-engineered parameters based on ATRs. Most professional traders know things intuitively from experience. However, we are all subject to different cognitive biases. Models help us keep an open mind and guard against biases. They differ from mechanical systems but are an integral part of the trading process.

Some of the best work was modeling optimal exit strategies for specific structures. We also did unique time of day work showing the distribution as to when the highs and lows were made for various markets. We found ways to quantify the degree of trendiness and create actuarial tables for individual markets. I have volumes of code and strategies and testing runs. About 90% of it led to nothing, but the other 10% was gold.

All you need is one good idea.

35

WAR HORSE

Where is the line delineating between our day to day lives, the markets, and trading? Over time, it fades into a fuzzy blur and our common-sense fades with it. Efficiency becomes a part of every decision. I built my stable next to my office so as not to waste any time once the markets closed. I could be on top of a horse within five minutes, and that includes changing into my britches. My barn hand would be waiting for me, ready to hand off one horse and then the next. These magnificent steeds were gracious saints to put up with me vaulting from my war desk onto their backs.

The discipline of dressage is about relaxation, suppleness, and eliminating tension from the horse. Imagine your ballroom dance partner shows up for a competition after getting caught in a major traffic jam. You are attempting to dance a graceful waltz, two beings becoming one, but your partner is anxious and upset, and keeps stepping on your toes. The poor horses.

My barn was directly across the street from the major showgrounds in Wellington. I was competing that weekend, but the shows started on Fridays. Since my ride time was around 11 AM, who would notice if I slipped away, rode my test, and came back 15 minutes later? I was already in my shad-belly and white britches. All I had to do was to put on my white gloves, top hat and zip up my boots. My barn hand had the horse braided and tacked up and I was planning to sneak in a ten-minute warm-up.

The day was March 20, 2003. One hour before my ride time, the US announced it was invading Iraq. Nobody had prepared for this. What to do? I was not ready to trade the markets in the heat of battle. I might as well slip across the street, ride, and see how the dust settles when I get back. I hopped on Black Beauty and trotted over to the show ring. If you have been so fortunate as to witness the expressive dancing horses that compete in dressage in the Olympics, you are familiar with their distinguished decorum. Dressage on a 1200-pound animal is like coloring within the lines with a dull crayon; there is no room for error.

The Dressage Test: Enter at A, at X, Halt Salute. The rider bows their head, the horse stands frozen, and both show respect to the judges. I entered the ring on Black Beauty, his dappled ebony coat glistening in the sun. X Halt Salute. Black Beauty reared straight up on his hind legs. In front of the judge. In the middle of the dressage ring. For all the world to see. There was nowhere to hide. Fuck a duck. There was so much tension in my body that he must have felt an electric current pulsing down all four legs as if he had been stung by an oversized wasp. The wasp was me, thinking about the implications of the War in Iraq on the markets.

After a mortifying ride, we slunk back to my barn. Back in the office, I might as well focus on the Iraq invasion gyrations. I surely couldn't ride.

The stock market, metals, crude oil, the Euro currency, and most commodity currencies began a multi-year rally after that announcement. I don't subscribe to the belief that news and events like war drive market trends. At the time, the bearish sentiment readings were sky high. This implied that there was an excess of cash on the sidelines—the number one variable in my book that drives trends. Over the next four years, the DOW went from 6100 to 10,850, gold from 580 to the 900s, copper from 70 to 400, and crude oil from 30 to 120. These look like historical moves on the weekly charts, but the fact is that the last four decades that I've been trading have all had crazy periods, to the upside and the downside. This was no different from the blast off in stocks that started in 1982. Despite having traded through many big moves in the past, there still is no way of knowing that this, too, is going to be that type of move. I still have to take things one day at a time.

The energy of the markets controls our entire lives. It is subtle and insidious, so we are not aware of how we come across to others. Can you shut off that electric current when you walk out of your office? If not, those around you may be getting zapped more than you realize.

36

HURRICANE FRANCIS

In 2004, two back-to-back hurricanes hit Wellington. It put our stringent backup and redundancy planning to the test. The last major storm to pass over Wellington was in 1964 and damage had been minimal. Who would even think hurricanes would be an issue 22 miles inland from the coast of Palm Beach? Since my house seemed to be the best prepared, I ended up with 10 people under my roof. Nigel, interns, my daughter and different folks who worked for me bunkered down in the office when Francis hit. We had plenty of time to close our positions "just in case," but the winds were not forecast to be severe. What was not predicted was how much rain would fall. The supersaturated ground along with 90 mile-an-hour winds toppled trees on top of the power lines. It took 10 days to restore the power to my block.

The backup generators kept the computers running. Quotes came in from the intact satellite dish. But the Internet was down, and the cell towers had blown over. Cut off from civilization despite being able to monitor every tick! A foot of water flooded the roads so nobody could leave town. The empty gas stations remained boarded up. A few adventurous people took canoes to the streets. Our big problem was that the generator was not hooked up to the main house or the well pump. August is the most humid month in Florida. Imagine ten traders living under one roof for a week and a half, no air conditioning, and no water for showers or toilets. Yet we watched the market move like any other day. There are only so many poker games and jigsaw puzzles a group can do before each person starts eyeing another's jugular. Debris filled the swimming pool ruling out refreshing dips to cool off. A sole rice cooker plugged into the office outlet heated up cans of soup. I wish I had taken delivery on those oats! The barn hands filled trashcans with water from a neighbor's barn so at least the horses could drink.

The day the airports reopened, our intern left Florida for good. I am sure he never returned. The stores were not prepared for a power outage, and refrigerated foods spoiled. South Florida was a mess. Now, here's the kicker. Two weeks after life returned to normal and electricity had been restored and refrigerators restocked, hurricane Jeanne hit. Nobody predicted the crazy path it followed. It veered away from Florida, made a 360-degree loop over the Atlantic Ocean and then circled back again. There are sophisticated forecasting models for weather systems which run off supercomputers, and they can't even get a gigantic hurricane's path right for the next 48 hours, let alone 24 hours. What makes people think we can do any better in the financial markets?

Two major hurricanes within three weeks hit my house, and there had not been any with winds that speed for over 60 years. Coincidentally, Hurricane Jeanne made landfall 2 miles from where Francis had hit. David Hand wrote a thought-provoking book called *The Improbability Principle—Why Coincidences, Miracles and Rare Events Happen Every Day*. He presents the theory and math why rare events happen more frequently than traditional logic would dictate. Like the death of pet animals, for example. People have a tendency to underestimate risk in their models. It is easy to model for events which have occurred in the past but impossible to know what type of new events will happen in the future. And there will always be new events.

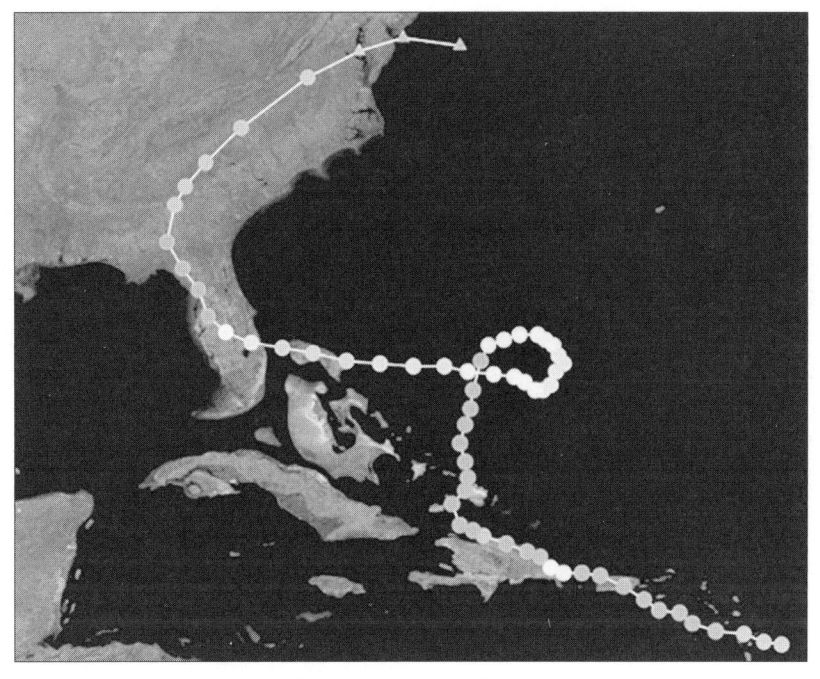

A rare chart formation – the hurricane "pivot."

Where's Waldo?

37

TRAVELS WITH ERIKA

I continued to have the opportunity to travel the world on business. Erika became my travel companion. We went to Paris for a conference shortly after the Iraq War invasion in 2003. Angry protestors flooded the streets. I told her to say we were Canadian if anyone asked because parts of the world were furious at America. She looked down at her hoodie that had the Ramones presidential seal on it.

I took her to Japan for a week when I spoke in Tokyo. We stayed with a prominent trader and his family in their house on the outskirts. It was a narrow concrete structure, six stories tall. Erika and I were on the top floor where we slept in a traditional tatami room, which is a glorified way of saying we slept on the floor. Erika had to go to the bathroom in the middle of the night. When she went to flush the toilet, she noticed a keyboard where the flusher should have been. All of the characters were in Japanese, so finding the "flush" button was hopeless. Not wanting to leave a surprise for our hosts to find in the morning, she woke me for help. I stumbled into the bathroom and looked down at the keyboard. Unsure of what button to push, I started pushing all of them. One of them had to be the right button. As I was button-mashing, I managed to find the bidet feature and the toilet immediately squirted at me. I shrieked and vowed to avoid that toilet for the remainder of the trip.

We went to the fish market which opened at 3 AM. This was not just any fish market, but the Tsukiji Fish Market where the tuna auctions take place. Before the auction begins, the buyers inspect the fish by swinging big meat cleavers into them to test for the fattiness. Trading pits form around each group of tuna and the head auctioneer stands in the middle. There is no distinguishing the traders there from the traders in the CME pits. The fish traders wore colored jackets with individual badges, too.

Tuna auctions are serious business. The tunas are flown in fresh on ice from all over the world every morning. Each fish weighs between 700 and 900 pounds. This year (2018) an auction fetched $323,000 for a prime bluefin tuna.

We went out to dinner with two dozen Japanese traders. Erika sang a song in Japanese she had learned at school for them after the meal. She was not shy and learned to sing opera anywhere, to any group of people. As a proud Mom, I used to ask her to sing to riders in my barn, which she obliged. I am sure the conference attendees forgot what I talked about but I doubt they will forget Erika's singing.

Many of my company office trips were organized around Erika. Most corporate events involve outdoorsy physical events that lead to "bonding" or a setting that demands plenty of drinking. Instead, we had group outings to Disney World or swimming with the dolphins in the Keys.

Erika met my colleagues, acquaintances, and clients; ultimately, 99.9% of the people in my universe were industry related. She even ended up playing tennis with Victor Niederhoffer.

The *Street Smarts* book I co-wrote with Larry Connors sold well. For the next few years, several publishers pursued me to write another book, but I did not want to write. I only wanted to trade. Despite this, Pam, a fiery, energetic dynamo who was the head editor at Wiley, had become a good friend. She finished publishing Victor Niederhoffer's book and invited me to a New York dinner at a fancy French restaurant to meet him. It was a bleak, cold February evening with a powdery dusting of slippery snow. The wind-chill knocked the temperature down another 15 degrees. Outside the restaurant, oblivious to the blustery conditions stood Victor. His blue pinstriped seersucker suit, the kind one wears in July when it is 90 degrees, drew attention away from his disheveled hair. Another ill-advised snappy dresser I can relate to in more ways than one.

I grew up wearing a plain green plaid uniform in grade school and did not own a pair of blue jeans until eighth grade. My grandmother bought me Lacoste dresses to go to the cotillion dances my Mom insisted I attend. I might as well have worn a crown on my head that said, "Puberty nerd, keep a healthy distance" at the dances.

Should I be grateful that Victor was another kindred soul who did not know how to dress or should I be wary and keep a healthy distance? During the dinner, I sat next to Pam and hoped if I sat still enough, nobody would ask me any questions. I feigned interest in the conversation between Victor and the female bond journalist who wrote for Bloomberg. The food was excellent and expensive. I do remember that.

A few months later, Victor flew me and Erika to Connecticut for an annual barbecue he held at his house. His house was a sprawling testament to previous trading successes, replete with a pool, a tennis court, *and* a squash court. Erika was a decent tennis player for her age and Victor took her outside to play tennis with her. Afterward, everyone gathered in the living room to listen to his friend Laurel play the piano. American art adorned the walls. There was not one square inch that was left uncovered. The whole scene might have been a backdrop for a Fellini movie.

The best trip Erika and I took together was to South Africa. Most of the investors in my fund were Fund of Funds or pools of money. Adam, a talented manager from Johannesburg, ran one such fund in London. We became good friends, and he visited my office in the States many times. In return, I often connected with him when I traveled to Europe. He was getting married to an American girl he met at college. The wedding was in Cape Town, Africa, and Erika and I were invited. We stayed at the Nelson hotel in Cape Town, an elegant British colonial landmark. Erika is still upset with me for limiting her indulgence of sweets displayed on the long tables at tea time.

My client's father flew us on a private plane to the Londolozi game reserve where we enjoyed a four-day safari in five-star accommodations. It is my most memorable trip of all time. This is why we work so hard, so we can experience fabulous travels and adventures, build memories, and occasionally even forget about the markets.

38

GIRLS' NIGHT OUT

People don't see many female faces in the financial industry, but that is because many of them are working behind the scenes. Back in the early nineties, before I started managing money, a friend from the MTA introduced me to a gal who was trading a system for him. He had designed the system which was marginal at best, but then he paid her to trade it. Go figure. Who are you going to get mad at if there is a losing period? The system you designed or the person pulling the trigger? She said it was a thankless job. The plus side was that we became friends. Cheri and I would talk on the phone commiserating over our trades.

"Hey! Why don't you come down to New Jersey for a week? It would be fun to have someone to trade with!" Before the days of the internet, texting and Skype, our choices of socializing were by phone or in person.

"It would be great to get out of Chicago this summer. How about in three weeks?"

"It's a deal! Looking forward to meeting you!"

Cheri arrived three weeks later, a teeny tiny person wearing big earrings with an even bigger personality. She was well versed in the markets and in trading.

Her father was a trader in the currencies on the floor of the Mercantile Exchange. He had sold his grocery store business and bought exchange seats. Cheri could read a chart better than anyone and was a natural in the markets. She became part of my clique—friends with Steve Moore, friends with my brokers at Gerald, and friends with Damon. I admired the way she could make friends so quickly with anyone. Damon gave her his "numbers," the support and resistance levels he worked up for the floor traders each day. I called her on the phone each morning, "Did Damon give you his numbers?" I was mildly jealous, not because I wanted the numbers, but because she could develop an instant rapport with anyone.

For many years, any time I traveled to Chicago I stayed with Cheri. She showed me great spots to eat, we went out on her boyfriend's boat, and she had the best wardrobe: colorful jean jackets, giant earrings, and cute T-shirts. Female trading buddies can be fun! Over time, I went to her wedding, watched her become a mom, and go through a divorce, all the cycles of life. And then we slowly lost touch, talking once a week, then once a month, then once a year.

Laura was ready to move on. Her husband was approaching retirement, and after living many years on a military base, Laura had had enough. Who could pick up the slack as our business manager? Cheri came to mind. She was not crazy about where she was currently working, so what better way to get back in touch?

"Just think, you'll be able to work from home and see your children off to school!"

Cheri had no idea what she was getting into. She had been handling the compliance for a registered RIA on the securities side of the industry, but now I was throwing her into the world of the NFA,

CFTC, CTA, and CPO. An array of acronyms well beyond RIA (Registered Investment Advisor). Laura had been so exceptional at her job that I had no idea just how complicated it was. She graciously agreed to work a few more months to train Cheri, but I bet people are ignorant as to how many moving parts there are to operating our business. Cheri had to navigate our sea of attorneys, accountants, auditors, clients, me, and my team with a very short learning curve. Completing the ice bucket challenge, the markets turned dramatically south in 2008, shortly after she started with us. Cheri told me later that Laura called her to give her a "heads up" that MFGlobal was about to bite the dust. I don't know if that meant to pack her bags or stock up on extra bottles of ibuprofen or wine.

Girl's night out with Cheri, Sue, Lisa, and Erika

Cheri and I started a once a month girls' night out comprised of—what else—female traders! Damon had introduced me to Lisa, a tall, blond ex-professional volleyball player who was the first female in the NASDAQ pit. She had started out clerking for her brother-in-law, and before long, she was swinging 100 lots in the NASDAQ futures as well as bonds. Sue was another tall blond who traded in the Russell futures before the ICE exchange snagged them. And then there was Carolyn who occasionally came into town, as well as one or two other gals. And Erika had moved to Chicago and was working for me for a year.

Do you think we talked about the markets? I will never tell.

39

DAMON

It was not too long after that I started dating Damon, my original SP broker. "Dating" is not quite the word when one person lives in Chicago and one lives in Florida, but after our paths kept crossing at industry conferences, his visits to Florida became longer.

Damon first visited my Florida house in 2002 with his six-year-old daughter. I put her on Erika's white pony, and she thought everything was grand. But then Damon saw the dogs, cats, birds, and horses, and it's no wonder I did not see him again for two years. He must have assumed there was no room in my life for him and at the time, he was right. There was no room for anyone other than Erika and other assorted mouths to feed. The markets were my preferred companion. We had great date nights every night in my office, just me and my charts, chill out music, and dim lights. Tosca, Peace Orchestra, Zero 7, Air, and Blue Six. So romantic.

One time we met up in Las Vegas at a conference when I was still dating another person whom Damon had come to know as well (*awkward*). Damon brought his dad along for the trip.

"Hey, I'm here in Vegas! Why don't you and your dad join my boyfriend and me for dinner?" This was a typical interaction between Damon and me, even though the subplot was already brewing.

Naturally, he didn't bat an eye at this motley crew dinner date. "Sure, where do you guys want to meet?"

The only thing was, I didn't have any reservations. At least not for dinner. "It's Vegas. We can find a spot!"

Damon recognized my naiveté because he immediately set to work finding a place to eat. He called one of his Chicago restaurant business contacts to make some calls. Soon enough, he texted me and said he had a reservation for four people at the steakhouse at the Venetian at 7 PM.

We all met outside; me, my boyfriend and Damon and his blue-collar Chicago-bred dad. Everyone was gracious enough, but it was clear Damon felt like he had to wrangle his father a bit in the present company and upscale Las Vegas restaurant. We walked in and saw a long line of people. The hostess was telling everyone it was a two-hour wait, which was mostly her way of getting people to leave. Damon slid past the line and gave them his name and the hostess beamed at him.

"Oh, Jimmy Bannos' friend! Right this way!"

Damon ordered a $250 bottle of wine because it was a 'business dinner.' After the waiter poured the wine, Damon's dad asked in his booming Chicago voice, "Can I get an ice cube for my wine?"

Damon was visibly distraught. He tried to whisper, "Dad, that glass of wine cost sixty dollars. Don't put ice in it."

His dad had no interest in whispering.

"I always put ice in my wine!" Damon was redder than the wine itself.

I had to interject, so I gave him a look and said, "The man. Wants. Ice. In his wine." My boyfriend did not even drink wine, which was another sign.

Damon was still red in the face, and one of the guys from *Everybody Loves Raymond* was a table over trying not to laugh at us. It was a memorable evening and one we still laugh at.

* * *

The first two Florida hurricanes had come and gone when Damon came up with the ultimate pickup line. "Why don't you come up to Chicago and I'll set you up with a backup hurricane office."

I was no longer dating anyone, so his ploy worked. Little did he know that he would get suckered into helping me put my house back together after the hurricanes hit. The pool solar panels ricocheted into the yard, taking roof tiles with them. The wind shredded the barn's ceiling fans into mangled modern art. Rain gutters bent at unnatural angles. There was an endless list of minor dings too small for a professional service, but they would be glaringly noticeable when it comes to putting a house on the market. That thought was crossing my mind as we spent more time together and Erika was getting closer to leaving for college. Each month, I spent a week in Chicago and Damon spent a week in Wellington.

Rumble rumble. Pitter-patter-pitter-patter. Raccoons in my attic? It was bad enough that I was not getting enough sleep from whatever world market event was going on at the time. But these damn critters were partying above my bedroom at night. I could hear their little feet. Damon had been staying for the week, and he swore he could not hear anything. This made sense since he had blown out his eardrums playing lead guitar with his band in his twenties. I still made him climb up into the attic. I *would* have done it myself, except I'm a girl?

No, it was a huge attic and I tried once, but it was impossible for me to get over to the section above the bedroom. You had to tiptoe across the rafters while holding a flashlight and hope you did not make a misstep into the fluffy insulation. Damon's manhood was on the line. He made the trek in the sweltering Florida heat and waited for the raccoon to jump out at him. Any moment. It never did. He found nothing, not even animal droppings. We concluded after much discussion that there must have been squirrels running around on the roof tiles. Which is weird in Florida when you only have palm trees. Where did the squirrels come from and how did they get on top of the roof? We will never know, but Damon proved his chivalry that night.

I was trading from the Chicago office when Hurricane Wilma hit the following year. Nigel was a genius when it came to setting up infrastructure. Our systems and positions were backed up each day across a network of multiple CPUs at different locations, including Wellington and Chicago. LBRGroup had full redundancy every which way up and down. It might sound like overkill, but my share of outliers was beyond random.

Nigel, Damon, and I in our new Chicago office.

40

JUDD AND THE START OF REALLY BIG THINGS

Judd is another trader I came to know through our online trading room. He started clerking on the floor of the CBOE in the equity options in 1992. The next year he moved to the CME exchange to trade in the LIBOR pit. Traders do not usually go out of their way to seek out the dullest market on the planet, but when you are young and eager to trade, you go where there is a job offer. Judd said the LIBOR market was in a 2-tick range for one year. 9680 bid, offered at 9681. The next year: 9681 bid, offered at 9682. Talk about a patience game. How does one trade a market like this? Contracts are spread between months or hedged with Eurodollars, and there are lots of scratch trades. At the end of 1994, Orange County, California, declared bankruptcy after losing 2 billion in over-leveraged bad investments. The LIBOR market had a 40-tick jump. One could say every dog has its day.

Long-Term Capital Management's fall also brought volatility to the LIBOR and Eurodollar markets. LTCM was a hedge fund with $126 billion in assets. The long and the short of it (no pun intended) was when Russia defaulted on its bonds in 1998, there was a squeeze in the derivatives markets. LTCM's pickle made the Libor market go wild. Once again, "It's never a problem getting into a market, it's always a problem getting out when you need to."

LIBOR stands for London Interbank Offered Rate and has long been the world's most popular benchmark for short-term rates. It has also been one of the most manipulated markets. As the CME went electronic, the 24-hour order flow started going to the screen. Judd left the soon to be defunct pits and began trading from upstairs. He came to a seminar I did in 2001 and was familiar with the basics of many of our strategies. We chatted online throughout a year and shared research ideas and charts.

When I came to Chicago, Judd offered to introduce me to his trainer, Crazy Bob. That was one of the first things which made an impression on me when I considered moving. I could live without the horses, or so I thought, but I could not live without a good trainer. Crazy Bob was genuinely crazy. He trained one of the gals on the American Gladiator show. He relished drilling using the grittiest, hardcore HIIT (High-Intensity Interval Training) techniques. Judd picked me up in his BMW, handed me a Red Bull, and we drove to an obscure gym in a building's basement on the outskirts of Chicago. Bob had us strap on weight vests, run and up and down stairs, and lift 100-pound medicine balls above our head. Before you knew it, all the bad trades of the day melted away into the drops of sweat. It took burning calories to a whole new level and built up a genuine camaraderie between Judd and me. You know you can work with someone in an intense office environment when you see each other in your sweatiest physical moments. Bear crawls and crab walks are the least glamorous exercise out there. I loved traditional bodybuilding. I thought I was in shape when I won the South Florida middleweight championship. But Crazy Bob took things up a notch.

Working out is an integral part of the process. It is essential to have good stress relief and stay in top shape. A sharp mind needs a fit body. And, when all else fails, it is better to take it out on a dumbbell than an intern or to fantasize about murdering defenseless rodents.

* * *

The Chicago office was firmly established, and I asked Judd to join LBRGroup. He held down Chicago while Nigel staffed the Florida office. Eventually, I sold everything in Florida—the horses, the barn, the furniture, and Nigel and I moved to Chicago. The stallion in my life, Damon, was winning out over the dressage horses.

Judd was a great sport. Nigel and I went to New York the following month to give some presentations at an investor's conference. We left Judd alone with the positions.

"Hey, Judd, keep an eye on the fund," which now had an 85 million dollar trading level and was growing.

In 2007, Nigel and I had to travel to New York to raise capital for the fund. I invited Damon so we could meet 'in the middle,' and both of us could work and also have some fun.

"Do you want me to book the hotel?" he asked me. He knew that I was best left to focus on trading.

"No, I'll do it!"

Damon checked in a few days later. I was pleased to report, "I got this great deal, and it was like $260."

"That can't be a good hotel."

"Oh no, it's a good hotel. It's three stars."

Damon knew that a three-star hotel in New York was not like three stars in Florida. I did not. He made a grim sigh and accepted his fate.

None of us went straight to the hotel because we had appointments right away. So, when we met up afterward, it was pretty late at night. We all met out front and went down the narrow seedy corridor to check into what looked like something out of *The Twilight Zone*. One guy manned the reception booth, and there were little bars in front of him.

"This is it?" Damon asked.

Nigel didn't say a word, but his lower jaw shifted a little bit as he looked around.

"We're just sleeping here. It's fine." I tried to look nonchalant.

Nigel is a bit of a clean freak, and I saw him look over at Damon knowingly. I couldn't admit it yet, but the place was a disaster, and we hadn't even set foot in our rooms. The hallways were not up to code, barely wide enough for two people to pass. Nigel opened his door first. There were no windows and no closet. All that was missing was the chalk outline of a body. You couldn't escape if there was a fire, which was a real possibility, because the room was heated by a cheap plug-in space heater. So, you had to decide between freezing and trying to sleep with a fire hazard. We agreed that it was crazy, but we weren't going to find another place at 11 PM at night. The showers were so dirty, that none of us showered, which was mostly hilarious in light of our professional itinerary in the city.

The next day we gave our presentations. It was followed by a private viewing of Christie's auction items. A four-course dinner took place in an elegant room brimming with flowers. One of the New Edge's partners had flown back from France that afternoon and brought numerous wines to sample. The juxtaposition between the reality of our horrid, seedy sleeping quarters and fine dining among millions of dollars of art was surreal.

Nigel and I sat at a table with some of the larger Fund managers, traders managing billions. I started the conversation sharing our research instead of asking questions. Showing my cards at the outset compels others to open up, and they disclose things that they might not otherwise share. We were small fry and no threat to anyone's business. We found out everyone was using similar time slicing algorithms to do their execution. It is what I had always done in the nineties; giving orders to the brokers in the pits to work a specified number of contracts over a specified period.

Time slicing is a way to say to the execution platform, "Buy 1000 contracts at random time intervals in random quantities, half the time work a bid, half the time take the offer. Do this over a three-minute period."

That is an example, but the point is nobody can see the size worked or detect what is going on. Traders think they can read the book or order flow to make a trade. But it is impossible with iceberg (hidden) orders and different algorithms running amok, often fighting each other. Plus, most large operators place orders through many firms across many accounts. Our research on trade management and execution algorithms could fill a book. In the grand scheme of things, it means little, so long as a trader follows one simple rule: never let a loss get too big.

New Edge sponsored the investors' conference. They brought together asset allocators and introduced them to 2-3 CTAs in the hopes of increasing their business. The majority of New Edge's business was institutions and hedge funds, very little retail. We attracted the attention of several large asset allocators, including Mann Financial. The problem was they only allocated in minimum units of 50 million dollars. And they didn't want to be the largest investor in the fund, which ruled us out. Too bad for us, we weren't big enough.

***

The "carry trade" was a popular strategy from 2002 to 2007. Investors borrowed money in yen where interest rates were low and invested it in higher-yielding currencies. It was a crowded trade, meaning too many people were in this same position. What was going to happen when people needed to unwind? I trade by technicals since

I have not had much luck using fundamentals. But I am aware when there is a market imbalance implying a crowded trade. The yen was a ripe situation. It had left a bear trap or false downside breakout on the weekly charts. I tried twice to put on a position, both times unsuccessful. The third time I knew I got it right. It was our cue to load up. I don't mind trying a few times if there is a basis for a position but the timing is off. The real key is to make it pay and use maximum leverage when the trade starts working. I told Judd to keep buying yen, and the ensuing rally made our year. The yen went straight up for the next five years as global interest rates came crashing down.

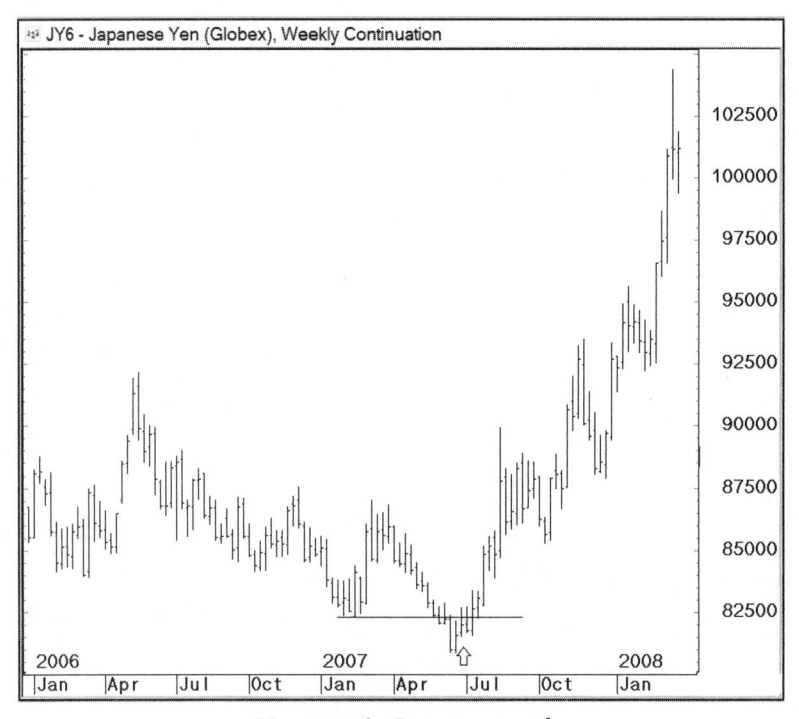

Yen-2006: Carry unwind

One morning, Judd came into the office with Ninja shirts for us. It was his way of saying he felt part of the team. We had also put on a significant short position in FXI after it spiked to 73 in the fall of 2007. It ended up trading below 20 a year later. It was the best stock trade we ever made. I am sure Judd thought our hedge fund was one big party. Just like the Las Vegas casinos that suck you in with a few winning trades and pure Oxygen piped into the gambling halls, every soaring high tempts you to push your luck just a bit farther.

The Dow had been rallying for five years off its 2002 lows and made a high in October 2007. The broad market was showing marked signs of deterioration for the next three quarters. By September 2008, it looked like it was ready to fall off the cliff. I like going home short at the end of a sloppy week. On this particular Friday, I stepped out on a limb and put on a big short position in the afternoon—over 600 SP futures and 600 Russell futures. I had to leave the last hour of the day to have a dentist fix a cracked molar. I was in the dentist chair when I got a call from Judd.

"Hey, Linda, the SPYs are trading up the equivalent of 22 SP handles after the close."

"Aghh a aghh."

"Okay... I just thought I'd call and let you know."

"Aghh a aghh."

It is impossible to yell "Fuck!" when the dentist has your mouth propped open and your jaw is numb.

The sub-prime mortgage crisis was heating up. The U.S. Treasury announced after Friday's close that it was stepping in to take over Fannie Mae and Freddie Mac. The market appeared to wildly approve of this move. It looked like the SPs were going to gap up at least 40 points higher on Sunday evening's reopening. There was nothing one could do except wait for the market to start trading again. And try to get a good night's sleep in the meantime.

Come on. Let's go. You can do this, AGAIN. Fight. Fight. Gotta get that money back.

I am going to get that money back out of sheer concentration and focus. Keep my head in the game. If I check out for one minute, I am dead.

How many times have I had to fight to make back a crazy blip?

Okay, so this was more than a blip, but I always tell myself, if I did it once, I can do it again. I am a racehorse, lining up at the gate. Turn off the mind, put the blinders on, and wait for that starting bell.

When the index futures re-opened in the Sunday Globex session, the position was showing a loss shy of $4 million. Bummer. The first thing I did was to cut the size in half. Whenever you have your back up against the wall, you have to get smaller. Reduce your size to the level where you can start trading again, because in these types of situations when there is uncertainty or unprecedented volatility, there is lots of money to be made. But you can't do it if you are frozen or stressed, so figure out the level where you can function and trade freely again.

I did some quick calculations. I figured if I could make $200,000 a day for the next 20 days we could make back the loss before the end of the month. It put things in a manageable framework. There was a strange energy in the air, though. I had a pretty good idea that Mr. Market was bluffing. This was a patience game now, waiting for that opening where momentum was poised to shift back down. That would be the signal to reestablish the position.

I had the best two guys in the world on both sides of me. Their faces were expressionless. I am at the helm, but I am not alone. I might be the one giving myself my own pep talks, but we are a team, and I had to prove to them we were going to make money. A lot of money.

"Ding Ding Ding." Monday morning, and "they're off." Look neither left nor right, only straight ahead and play your game.

As it turned out, we made back the loss in 5 days, and the Granat Fund went on to end the month up 3%.

My friends always want to know, "What did it feel like to lose that much money overnight? What were you thinking? Tell us your emotions."

Of course, it sucks for sure, but I did not feel much. Over time, the markets desensitize you to the point where you nod and mutter, "Oh. Okay."

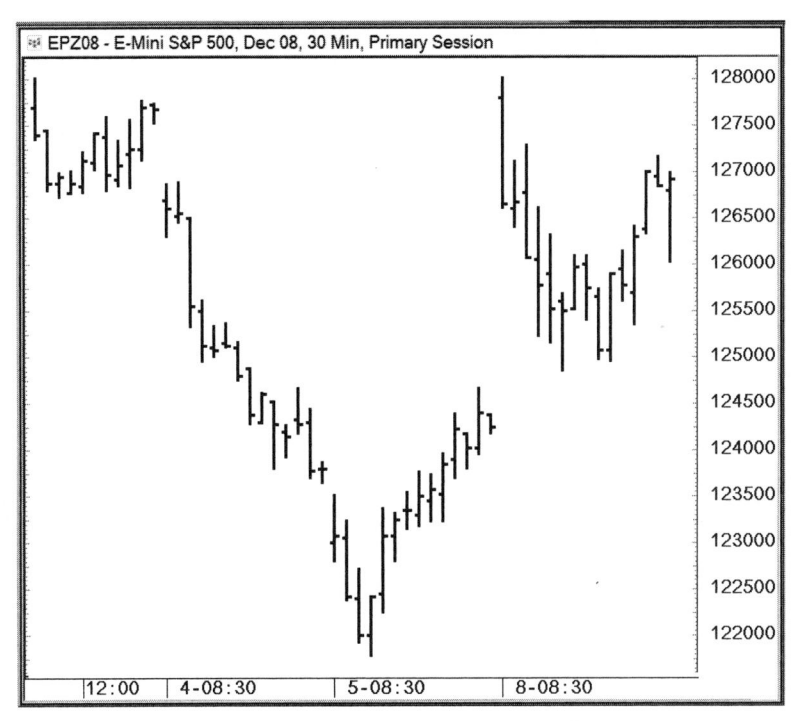

SP-2008: 50 point opening gap loss

Other traders might slam the desk in anger and get REALLY MAD. I had already practiced throwing paperweights through the door 20 years earlier. I had been sent to jail thousands of times playing Monopoly and bumped in Sorry even more. "It's just a game," I tell myself. But this game was my life.

* * *

My knack for being on the wrong side of outliers or, mini black swans, only seemed to increase after that. Nassim Taleb coined the term "Black Swan," which he defines as, "The disproportionate role of high profile, hard to predict, and rare events that are beyond the realm of normal expectation." It is right up there with flying pigs and the Chicago Cubs winning the World Series.

Two months later, Damon and I traveled to Hong Kong. The bond market had been lots of fun to trade because the Global financial crisis was creating beaucoup volatility. "Fun" in this case is a tongue-and-cheek term, as on any given day the bonds could be either my best trading market or my worst. It was a lasting love-hate relationship. We were short way out of the money bond call options. They were set to expire in a few days.

In Hong Kong, I set up my trusty laptop in a swanky hotel. Our wood-paneled suite on a high floor faced the harbor, which was obscured by a thick haze of smog. This did not matter because I mainly cared about Internet connectivity so I could keep an eye on our positions. Unfortunately, that night (I was now in the opposite time zone), the Fed announced the start of QE (quantitative easing). It consisted of $800 billion in asset purchases. The bonds jumped 24 handles over the next few days. They were ticking up like they overdosed on Viagra with some steroids tossed in. Who needs sleep anyway?

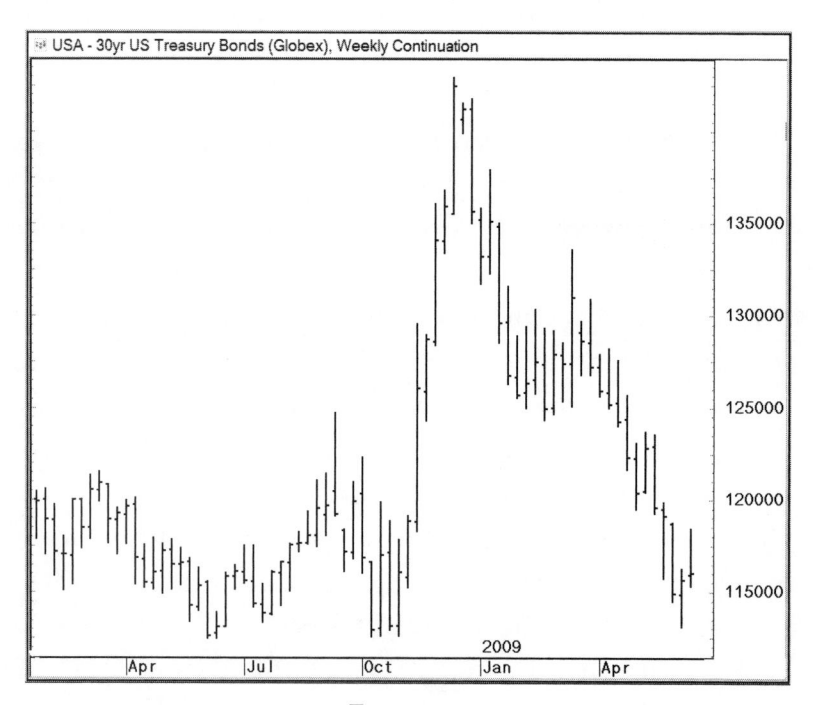

Face ripper

Pay no attention to the man behind the curtain. Slow the breathing. What do I do? Get smaller. The first course of action in a bloodbath is always to get smaller. When the price stops going up, I can sell back out again. Taylor is forever chanting in my ear: "Take it back when you are wrong, put it back out again when you think you are right." Clearly, I was wrong. I had to relax my body. Count, one, two, three, four. Get my bearings. Keep paddling over the rapids and focus on something on the horizon.

It did not matter how far out of the money those options were, it was still a bloodbath. I am not sure how but we managed to minimize the damage after a few days of high-anxiety trading, but we did. These situations are the type of events where even if a trader can break even or make money, it extracts a toll from your psychological capital. The streets of Hong Kong had rows of shop fronts with dead ducks strung up by their necks in the window. I was starting to feel like one of those ducks.

I lie to myself that I am the best game player around. I love to win. I love playing games. But when you lose, do games cost this much in psychic capital? This is a much bigger pot than even TV poker. I talk to myself—*Be brutally honest. Did those rose quartz crystals help? Did my James Allen books help? Did the 5 thousand herbs and vitamins help? How about the binaural beats and mediation?* My miracle books say, brainwash the mind and it will believe. Tell it enough bullshit and it believes.

Face ripper [fays rip-per] -noun 1. A market advance with extreme intensity, so much that it takes skin and hair along with it from the facial area. Difficult to detect in advance, but upon arrival the feeling is instantaneously recognized. 2. Common situation typically experienced by those who are "short in the hole."

41

BULLS AND BEARS MAKE MONEY AND PIGS GET SLAUGHTERED

The majority of my clients were Fund of Funds. These are more substantial funds that allocate to individual managers and funds with the goal of building a diversified, non-correlated portfolio. My program fell under the dubious title of "short-term systematic." "Discretionary short-term systematic," to narrow it down even more. Which is a catch-all term that meant we were not trend followers, mechanical quants, long/short, or event-driven. There is a fine art to blending managers, so there is non-correlation between programs. We always seemed to do best when the other funds were doing worst, but this was random. One year the grains might be our best performing market, the next year the SPs and another year the Bonds or the yen.

Galen Burghardt wrote a research paper explaining the blending of managers in a Fund of Fund portfolio. "One of the most powerful tensions in the world of money managers is the pull between assets that perform well on their own and portfolios that perform well. What we found was that team players outperform superstars." Managers with low correlations to others produce the best possible Sharpe ratio for the Fund. It was more important to find programs which complemented each other as opposed to seeking out the one-two superstars with superior performance. A Sharpe ratio is one of many measurements of risk.

What astounded me was that some of the allocators kept even better stats on our positions than we did. They usually dropped by our office once or twice a year for a due diligence check.

One time a client walked in with reams of sheets. He had it down to daily and monthly statistics. Which markets had been our best and worst performers? By how much? What was the average margin used for each market? How much time did it take to make back drawdowns in each market? What could I say? I was under the microscope twice a year.

"Yup, that looks about right to me," I'd say as I tried to remember when we lasted traded rough rice. Our fund had one of the best statistics on peak to valley drawdowns. This is the time that elapses before making new equity highs. If only we didn't have those pesky drawdowns at all.

Allocators wrestled with when to cut a manager loose for lack of performance. What should they do if the drawdown for a trend follower was more extensive than usual? How long should they keep a CTA who was not making back a loss? The last thing you want to do is ditch a trend following program at its lows because that is probably the time it is due for a big win. But, how do you know for sure they are going to come back this time? It was no different than a manager debating which stocks to prune from a portfolio.

How do you know the markets have not changed? Perry Kaufman was firmly convinced the increase in noise levels over the years would doom the traditional trend followers who raked it in in the early eighties. So far, the statistics for the past decade have proved him right.

We had loyal clients. They were sharp, well-capitalized, and seasoned in the business. Unfortunately, 2008 bought trouble to some of our best clients. We had large allocations from RBC (Royal Bank of Canada), but they closed their entire managed fund programs due to losses from other managers. The volatility in the financials was extreme. Up until 2008, they had never had a losing year for their clients. Schoenfeld had monies placed with us, and we had done well making money for them. However, they ended up shutting down all their managed account programs. And so on and so on down the list.

Our private individual clients were okay and grateful we were an offset to the drawdowns in their stock portfolios. It was a coincidence that it seemed like we did best when the markets were falling out of bed. I liked to trade from the long side as much as I liked to trade from the short side. Unfortunately, we lost a third of our assets under management the very year we had our best performance—2008. We had $145 million under management, and in one fell stroke, we dropped to $100 million. It takes a lot of work to build up client relationships. It involves establishing both trust and rapport, and this takes time. So, it was a loss not only of a good chunk of our management fees but the intangible friendships that come when developing business relationships.

It is natural to want to protect your children from the most stressful professions. I made sure my daughter had no interest in trading. She went to a performing arts school in music and chose to go into vocal performance to become an opera singer.

"Erika, your job in life is to sing beautiful music and make everyone forget for two hours just how crazy and stressful the world can be." What a noble calling!

* * *

Damon and I flew to Miami in the spring of 2009 to hear her sing the lead in an opera at the University of Miami. It was a long overdue weekend getaway.

Seasonal patterns generally work well in the meats and grain markets. Lean hogs tend to have a nice rally in the spring. I don't trade the meats unless there is a compelling chart formation or a strong seasonal. There has to be a basis for a position trade. That week I put on a sizable position in the hogs for the first time in many months. Damon and I were walking through the Miami airport on Sunday afternoon to catch a flight back to Chicago. We walked past a kiosk with freshly printed newspapers that were piled up to waist level. On the front page was a picture of a cute baby pig holding a hypodermic needle in its mouth. Swine flu had struck the U.S.!

I knew nothing about swine flu. This new virus originally came from a strain that lived in pigs, but it was a human transmitted virus which required no contact with pigs. Still, nobody is going to touch pork when you have emotionally charged buzzwords like "killer swine flu" circulating in the media.

Monday morning back in Chicago, trading was no fun. The front-month hog contract opened down limit. What a drag. Not only did we have a substantial long position in the meats, but we were also long the grains. Every agriculture market was coming under liquidation pressure. Hogs got slaughtered. The front-month hog contract continued down limit for several days, like water draining down a giant vortex. It was a crummy week for pigs and those who owned them.

I followed my now standard game plan for dealing with unforeseen events: *Get Smaller.* Reduce size down to the point where the eyeballs stop bulging out. Jesse Livermore has a quote, "Sell down to the sleeping point." These same events can then create opportunity, though it may come in a different market. You don't have to make money back in the same market you lost it in. That has more to do with ego.

In the markets, it is essential to stay in the game mentally. Sometimes it feels like running a marathon. There is the temptation to give in when you hit the wall, but once you check out mentally, you are quitting.

I say to myself, "I am going to make back a drawdown because I can concentrate better than anyone else." However, you can't force an opportunity to happen. It is a matter of faith that your routine and rituals will eventually give you the edge again.

The game is more important than anything else in the world. Until I walk out my office door. Then I am focused on tennis, weightlifting, gardening, riding—anything except the markets. It is as if a giant switch clicks off in my brain. Unless I am in a drawdown in which case I can only keep that switch clicked off for so long before it starts to creep back in the form of anxiety. I wonder how I can be playing outside when I should be fighting to make money back. Damn. There is no worse feeling than being in a drawdown, even though you know it is part of the game. It is just a cycle, but it still stinks.

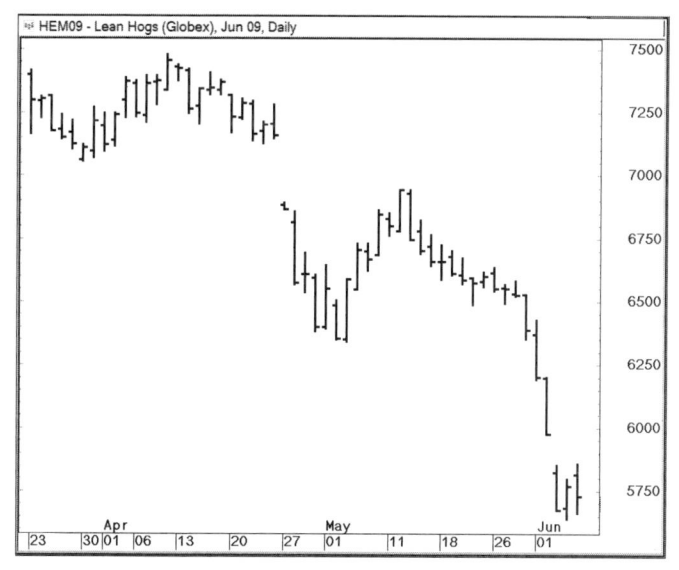

Swine flu. Guess which way we were positioned two days before the news broke.

We managed to finish that month plus, with a capital "P" for perseverance. The best trades are often making back losses.

Throughout our journey down the road of outliers, Judd and Nigel never once questioned my process even though I made plenty of mistakes. They were the ultimate support network. They were sharp, thoughtful, and above all, amazing friends.

Fast forward to May 2010. The SPs had rallied through 2009. They made a small low first quarter of 2010 and were now correcting an overbought condition. I was looking for a spot to buy.

There are three guidelines to tape reading.

The first is: always watch price relative to a reference point. It can be another price such as the day's opening, a daily swing high or low, or the level at which one entered a trade. In this case, the reference point is static. If you are watching price relative to an oscillator or another market, as you would if you were monitoring for a momentum divergence, the reference price is dynamic—always moving.

Tape reading is about relationships. What is the length of the previous downswing or upswing? What is the length of the current downswing relative to the previous downswing? In this case, the last daily corrective swing had been about 100 SP points. The current correction was approaching this same length.

The second thing I watch for is the moment the price stops going down (or up). You do not want to try catching a falling knife. Wait for the momentum to slow and for the price to start trading in a few ticks' range. It needs to establish support. Below this support is your initial risk. A reaction must start quickly in the opposite direction.

Tape reading is also about watching for aberrations—unusual activity, heavy volume, significant gaps, anything out of the ordinary.

The previous week, the SPs had been trading in the low 1200s. Now the market was approaching 1125 to 1130, down 90 points. I started buying 100 lots at a time, expecting the price to begin reacting up a bit. The trade was good for about 1 minute.

Before you could say "Cowabunga," the price dropped eight handles in 10 seconds.

My first instinct was, "Oh crap. There must have been a nuclear explosion somewhere." I hit the FLATTEN button so fast, I felt blessed we got filled with only six points of slippage from 1122 – 1116. It was the most amount of money I had lost in the least amount of time, other than a substantial overnight event gap. Over the next five minutes, the SPs dropped another 70 points. This time the price really stopped falling and started to act a bit bouncy. We still had no idea what was going on, but there was an opportunity to trade from the long side. I re-bought and then bought some more, doing a bit of trading along the way. At the end of the day, we were back to break even.

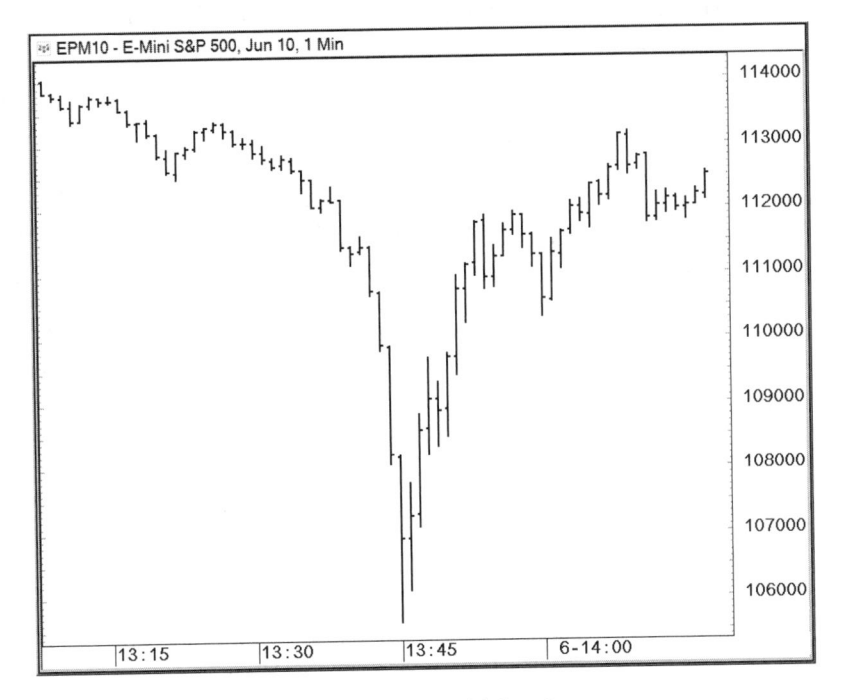

Any number of evenings sounded like this:

"Hi, honey. How was your day at the office?"

"Ahhh, it was okay. The market ended up unchanged."

"Did you make any money today?"

"No, it was another flat day."

We joked about this a lot. Sometimes there was so much volatility that you felt like a genius for not losing money.

I have to separate whether or not I did my job from whether or not I made money. There are plenty of days I made money but felt I was sloppy and didn't follow my plan as well as I could have. There are also days that I thought I was crisp and precise but didn't end up making money. It's important to focus on the process and realize that it will lead to the profits longer term. Don't look at the P&L, look only at the price structure and trade it. It is beneficial to have a spouse or partner who is also in the markets. It's tough for people outside the markets to relate the crazy things that happen. Not to mention the stress! What does a heart surgeon talk to his partner about when he gets home? How does a fighter pilot speak to his wife when he comes back? There are lots of fields where it is hard to relate to if you are on the outside.

Damon, my original SP broker, and I got married in 2008. We rarely talked about my positions, the markets, or the fund. Still, it's nice to know you have a partner in a very time-consuming lifestyle. My first husband was a trader when we met, and we never talked about the markets. If we had, I am sure our marriage would have ended sooner than it did.

Focus on the process and it leads to profits in the long run.

42

JINX

One day, the mail came while Judd, Nigel, and I were in the office eating lunch. We always ate at our desks. Judd's wife packed him a healthy fare of hard-boiled eggs, tomatoes, avocados, and raisins. Nigel had a personal chef who cooked him two weeks' worth of gourmet meals and shrink wrapped them into individual packets. Nigel's lunches were five stars every day.

In comparison, my generic water-packed can of tuna looked mighty sad, but it was quick and easy. Most of our mail went to our business manager. On this occasion, a big fat manila envelope managed to find its way to us. There were several copies of the latest BarclayHedge quarterly newsletter. It supplies research and rankings on CTAs and Hedge Funds. Inside, it showed the Granat Fund ranked 17th out of 4500 funds for best 5-year performance. Our fund was in the top ten rankings for many other categories as well.

I never looked at these rankings. Our business manager was in charge of supplying the data from the accountant to the research firms. She was my interface with the outside world. If I look at these types of things, I risk them messing with my head. It shouldn't matter when you believe in your models, but I was superstitious of outside influences. I do best when I can keep my game as pure as possible.

In this case, though, I felt a sinking in my heart when I saw the BarclayHedge reports.

"Wow, look at this! We're right at the top of national rankings!" Judd's voice was a notch up in decibels.

"Oh, great. This is worse than being on the cover of Sports Illustrated." I felt jinxed.

My mother was a huge believer in "whatever thoughts you put in your head have a way of manifesting themselves." This came from her mother who believed in Parking Fairies. When I was growing up, anytime we drove downtown and needed a spot for the car, my mom said, "You just watch, the Parking Fairy has a spot just for us!" And a car would pull out in front of the opera house or theater. Mom zipped right in, smiling.

My great-grandmother emigrated from Germany when she was 21. A Mormon family sponsored her. On the boat over, her luggage was lost, so she boarded a train by herself with no possessions and headed out to the Wild, Wild West. She had an incredible ability to see the silver lining in every cloud. This is how I grew up. My mom lectured every day, "The glass is half full, if life gives you lemons, make lemonade, and wear rose-colored glasses."

This is the power of positive thinking, but if you let doubts sneak into your head, it can work in reverse.

Not too long afterward, I was working out at the gym with my trainer, a different gym and a different trainer. He was a top gymnast from Romania and had become a renowned natural bodybuilder. We always followed one of four routines with lots of stretching. On this day, he decided to do something different: high-speed drills in a semi-lit room with a slippery wooden floor. I was wearing the wrong type of shoes for this. While shuffling sideways at breakneck speed, I tripped over my own two feet and went flying sideways across the room like a cannonball. I landed full-force on top of my right shoulder. The fracture was so severe that even after reconstructive surgery and multiple pins and screws, it took ten months of physical therapy before I regained some range of motion. I am right-handed, so it was impossible to use a keyboard, mouse or even a pen to log my numbers. My thirty-year routine was interrupted.

It is unavoidably embarrassing to walk around with your arm in a sling and get sympathetic inquiries as to what happened.

"I tripped at the gym." An inevitable pause.

"Oh..."

* * *

The silver and gold markets had a fabulous long-side play underway but not without wicked volatility. I loved trading the silver market. The swings can be wild. It is one of those markets that is exceptionally good at driving the most amount of people crazy before it makes a nifty move. It was darned near impossible to concentrate, though, when I was running to a doctor's appointment or physical therapy every other day. My shoulder became infected. Why did I have to deal with this inconvenience? I was not working out, and when you are addicted to physical exercise, it's easy to become depressed. I no longer had my horses to ride either. And the precious silver market was driving me bonkers.

Wine? Too obvious. Vodka? Too tasteless. I got a dog. A six-month-old Puli, a Hungarian sheep herding dog. Taking the puppy down the elevator and outside into the snow was my exercise. OK, I drank wine, too.

I decided to trade out of our condo for a bit. Nigel wrote me a program for the X-trader hotkey pad. It interfaced with the Photon platform's API. I could place orders using any one of 120 hotkeys with one click. My own set of nuclear buttons. Way better than my old batphone. No more mouse or keyboards to deal with, I could make trades one-handed.

Programmed to taste, the hotkeys worked like this:

"A1" buy 300 SPs at the market. "A2" sell 300 SPs at the market.
"B1" buy 100 Gold on the bid, showing 20 at a time.
"C1" buy 100 bonds, join the bid.
"F1" Do not touch that button. Stay away from the F1 eject button.

One morning when I was trading, my cat jumped up on top of my desk. Toni was a scrawny barn cat I had adopted in New Jersey. I brought her with me to Florida, and she now lived with us in Chicago. She was a Hemingway cat with six toes on each foot. I scolded her in a pet-mom voice, "No, Toni, you are not allowed up here," and picked up all six pounds of her to throw her off the desk. With my bad arm and awkward angle, her fat toes touched down and hit my hot-key pad.

Bleep Bleep. She executed several trades.

Trading makes me tired.

Toni decided to make a trade in Bean Oil, a market I had stopped trading. Thus, I had not rolled to the new front-month contract. It made fixing it extra tricky. It was one day from going first notice. This was the market my cat chose to trade with her twenty-four fat toes—100 contracts, no less. It took a bit of patience to get out of that snafu. She jumped up once again and executed two more trades for me before I shut the office door on her. The funny thing is, all three trades ended up being small winners. Fortunately for her, she had several lives left.

Fix mistakes immediately.

43

A WALK IN THE PARK

"Arab Spring" was the name given to the tumultuous events in North Africa and the Middle East in the winter of 2011 and 2012. The last time the market saw this type of volatility and expanded ranges in the SPs futures was in the fall of 2008. Many of the gyrations from the Arab Spring discord happened in the European session at night (when U.S. traders are supposed to be sleeping). I set my clock to wake up at 2:00 in the morning, sat in front of the monitors in the condo and then squeezed in another hour of sleep before heading off to the office in the morning. All the recent studies show sleep is the most important thing for one's health—more important than diet and exercise. And it is even more critical for one's ability to think. Of course, when you are tired, you are not thinking about this.

In 2008, I could do no wrong. However, in this volatility, I could do no right. I was zigging when I should have been zagging. Whipsawed with a wet leather cattail.

"Thank you, Sir! May I have another?" The market sucked me under in the riptide, and each time I came up for air, I was hitting the crest of the wave instead of the trough.

In a few days, I dug a seven-digit hole. I was well on my way to digging to China. Every trader has been there.

"Can I start the week over again? Please? I promise not to get out of bed this time."

I was feeling demoralized when my daughter called me. She lived a few miles away in the West Loop of downtown Chicago. I told her I was super bummed at my loss of discipline and that it had cost me dearly. There have been many times during my career where I made mistakes and ended up depressed for a few days. I know the routine well by now. There is little one can do to shake it off except to wallow in it until it disappears, like a thick San Francisco fog finally lifting. Time, the magic cure for everything.

Erika told me she had a present for me. She was going to come to meet me at work and then we could go back to the condo together which was a mile away. She brought me a bright pink Victoria's Secret cape made out of sweatshirt material. Soft and comfy except totally wrong for a trading office filled with guys.

When we got back to the condo, she showed me her other present. It was something her college roommate from the University of Miami had given her a year ago. She had saved it for a much-needed occasion.

We decided to go for a long walk. Our condo was a penthouse on the corner of Lake Michigan and the Chicago River. It was next to Millennium Park. We walked and talked for four hours, exploring all the statues, gardens, and unique icons in Grant Park. We trekked around the Field Museum, along the edge of the lake, and through the grassy soccer fields. I can't ever remember babbling so much. Hiking for hours with Erika rivaled the endorphins I felt on my first seven-digit trading day. Except, unfortunately, my account balance had gone in the opposite direction.

It turned out to be such an amazing day. A long walk with my daughter and nature sure beat wallowing in depression for a few days until I got my act together again.

When people experience chronic sleep deprivation, they become too tired to realize how tired they are and their cognitive abilities are much worse than they think they are. There are adverse severe performance consequences. It is like the happy drunk at the party, too drunk to admit that he's had too many, who insists he can drive himself home safely, oblivious to his cognitive deficit.

Don't trade when tired. PERIOD.

44
THE BIGGEST LOSS IS YET TO COME

It was a considerable pause to realize that I had built a multi-million dollar business that was dependent on my ability to function at all times. Thus began a new chapter down a big expensive rabbit hole. I thought it time we move towards automated functions and algorithmic trading. It requires an intensive infrastructure. I loved the pure, simple trading game I had developed over the previous three decades, but how could I do justice for my clients if I something happened to me? What if I was out of commission? Or set 2 AM alarms thinking I might find exciting trading opportunities in Europe? Our team had the brains and research to develop strategic algorithms. At the very least, HFT, high-frequency trading, could make an attractive profit center.

When I had my accident, I brought another talented colleague on board as a partner. I had known Mark for the previous decade since he, too, had been a chat room member. He was a consultant with McKinsey and was proficient in system development and coding. So I made a not very well thought out decision to buy a technology firm that I had invested in a few years earlier. The firm had 144 servers and was writing its own gateways. We were in Chicago in 2009 and the time seemed right. I had always thought it impossible to create mechanical systems and HFT (high-frequency trading) algorithms that were robust. Now there was a glimmer of light at the end of the tunnel. There were no certainties, but at least there were possibilities. The Fund was up to a trading level of $145 million. It was difficult putting more monies to work with my current style of trading.

When I started in the business, my initial area of study was delta, theta, gamma, and beta. Now I had graduated to a different school of acronyms: API, FIX, TCP, SSL, and DMA. Colocation, cost of racks in data centers, failover, and requests per second. My head was swimming. I hired a new CTO on the recommendation of my brother. The costs for writing new gateways entered the parabolic stage. The CME was building out new data centers in Aurora, Illinois. Was this essential for our business?

I set out to steer a new ship with one left arm. Little did I know the ship was about to collide with an iceberg that nobody could see. (Spoiler alert.)

The firm I purchased had most of its customer accounts at MF Global. The revenues from these accounts covered the costs of offices and 17 employees. It was a big monthly nut to cover the CTOs, CFOs, programmers, and compliance officers. It does not take long to get the picture of what happens when client business goes away and the expenses remain.

This is a complicated story because Granat Fund was tangled up in this too. Its main trading account was at MFGlobal.

A few years earlier, Man Financial purchased the customer accounts when Refco declared bankruptcy. The CEO of Refco hid $430 million in bad debts from the auditors and investors. When his scams came to light, Granat Fund's accounts moved from Refco. Man Financial then spun off the brokerage division and named it MF Global. It was only six years later that MF Global declared bankruptcy as well.

The week before, MF Global's stock was acting crappy. Having already been through Refco's debacle, we moved most of the funds out of MF Global, leaving $1.2 million for margin to cover bond futures and options. Friday, the CFTC went into MF Global's offices to talk with them. By Sunday, there were rumors of bankruptcy.

That night, Damon and I were driving back from Indiana where we had heard my daughter sing in an opera at Indiana University. Damon was driving in the pitch black past windmill farms and corn fields while I was trying to find news on my iPad. The fierce wind was driving the turbines full tilt boogie as fast as 120-foot blades can spin. Schubert piano music wormed its way into my consciousness. *Der Erlkonig* (The Elfking) is one of the most beautiful pieces of German song ever created. It is in German which is already a pretty terrifying language. Even the words, "I love you," *Ich Liebe Dich*, are difficult to say without sounding sinister. Said emphatically, you spit all over the person you love, literally showering them with affection. "Iccchhhh liebe diiicccchhhh!"

The poem is by Johan Wolfgang von Goethe, the God of German poetry in my opinion. As an aside, this poor man is doomed to have his name mispronounced for all of eternity. GETH, GETHA, GETTA, GURTH. Chicago even had the audacity to name a street after him, which people pronounce GERDA as if they were pronouncing the word for chronic acid reflux. There is only supposed to be a shadow of an R pronounced in the middle of his name. It's pronounced GEr-ta. You glide over the r as gracefully as you can. You may think this is picky, but I spent a lot of money for Erika to learn that, so I feel it is worth mentioning.

The piano part starts, trembling agitatedly in the right hand which creates a sense of urgency and anxiety. The left hand mimics the racing hoof beats of the horse. After 14 bars, the narrator sets the scene: "Who rides so late through the night and wind? / It is the father with his child / He has the boy well in his arm / He holds him safely, and he keeps him warm." There are four characters in this poem: the narrator, the father, the son, and the Elf King. That's what makes this song challenging to perform for the singer—he has to change characters with his voice and expression. The father is deep and comforting, the son is youthful and frightened, and the Elf King must sound so supernatural that you get chills down your spine. The Elf King symbolizes death. Was MFGlobal the Elf King? At the end of the story the child dies. I did not want to die. I tried to conjure up images from Children of the Corn to see if they could do battle against the Elf King.

A broker friend who worked at MFGlobal called us on the phone to give us updates. The rumors were flying. It is incredible how all the adverse events happen on Sundays. Not only was it Damon's birthday, the next day was our anniversary.

There were two suitors lined up to buy MF Global, but on Monday, the deals fell through. The CFTC closed the firm in the middle of the day. This was unheard of. They shut down MF Global's servers, so execution platforms no longer worked. Then they told everyone they would have to exit their positions by phone. Imagine one trade desk trying to take orders from all the customers to exit positions. Fortunately, our offices were one block away, and we got permissions for FuturePath's employees to timestamp our orders and walk—no run—them to the one trade desk MF Global reopened. Nobody could get through by phone. Who cares where we got filled? We wanted out. "Please, God, tell me I am flat." It was a very perverted case of "It's never a problem getting in, it's always a problem of getting out when you need to." It still cost us dearly to exit our positions in a panicked market.

The CFTC chose which brokerage firms to transfer the customer accounts. A week later on Monday, 60% of the clients' capital was freed. It took three years for most to recover 98% of their funds.

It was not a pretty picture because the CEO, whom I will not dignify by name had dipped into millions of dollars in segregated customer funds. Some of these funds came from my technology firm's clients. This means that overnight my firm lost 90% of its clients. Everyone's account was frozen until funds could be recovered, a process which seemed like an eternity.

At least with a bad trade, the market has the decency to take your money unequivocally and immediately. In this case, worse than the monetary loss was the complexity and dragged out timing of it. It was like Chinese water torture. I far prefer–"rip the Band-Aid off" and move on to the next trade.

Talk about depreciation....

My loss from the purchase and running of this technology firm exceeded the enormous overnight loss from the SP gap caused by the Fed's takeover of Fannie May. The once costly servers became outdated. New technology allowed a more efficient way to connect our platform to multiple exchanges. The gateways were prohibitively expensive to write and maintain. Far less costly ways to connect to overseas exchanges became available. My multi-million dollar investment in technology and data centers and programmers went up in dust. *Poof.*

Oh well, all I wanted to do was to trade anyway. I never wanted to own a business or manage employees. Was I really back to square one? Hadn't I come to this conclusion 20 years earlier when I built my business up too big with too many people? The Granat Fund had a stellar performance record, my trading methodology worked better than ever, and the market volatility was exceptional. I loved the game more than ever. There was one problem—I was feeling tired. Profoundly tired.

45

WHAT DO YOU DO FOR FUN?

I was still working out and had an excellent trainer. His name was Ronnie Coleman, like the professional bodybuilder but with an "ie" instead of a "y." This Ronnie must have been his twin. He, too, was massive and had competed in the past. Each trainer I worked out with had all sorts of unique tricks. Ronnie liked to do lots of heavy reps to the point of failure which was my favorite style. He said, "Now give me 30" and started counting. After 22 reps he stopped and moved on to another exercise or started over again. The brain tends to quit right when it knows it is getting to the end, but Ronnie always stopped midstream when you were still giving your maximum effort.

At the end of our sessions, I had to carry a 25-pound weight up the stairs of the condo building where I worked out. Ronnie said, "OK, I'll see you on the 34th floor!" And then he took the elevator up while I sweated in the stuffy stairwell. Right when I thought I was going to pass out at floor 28, he stuck his head in the stairs on the 29th floor. Mercifully, I would get to ride the elevator back down.

When I was in the midst of a depression after my shoulder injury, I called Steve Ward who was a super friend. He is a trading coach in London and had given lectures for clients of mine.

"Steve, I am not sure what is wrong with me, but my usual motivation and energy are gone."

"Well, what do you do for fun?"

"Fun?"

"Yes, F-U-N. What did you do when you were living in Florida?"

"Well, I would go out and ride my horses every day after the markets closed."

When I moved from Florida, I sold my horses, my barn, and my saddles. Closed out all my equestrian positions. I had moved on to my Greek stallion (Damon). City traffic can be a bitch in Chicago, and it was pointless to own and train a horse unless I could ride 5-6 days a week.

After that call, I found a newly built barn outside of Chicago which was less than an hour commute away. I had to get a horse again. I called several horse trainers I used to work with when I had been showing in Florida. One called me back the next morning.

"Oh, Leeeeenda, I just returned from Germany last night and was looking at horses for clients. I saw the perfect horse for you, even better than Monopoly."

Monopoly had been my Grand Prix horse, and there was no better horse than Monopoly. However, he saw the big red X on my back. "Easy sale, check here, big commission."

I knew this but it was okay, so I took Marco at his word. I did not have the time or energy to shop around for horses.

"OK, Marco, send me the video, and I will look at him." His 13-year old son he took along on the trip had shot the video. It was either out of focus or filming the dirt footing. I did not care. I was feeling desperate.

"Marco, on your word I will take him. But your word is on the line here." He was ridiculously expensive, ridiculously worth it, and his name was "Richie Rich." Seriously.

Despite staying fit and having a hobby back in my life, I was sure I was getting early-onset Alzheimer's or dementia. What else could explain the horrible fog blanketing my mind? I took a trip to Florida to see a physician friend who switched his specialty from surgery to a wellness practice.

His name was Alan, and he walked into the room after I had some tests run.

"Holy cow, Linda, your cortisol levels are off the chart. I have never seen readings this high."

I did not know what to say. You mean the tightness in my throat that only goes away for a few sweet minutes when I'm lifting weights?

"Are you referring to stress?"

My body stopped producing needed levels of hormones, including testosterone, estrogen, and progesterone. I had severe hypothyroidism. Even though I had a healthy diet, exercised, and did not have a family medical history, my body chemistry and metabolism were pretty messed up.

Alan told me to read a book called *Adrenal Fatigue: The 21st Century Stress Syndrome*. I started taking compounded hormones, dozens of herbs, vitamin D, and thyroid medication. I made a concerted effort to get at least 7 1/2 hours of sleep each night—something I had thought I could live without. I never realized how important it is. For me, sleeping robbed me of precious time to do things. Lost time, but I found out I could not do anything well if I did not get enough sleep. It was an agonizing Catch-22.

Besides my limited right shoulder, I destroyed the cartilage in my right thumb joint from overuse of the mouse. Do not sit with your hand on the mouse all day! Basal joint arthritis is only remedied by a nasty surgical operation which has a long recovery time. I have not had the nerve to proceed with that. Yet.

I moved into a new office downtown Chicago. Nigel, Judd, and Mark had all moved on to do their own things. Perhaps my physical demise was the perfect excuse for them to leave the coop and spread their wings. Mick became my new assistant. His father had been in the wheat pit for 30 years, and Mick knew everything about the grains. Before he came to me, he had been working on a desk executing grain spreads in the night markets –no easy feat considering the lack of liquidity.

My new office was set up for ten people and I only had four. Room for interns, right? I did not go looking for this, but someone from overseas came begging me for a place to park two French students. They were getting their masters in quantitative finance and needed an internship. I was familiar with Nicole El Karoui, a professor of applied mathematics. She became famous for creating and pricing financial derivatives. Let's say she achieved cult goddess status without ever working a real job in the corporate or institutional world.

I spent several weeks outlining the quantitative projects our two young French geniuses could work on. When Mutt and Jeff showed up, they staggered into the office every day around 10 AM, half hungover. Initial optimism gave way to serious doubts.

I wanted this to work out because if I kicked them out of my office, they had nowhere to go and would have to leave the country. So, I resigned myself to making the next six weeks pass as fast as possible. They knew nothing about the markets, trading or technical analysis. I was not about to teach them. So I schemed up a contest—everyone likes healthy competition! I gave them each a Photon simulator execution platform with charts. I told them they would each have one week to come up with their own method. Then they were going to have a contest with each other for all the marbles. They could trade no more than 25 contracts of whichever markets they wanted to trade (I had to put in some limits because these dudes would have done 100 lots). They still managed to stagger in after the markets had opened, green and hungover, but at least they were quiet the rest of the day. The only obnoxious thing was they spoke French, so I was not sure what they were saying behind my back. My high school French was no match for their accents.

The trading contest began in earnest. At the end of each day, they wrote their P and L up on the blackboard–how much they were up or down (They were up about 90% of the days). The big reveal was at the end of four weeks. They had to give me a presentation on what they did and how it worked out.

They impressed me. Each treated me to a professional two-hour PowerPoint presentation, complete with a detailed explanation of their chosen style of trading. They included stats and pie charts. Shoot, if I had been doing their trades in real time instead of on the simulator, I would have been up an additional 500K. It was a steady equity curve, too! These were two of the un-brawniest human specimens, but they had a brain and could concentrate, even with a hangover and food poisoning from eating out in China town (another common excuse they had). Woe is me—entering the next decade competing against young lads in their early twenties.

So, you can't judge a book by its cover. Now the reader says, "Tell us what they were doing. We want to know the secret!"

The secret is—each focused on doing one thing and one thing only once they sat down. No internet, no social media, no talking, no T.V. Game mode only. The first intern used Bollinger bands on 5-minute charts and made countertrend trades in the SPs. He waited until the middle of the day when the volumes were lighter and there was no risk of getting run over by a strong morning trend. The second intern had the opposite strategy. He entered early in the morning, using a MACD oscillator. Sometimes he took a little bit of heat, but he played to capture the sweet spot of the morning trend. He traded SPs, the Euro currency, and gold.

Both did well with two opposite styles. Neither looked for confirmation from the other or anyone else. Both stayed off the internet and refrained from other distractions. It goes to prove the power of concentration and tape reading as well as staying methodical in whatever you do. One market, one strategy and voila–even a neophyte Frenchie could do just fine. Day trading, no less.

They did so well, it made me feel old. Old and slow. It was not long after that I moved my office out to the suburbs.

A time to work, a time to rest.

46

FULL CIRCLE

I closed the Granat Fund and deregistered as a CTA and CPO. I was one of the original investors in my fund. I did not believe in trading a separate personal account while managing money. I was just another client. Hank Pruden's lecture in Santa Barbara forever echoed in my ears, "Be your own best client and do your analysis in a room with no windows or doors." The Fund had a class of 2 x 1 leveraged shares, and this is where my money stayed for nine years. When I shut down the Fund, my account had increased by more than 900%. Through the power of compounding, I had become the largest investor.

I moved to Florida for six months out of the year. I did not want to spend cold, miserable winters in Chicago. A bona fide Snowbird. I bought another barn in Wellington and took the horses down to compete in the winter dressage festival. And, I started working out with Mr. Bill again. My friend with whom I won the bodybuilding contest with 15 years earlier is still at the gym every day. He is now

84, and continues to be a role model to all around him, and most importantly to me.

Traders are always looking for the secrets. Strategies, indicators, algorithms, anything to make money. Most do not recognize the hard work it takes to do research and development. And even more underestimate the countless hours required to gain experience. Few have the perseverance and attitude to stick out the tough times, but none of this matters if you don't have your health and can't control the stress levels.

The dust settles. Trading continues. The Earth does not stop turning. New players enter the arena convinced they are going to be smart enough to figure out the markets, create new algorithms, and reap the lucky fruits of a mythical printing press. "Luck is the residue of effort." I am sure that most underestimate the time and energy required to achieve consistent profitability. If you believe, never give up, and focus on trading above all else, the markets provide unlimited abundance. I am living proof. I have been on the wrong side of every type of black swan, crazy adverse move, and tough break. But here I am, in front of my screens every day and playing the best game in the universe!

I am ever so lucky my daughter stayed out of the trading business and is an excellent singer. I have four magnificent dressage horses, barns in Illinois, and farms in Wellington. Above all, I have the most wonderful husband, Damon, my original SP broker from the eighties.

Give, and everything you give will come back to you tenfold. Stay humble but remain confident. And never forget, if you don't know who you are, the markets are an expensive place to find out.

"Life should not be a journey to the grave with the intention of arriving safely in a pretty and well-preserved body, but rather to skid in broadside in a cloud of smoke, thoroughly used up, totally worn out, and loudly proclaiming 'Wow! What a Ride!'" —Hunter S. Thompson, *The Proud Highway: Saga of a Desperate Southern Gentleman, 1955-1967*

EPILOGUE

I am supposed to write on how the markets have changed, how my style of trading might have changed, but all that is garbage. The game has not changed: the markets are going up or they are going down or they are chopping endlessly in noise. Period.

It occurred to me that writing is much like composing music. My initial writing efforts were like those of an eight-year-old writing a few lines for the piano. Mozart, I am not. I have had six books outlined for fifteen years, but I never found the time to write because trading took priority. The markets don't stop for anyone.

Fast forward four years after my daughter graduated from Indiana University with a masters in vocal performance. She could not officially graduate until she gave her master recital which she had put on the back burner. So we made a pact: I would write a book by the time she gave her concert. That was a three-month deadline. As fate always has it, those were three exceptional months of volatility in the market. The book stalled again because I could not pull away from the screens.

I learned several lessons from this. Trading is crazily addicting. I took it for granted the markets were my sports court because this is the main game I have always played. I did not think of it as an addiction because it was my life, what I knew, my medium. Take me out of my game and I flop on the top of my desk like a fish out of water. So, this book brewed for several more years never getting written. It is not even one of the original ones I outlined.

The second lesson I learned is how difficult it is to learn a new craft. I have written many articles over the years, even half of a book 23 years earlier. This project was different. With a family history of Alzheimer's and dementia, I didn't want to take it for granted that I will remember things in another ten years. Stephen King suggests reading and writing as much as possible. Like a newbie studying the markets and trading, I immersed myself in trying to figure out how to make words spill on paper. This took another 2-3 years.

I enlisted the aid of my daughter. Who knows me better than she? She was with me a good part of this journey, growing up in a house filled with market culture. All my friends and associates were uncles to her. She traveled with me, and I traveled with her. And she knows I really do use four-letter words but would not have had the honesty to write them if she did not put them back where I took them out.

PARTING SHOT

From one of the first Trading books written in 1688:
"Whoever wishes to win in this game must have patience and money, since the values are so little constant and the rumors so little founded on truth. He who knows how to endure blows without being terrified by the misfortune resembles the lion who answers the thunder with a roar and is unlike the hind who, stunned by the thunder tries to flee. It is certain that he who does not give up hope will win, and will secure money adequate for the operations that he envisaged at the start." —Joseph de la Vega – *Confusion de Confusiones*

"Fuck a Duck, get me out." —Linda Raschke

ACKNOWLEDGMENTS

This book would not be nearly so entertaining without the input from my millennial daughter, Erika. She encouraged me to study writing for two years and then showed me the way with her humorous rewrites. I hope she writes her own book one day because it will surely be a best seller.

Thank-you to John Montesi, my editor and so much more, (another millennial with a penchant for Joan Didion.) John was instrumental in adding color and conversation as well as being a positive and upbeat friend. Yes! I can see the light at the end of the tunnel too. Just one more switchback, one more hill, 3 more hours until the sun comes up and the manuscript will be finished. John is a fellow nature lover who does not own a TV. There is hope for the human spirit when my generation has passed. I know John has an important novel brewing inside him.

Many thanks to Terry Liberman for being my Yoda after I retired. Terry was my sounding board, never offering opinions but prompting me to keep rearranging the puzzle pieces to see which one fit best. No matter what I wrote, it was "terrific," "awesome," and "fabulous," even though I ended up rewriting things many times.

I made two wonderful friends while speaking in Australia: Mandi Pour Rafsendjani and Andrew Swanscott. Both saw the early manuscript and provided encouragement and helpful comments. These two amazing people prove that distance means nothing in today's world, even in opposite time zones. I am happy to call them best friends.

Thank-you to the following people for taking the time to make thoughtful comments and perceptive edits. It takes professionals valuable time to comb someone else's manuscript, and I am very appreciative: Greg Morris, Tom McClellan, Perry Kaufman, Tom Aspray, Steve Ward, Brett Steenbarger, Dave Landry and Jay Kaeppel.

A shout out to Rangan Padmanabhan, my on-line trading buddy in Texas for his demented comments and edits. "Now I get it. Now I see what you were talking about." He is on his way to becoming a top ranking hedge fund manager.

Thank-you also, to Larry Williams, Larry Connors, Victor Sperandeo, Judd Brody, Steve Moore, Carley Garner, Toni Hanson, and Mick Ieronimo. I am so lucky to have such great friends.

Erika and I, July 4, 2018 - Alaska

Special thanks to Hector Seda for transcribing my material from years past and telling me how "easy" it was to write a book. I naively believed him.

Soheil Zargarpour showed me the equivalent of how to run a 4-minute mile. I gave a lecture in which I mentioned my struggles in writing. He approached me and said he had a system for writing. "How to write a book in three and a half days by chunking it into 90-minute blocks." I believed him. It was actually a year later that I finished the book, but who is counting. Just knowing that it COULD be done is sometimes all one needs. And the word "system" struck a chord. He panned my early writing efforts. "No, no, NO. Pretend you are walking into the room. Now, what do you see?" Show not tell. He is destined to write a great screenplay one day.

My loving husband, Damon Pavlatos, made this story possible by adding so much to my life.

GLOSSARY OF TRADING LINGO

3/10 oscillator – Similar to the oscillator on the original Security Market Research charts. It is the difference between a 3 and 10-period simple moving average. A 16-period simple moving average of this is overlaid on top of the faster oscillator.

API – Application program interface, or the software that allows two applications to talk to each other.

ATR – Average True Range in an N-day simple moving average of the true range values.

Auction Theory – How people act in auction markets including supply and demand characteristics and initiating and responsive behaviors.

Big Round Number – Price levels for a market usually in increments of 100 and 500. For example, 2700 is a big round number in the SPs. 100 is a big round number in a stock. Big Round Numbers can serve as magnets for price where it then becomes a support or resistance level.

Box – a relatively neutral option strategy where a trader is long a bull call spread and long the corresponding bear put spread in the case of a "long" box, and vice versa for a "short box." It used to be a play when interest rates were high.

Carry Trade – A strategy where traders borrow money in a low interest rate currency (in this case, the Yen) and invest in a high-yielding currency to capture the difference between the rates.

City Service – An oil and gas company established in 1910. In 1964 it created the brand name, CITGO. It was acquired by Occidental Petroleum in 1982.

Colored Trading Jackets – Each clearing firm had its own designated jacket color. This allowed the floor clerks who collected the order tickets from the traders to know which traders cleared through which firms. Some of the larger clearing firms included First Options of Chicago, Speer Leeds, Merrill Lynch, and Drexel Burnham.

CPO – Commodity Pool Operator

CTA – Commodity Trading Advisor

Double Nickels – a price that ends in 55. The SPs were trading at 462.55, or double nickels.

Drexel Burnham – a leading US-based investment firm. It was forced into bankruptcy after inside trading violations and assorted other offenses.

FIX – Financial Information Exchange. The protocol used for real-time exchange of securities transaction and trade information.

Greenmail – The practice of buying enough shares in a stock to threaten a hostile takeover, forcing the targeted company to purchase the shares back at a premium.

Handle – The whole number for the price quote. The handle for bonds when they are trading at 132'16 would the 132.

LBR310 – the 3/10 oscillator on CQG's chart.

Long Liquidation Flush – The opposite of a "Short Squeeze." A rapid selloff in a market when most market participants are already long.

Open Outcry – The form of communication used in the trading pits involving verbal shouting and sometimes hand signals.

OPM – "Other People's Money." Slang used for managed accounts.

GLOSSARY OF TRADING LINGO

Opportunistic trading – Strategies that take advantage of short term market inefficiencies or directionally based trades.

Quotron – The first financial data terminal to display stock quotes on an electronic screen. The company was started in 1960.

Straddle – An options strategy which is long both calls and puts speculating that there will be a big move either up or down (long straddles), or short both calls and puts speculating that the stock will stay within a contained range (short straddles).

TRIN – the ratio of advancing to declining issues divided by the ratio of up volume to down volume. (Created by Dick Arms, it should be called the "Arms" index.)